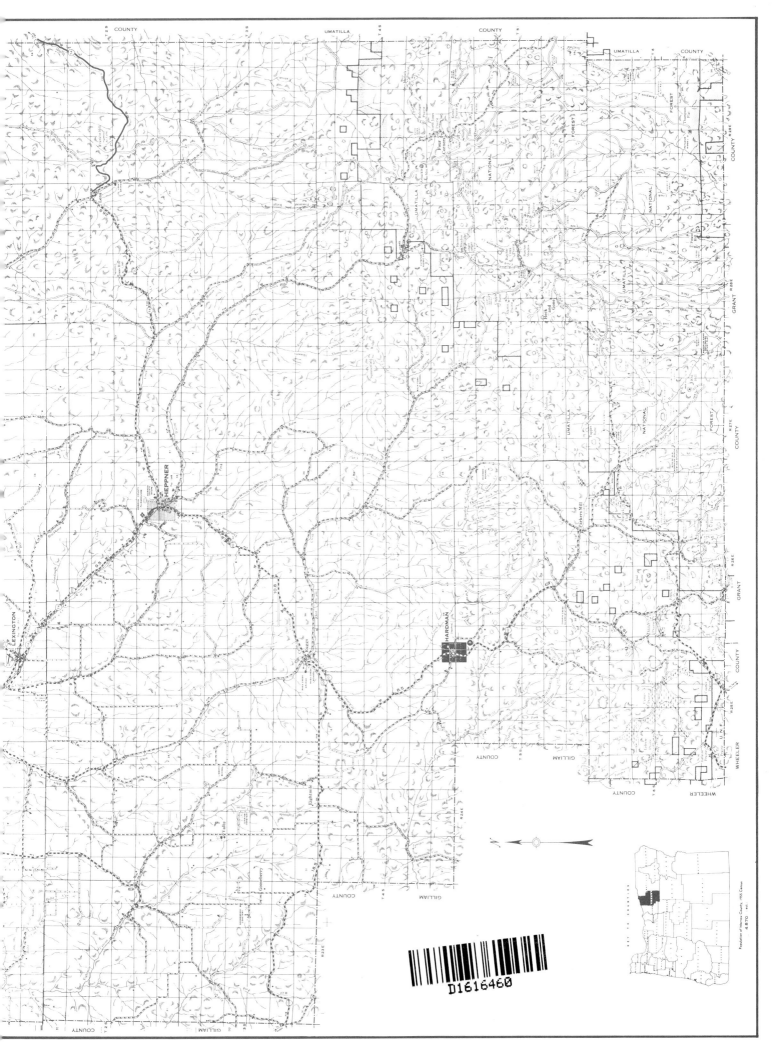

HOMESTEADS AND HERITAGES:
A HISTORY OF MORROW COUNTY, OREGON

Books by the Same Author:

The Golden Land
Cattle Country of Peter French
These Things We Note

Homesteads and Heritages:

A History of Morrow County, Oregon

By

Giles French

Published by

BINFORDS & MORT, *Publishers*

for the

MORROW COUNTY HISTORY COMMITTEE

Portland   •   Oregon   •   97242

INTRODUCTION

When Mrs. Harry (Amanda) Duvall donated money for the library and museum to Morrow County in honor of her departed family an increase in interest began in the Morrow County Historical Society.

Mr. Oscar Peterson, who describes himself as a stubborn Swede, cast about for someone to write the county's history and I was chosen. W. S. Shiach wrote a good history in about 1901 and the women of the county, led by Miss Esther Kirmis, wrote and published a booklet about early days which contained much valuable history and this whetted the appetite of natives for more accounts of early days.

Pioneers are my favorite people and I took up the history of the fine early characters who brought their herds and flocks to eat the grass from Morrow's hills with relish. Many are recalled in this book, not all however, were public figures and therefore noted in the newspapers from which this is largely taken.

Many Morrow Countians have helped with this history. Mrs. Rachel Harnett, curator of the museum, has been invaluable for advise and for the plain digging research requires. Mrs. Elaine Sigsbee George has given detailed information about events within her memory. Judge Paul Jones obligingly made the old copies of the county's newspapers available to me so I could peruse them at my home in Moro. Mr. and Mrs. Ralph Thompson lent a copy of Shiach, now rare. Harold Cohn and Frank Turner have been helpful with information about early times. Judge John Kilkenny has given encouragement and offered usable information contained in his long story of the Morrow County Irish. Orville Cutsforth, D. O. Nelson and Shirley Rugg have instructed me in modern methods in use in modern times. Pioneers have ridden with me up and down the creeks telling me tales of early days. Morrow Countians have been cooperative and courteous and I am thankful to all of them. Mrs. G. Douma typed the final copy and I am thankful to her for I cannot make a final copy.

Probably no two people have the same idea about what a county history should contain, some would like a personal history of the many families, something that should properly be done by some member of the family—a project we would encourage.

I have tried to include the events that had a material bearing on the development of the county, on events that changed the course of the county, about the men who influenced such events. We have commented where it seemed pertinent.

What will happen in the future we do not know although there is enough inventiveness and ambition among Morrow Countians to develop an industrial future while continuing an agricultural past if conditions are reasonably favorable. We did not come to speculate; we came to chronicle.

GILES FRENCH

CONTENTS

Geography   11

Explorers   12

The Cayuse War   15

Gold   17

Transportation — Communication   21

Why Stansbury Flat?   22

The Big Scare   27

People Are Coming   28

The County of Morrow   35

The Elements of Growth   38

The Lost Boy   43

Irish & Swedes   44

Grass Is Going   48

Morrow County Press   52

Early Schools   55

Ione   57

Lexington   60

The Heppner Flood   60

Mike Galloway's Story   67

Heppner in the New Century   75

A Time of Change   76

Mechanical Revolution   83

The Town's Afire   91

Wants Make Woes   93

The Great Depression   97

The Forties Were Terrible   102

Modern Times   105

Miscellany   113

Irrigation   117

Index   123

*This History of Morrow County was sponsored by the Heppner-Morrow County Chamber
of Commerce and the following individuals and organizations:*

Mr. and Mrs. Robert Abrams
Mr. and Mrs. Frank Anderson
Nellie G. Anderson
Mr. and Mrs. Ray Ayers
Mr. and Mrs. Jack Bailey
Mr. and Mrs. Henry Baker
Bank of Eastern Oregon
Mr. and Mrs. James R. Barnett
Mr. and Mrs. Wm. F. Barratt
Mr. and Mrs. J. G. Barratt
Mrs. C. H. Bartholomew
Bechdolt Bros.
Mr. and Mrs. Charles Becket
Mr. and Mrs. Harold Becket
Mr. and Mrs. Terrel E. Benge
Carl F. Bergstrom
Mr. and Mrs. E. William Bergstrom
Mr. O. F. Bergstrom
Mr. and Mrs. Rudy Bergstrom
Mr. O. W. Bisbee
Miss Opal Briggs
Mr. and Mrs. Howard Bryant
Mr. and Mrs. Edward L. Burchell
R. A. Campbell
Mr. and Mrs. Lewis Carlson
In Memory of
Mr. and Mrs. M. L. Case
Mr. and Mrs. Barton Clark
Mr. and Mrs. Howard Cleveland
Mr. and Mrs. Harold Cohn
Mr. and Mrs. Bill Collins
Columbia Basin Electric Co-op
Mr. and Mrs. Morgan Connor
Josephine Woolery Conway
Vera I. Cooley
Mr. and Mrs. Clair H. Cox
Mr. and Mrs. Winn Crist
Mr. and Mrs. Orville Cutsforth
Mr. and Mrs. Ron Daniels
Mr. and Mrs. George Davidson
Mr. and Mrs. L. E. Dick
Mr. and Mrs. Dan Dinges
Mrs. Amanda Duvall
Mr. and Mrs. Bernard Doherty
Mr. and Mrs. Charles Doherty
Lawrence P. Doherty
Mrs. Ray Drake
First National Bank of Oregon
Mr. and Mrs. Leroy Gardner
Elaine Sigsbee George
Donald F. Gilliam
Mr. E. E. Gilliam
Mr. and Mrs. E. E. Gonty
Mr. and Mrs. Herman Green

Mattie B. Green
Mr. and Mrs. Marion C. Green
Norman B. and Frances C. Griffith
Jessie Griffin
Mr. and Mrs. Everett Harshamn
Rachel Harnett
Marion Hayden
Mr. and Mrs. Walter Hayes
Vida N. Heliker
Heppner Gazette Times
Heppner Lodge #258 BPOE
Heppner Lumber Co.
Heppner Wranglers Riding Club
W. E. Hughes and Sons
Eugenia B. Huston
Ione Lions Club
Mr. and Mrs. Bob Jepsen
Mr. and Mrs. John Jepsen
Alva W. Jones
Mr. and Mrs. C. N. Jones
Dr. and Mrs. Gerald Jones
Judge and Mrs. Paul Jones
Jordan Elevator Co.
Mr. and Mrs. Rupert Kennedy
John F. Kilkenney
Mr. and Mrs. Lindsay Kincaid
Kinzua Corporation
Mr. and Mrs. M. N. Kirk
Pearl Padberg Kruse
Mr. and Mrs. Elmer Ladd
Mr. and Mrs. Conley Lanham
Mr. and Mrs. M. L. Leonard
Lexington Grange #726
Mr. and Mrs. Larry Lindsay
Mr. and Mrs. Robert Lovgren
T. W. Lowe
Mr. and Mrs. Raymond Lundell
Mr. and Mrs. P. W. Mahoney
Mr. and Mrs. Fred Mankin
Mrs. Norma Marquardt
Mr. and Mrs. Carl McDaniel
Dr. and Mrs. A. D. McMurdo
Mr. and Mrs. Clint McQuarrie
Mr. and Mrs. Edwin H. Miller Jr.
Mr. and Mrs. George E. Miller
Mr. and Mrs. Paul Miller
Katherine Monagle
Melvin Moyer
Mr. and Mrs. Rod Murray
Mr. and Mrs. Alfred Nelson
Bertha Nelson
Charles Nelson
Mr. and Mrs. D. O. Nelson
Kristin Nelson

Mr. and Mrs. Norman Nelson
Mr. and Mrs. Harry T. O'Donnell
Pacific Gas Transmissions Co.
Mr. and Mrs. Elmer Palmer
Mrs. Etta Devine Parker
Mrs. Frank S. Parker
Emma P. Peck
Mr. and Mrs. Harold K. Peck
Carl J. Peterson
C. R. Peterson
Mr. and Mrs. Oscar Peterson
Mr. and Mrs. Paul Pettyjohn
Mr. and Mrs. Gene Pierce
Johanna Rauch (Mrs. Fred)
Rhea Creek Home Economic Club
Victor I. Ritchie
Mr. and Mrs. Dave Reitman
Mr. and Mrs. Omar Reitman
Mr. and Mrs. Victor Reitman
Mr. and Mrs. Walter G. Roberts
Mr. and Mrs. W. C. Rosewall
St. Patrick's Church
Mr. and Mrs. Leonard Schwartz
Mr. and Mrs. Oral M. Scott
Mr. and Mrs. Harold Scritsmier
Mr. and Mrs. Walter Skuzeski
Mr. and Mrs. Wesley Sherman
Mr. and Mrs. Kenneth Smouse
Soroptomist Club of Heppner
Mr. and Mrs. Charles Starks
Mr. and Mrs. J. V. Stephens
Stone Machinery
Jack and Rita Sumner
Mr. and Mrs. Jerry Sweeney
Mr. and Mrs. James G. Thomson
Mr. and Mrs. Ralph Thompson
Mr. and Mrs. Herschel Townsend
C. W. Troedson
Mr. and Mrs. Verner Troedson
F. W. Turner
Mr. and Mrs. Jack VanWinkle
Mr. and Mrs. C. A. Warren
Mr. and Mrs. Dewey W. West Jr.
Mr. and Mrs. Dick Wilkinson
Wavel B. Wilkinson
Willows Grange #672
Willows Lodge #66 IOOF
Mr. and Mrs. Herman Winter
Dr. and Mrs. Wallace H. Wolff
Mr. and Mrs. John Wood
Mr. and Mrs. Albert Wright
Mr. and Mrs. Harold Wright
Mr. and Mrs. O. E. Wright
Mr. and Mrs. Raymond Wright

HOMESTEADS AND HERITAGES:
A HISTORY OF MORROW COUNTY, OREGON

Pioneer Stockmen—Picture taken in 1902. Here are the founders of Morrow county, many of them, whose pictures were gathered by Mike Galloway about 1900. This is the way an early day stockman looked when he went to have his picture taken. Many of these men had been on the Heppner Hills for thirty years and were prior to the Irish and the Swedes. (Courtesy Mrs. Elaine S. George)

1. Thomas Matlock	25. Matt Lichenthal	49. O. E. Farnsworth
2. William Dutton	26. James Jones	50. Dave Herren
3. Norman Kelley	27. Ben Parker	51. Steve La Lande
4. C. A. Petteys	28. J. W. Morrow	52. James Wyland
5. O. F. Thompson	29. Albert Wright	53. R. C. Hart
6. A. E. Wright	30. Harvey Rush	54. Press Looney
7. Henry Thompson	31. Henry Padberg	55. Andy Rood
8. W. O. Minor	32. All Florence	56. Hugh Fields
9. John Hughes	33. Henry Heppner	57. C. A. Miner
10. John Hayes	34. James Williams	58. Ed Day
11. Ellis Minor	35. James Hayes	59. Cas Matlock
12. Elisha Sperry	36. Ed Rood	60. Arthur Andrews
13. S. P. Florence	37. John Elder	61. John Ayers
14. Silas Wright	38. J. P. Rhea	62. Henry Blackman
15. William Ayers	39. C. A. Rhea	63. Thomas Quaid
16. A. G. Bartholomew	40. Alec Thompson	64. Thomas Marlatt
17. Wm. Hughes	41. T. H. Bisbee	65. D. O. Justus
18. Nat Webb	42. Frank Gilliam	66. Henry Jones
19. R. F. Hynd	43. J. C. Kirk	67. T. A. Rhea
20. T. W. Ayers	44. W. J. Morrow	68. William Barratt
21. Charles Kirk	45. William Penland	69. W. J. Backett
22. H. C. Gay	46. J. T. Allyn	70. James Adkins
23. Wesley Marlatt	47. Andrew Cook	71. George Conser
24. Holland Thompson	48. Press Thompson	72. E. L. Matlock

GEOGRAPHY

Morrow County is the 2069 square miles (1,317,760 acres) in northeastern Oregon lying between Township 23 East of the Willamette Meridian for the most part and extending to Township 29 EWM except in the northern part which joins Umatilla County midway in Township 27 EWM. It reaches from the Columbia River on the north to the seventh Township south of the Base Line, thus being five townships north of the Base Line, which crosses the county near Ione, and six Townships south, 66 miles in all. The average width is 40 miles.

Morrow County probably has the softest landscape of any eastern Oregon County. There are few of the tall, precipitous basaltic cliffs that distinguish the terrain of Sherman and Gilliam Counties, immediately west of Morrow, and the Blue Mountains in the southern part of the county are not so steep as in Umatilla and Grant. More canyons have grassy hillsides than rock cliffs or shale.

Willow Creek (Hohesna on some early maps) runs to the Columbia diagonally across the county from the Blue Mountains near Black Butte but its bordering rimrock is seldom very sharp or high.

Butter Creek starts in the southeastern part of the county and cuts a deep gash until it reaches the level land at the Umatilla County border and then runs through flat country before joining the Umatilla River some ten miles south of the Columbia.

Except in a few places the hillsides are grass covered with few outcroppings of shale, a distinguishing feature of nearly every other county in eastern Oregon. Morrow County gives evidence of being a part of an older geological formation, a more eroded, smoother, formation. The layer of volcanic rock is thinner, more worn.

Madison Butte is not the highest peak in the county but there is a road running clear up to the lookout at its top. Right on that point is an outcropping of rock resembling decomposed granite as if the rains and snows had worn the peak down to expose the solid granite framework of the earth. The Forest Service says Madison is 5707 feet high, Arbuckle rises to 5827 and Black Butte is the highest in the county at 5932.

Sand Hollow is a geographical feature of the county that is not repeated in any other county bordering the Columbia River on the south. It starts at Hinton Creek on a pass so low that a little erosion could cause it to drain that creek. It runs almost straight north for over twenty miles until it is lost in the flat land nearer the river, its sides steadily getting lower. Although it fits the description of a hollow as known in western geography it does carry a little water in the spring.

The county may be roughly divided into three parts by geology and geography and also by use.

The southern part is stock country and forest. It is the location of the 233,500 acres of forest land of which nearly all, 202,000 acres, are in the Umatilla National Forest. Much of it drains into the north fork of the John Day River where Monument has 1900 feet elevation. The streams are numerous, the soil a gravelly one that produces a stand of nutritious grass, tall pines and patches of beautiful wild flowers.

The central part of the county, the wheat belt, is typical of eastern Oregon wheat land, probably volcanic in origin which the southern part surely is not. It has low hills for the most part although some fields are steep. There are numerous dry creeks caused by spring run-offs that have gashed the country in the rush of water to seek its level. Most of the county's 372,306 acres of tilled land is in this belt.

The northern part of Morrow County lies low along the Columbia River, a large part of it is sandy with outcroppings of rock. Much of it is called desert and it qualifies. Recently, since average rainfall has increased—temporarily—part of it has been successfully sown to wheat.

Scientists say that once upon a time in the distant geological past a huge lake called Mazula in northeastern Washington broke its boundaries and overflowed down the Columbia River channel to send tons of sand to cover this area which was about the first place such a flood could spread out. A newer theory has it that the deposit of sand was caused by a natural dam in the big river that backed water up to cover the north end of Morrow County and thereby deposit sand.

Whatever the cause, this section has not been productive of crops for man except under irrigation which has been intensive near the Umatilla River. Several townships were taken over by the federal government as a bombing range and when no longer used much for that purpose were leased to the State of Oregon and turned over to the Boeing company as a missile testing base.

The Columbia gorge is not a gorge in Morrow County; there are no high basaltic cliffs bordering the river here. The land slopes gently to the river. Willow Creek comes to the Gilliam County border before it meets the river and Butter Creek at its terminus is in Umatilla County. But the bottom lands of both, while going through Morrow County, are irrigated and productive of a healthy livestock industry.

When high-piled snow on the southern hills melts quickly or when a cloudburst hits across a ridge, sending water down two creeks at once, floods occur in Morrow County. Winds are sometimes strong along the Columbia in the spring, the season of the chinook. But back in the timbered hills wind is not common.

There are examples of very high and very low temperatures, 20 below and 100 degrees above zero, and once in eight or ten years such may occur. In ordinary summers the mercury climbs into the nineties and natives expect some zero nights in winter. Rainfall is light, 8.6 inches in the north and 13.15 in the wheat belt and nearly 20 in the range area.

At the mouth of Clark canyon there is a geographical peculiarity that has attracted attention. It is a mound, perhaps 100 feet high, rocky and mostly barren, that rises from the Willow Creek floor with no connection with other hills and ridges. When the federal government in 1940 hired writers to go about describing the state they wrote of this mound: "At Lexington, State 207 unites with State 74 and turns left to Clark's Ranch 46 miles, the site of the remains of an ancient stone sepulcher, one of several in this region. Found nearby are pictographs and artifacts. Anthropologists have surmised that these graves contain remains of a Mayan people, ante-dating the American Indian, who left a trail from the Columbia River to Central America." American Guide Series, Oregon Pg. 262. No native has been found with so romantic a background for the mound and it will be remembered that in the depression writers were enlisted because of their imagination and indigence, not their knowledge of anthropology.

EXPLORERS

Lewis and Clark came down the Columbia reaching the eastern edge of Morrow County on October 19, 1805. It was a Saturday which didn't mean much to the explorers other than to mark another day. They had just completed the dangerous passage of the Bitterroots and spent enough time with the Nez Perce Indians to buy a small canoe and dig out some larger canoes from logs. Men of the party were better boatmen than horsemen and were happy to be on the comparativley calm of the water after their experiences of riding horses across the mountains.

Their canoes were filled with dogs, for in no case did the men of the Lewis and Clark party want to be reduced to eating salmon.

Clark noted that he left Yelleppit, the chief of the Umatilla Indians, after promising to spend more time with him on the return trip. Yelleppit was, according to Clark, a handsome Indian, about 35, well-built and dignified. Dignity was a characteristic of Indians, especially the chiefs, and they derived some of their authority thereby.

Clark noted a big island, now called Blalock, on

which he walked and visited some Indian habitations. He found the natives shy until he brought Sacajawea forward to show his peaceful intentions; Indian tribes in these parts, noted Clark, never took women on war parties and her presence assured them of his goodwill. He offered his pipe to the braves for a whiff of tobacco. He observed that the women wore shorter robes than did those of the Nez Perce and some scarcely any at all. And this was October.

The adventurers from the states did not set foot on present day Morrow County, neither then nor on their return. There was nothing to attract them. Even the sharp-eyed hunter George Drouillard could not spot a deer in that barren area, not anyway before he was seen.

The huge cliffs that border the lower Columbia begin to shorten at the big rapids at one-time Celilo and along the river through Morrow County there are no cliffs of consequence. Clark noted this and the few willows along the bank. There is about thirty miles of smooth terrain between the cliffs of the lower river and those that begin again in Umatilla County.

Neither did the voyagers who plied the river for the Hudson's Bay Company stop in present day Morrow. There was too little grass along its shores to attract deer or antelope and their hunters would have lacked cover for stalking anyway. The river had few rapids strong enough to require portages.

When Ramsey Crooks and John Day were captured by Indians at the mouth of the John Day River in the winter of 1812 and robbed of their rifles and clothing they made their way back up-river to the camp of the then chief Yeck-a-tap-em, who kept them until spring when an exploring party under David Stewart rescued them. They undoubtedly found the sands of Morrow County welcome to their freezing feet.

The part of Morrow County seen by the first white men to tread on it was unattractive. In 1843 J. W. Nesmith described it as barren sand, no timber along the river. In 1851 P. V. Crawford came through in August and noted "this day we traveled twelve miles, four miles down the valley brought us to the Umatilla Agency . . . . our company took the Welles Springs road and crossed a dry, sandy desert, eight miles to Butter Creek."

In 1853 Mrs. Maria Belshaw, also from Indiana, one of the women diarists of the overland trip de-

scribed the Morrow County part as "dust, wild sage brush, no rocks. Came to a spring this evening. It proceeds from a mound dug out in the middle, plenty of water but not good. This spring is 20 miles from Butter Creek." A difference in the estimate of mileage is apparent.

The emigrant trail was about fifteen miles from the Columbia; in fact, the emigrants did not see the river until nearly across Sherman County.

Before entering the Morrow County desert the emigrants crossed Butter Creek, and had it not been for Wells Spring, a fortunate bit of water comprising several springs, they would have had a most difficult time making it. There were no remarks about luxuriant grass for their stock as was the case before and after. This was, for some, the most desolate part of their trip.

No white men were living in present Morrow County when in 1847 the Cayuse Indians, disconsolate because their children were dying from an ailment—probably measles or smallpox—no doubt started by contact with white children on a wagon train that had gone through. The Cayuses had many complaints against Whitman, not all self developed.

The Indians, with native sagacity, discerned that the white men were divided in their religion and that some of them were more intent on discrediting each other than in converting Indians. The power was with the Catholics for many of the employees of the Hudson's Bay Company were of that religion. Whitman and the Presbyterians, especially Henry Harmon Spalding, were violently opposed to Catholics and the conflict between the two Christian faiths was often more intense than the efforts made to wean the savages from their animistic beliefs.

Whitman's medical art necessarily practiced on the far frontier and in a time when medicine in general was not much superior to the incantations of the aboriginal medicine man, was inadequate to cure the ills of the children and the Indians blamed him for their deaths. The white man's diseases wrought havoc among the native Americans throughout the pioneer period.

The Indians began to sense that the waves of white settlers that came over the Blue Mountains every fall in an almost perpetual stream boded no good for them. Politically Oregon was merely a settlement, not even a territory, and none of the blue-clad soldiers that represented authority were present. Indian orators—adept rabble-rousers—had no difficulty raising fears that white men would eventually take over the land that, although held in common, they felt was theirs by every right they recognized. There were but a few whites; why not end the threat before it grew. Few can argue with the Indians' reasoning.

To the whites the killing of eleven residents of the Whitman mission at Waiilaptu on November 29, 1847 was a massacre; to the Indians it was striking a blow for liberty. Four others died later, some from exposure.

The whites reacted quickly for if they were going to remain in Cayuse country they had to show they were powerful enough to overcome or at least, resist. It was profitable to stay. William McBean, factor at Fort Walla Walla (Wallula), sent a messenger to James Douglas, chief factor at Fort Vancouver, telling of the massacre. McBean was much criticized by the Presbyterians and called a bigoted half-breed, but his actions in this case were laudable.

The messenger arrived December 4 after making a part of the trip by boat below The Dalles. Douglas dispatched Peter Skene Ogden to Fort Walla Walla with a small party which left December 7 from Fort Vancouver.

The Hudson's Bay Company had good relations with the Cayuses as they usually did with all Indian tribes. They planned it that way. They provided the natives with a market for their furs and sold them blankets, muskets, some foods and decorations to delight the savage breast.

It took Ogden twelve days to reach Fort Walla Walla where he immediately called the chiefs together to tell them he wanted to take the whites held in captivity back to their people. Peu-Peu-Mox-Mox, the Walla Walla chief, was present and aided in the exchange as a sort of intermediary. It was not an act of generosity or mercy on the part of the Cayuses. They received 53 point blankets, 50 shirts, ten guns, ten fathoms of tobacco, ten handkerchiefs, and one hundred rounds of powder and ball. The prize for releasing Spalding was less, being 12 blankets, 12 shirts, 10 handkerchiefs, five fathoms of tobacco, two guns and 200 rounds of powder and ball and some knives.

Ogden left on January 1, 1848 by boat and arrived at Oregon City January 10. By that time the provisional government had organized to punish the Cayuse chiefs responsible for the murders. Governor George Abernethy called for volunteers, who were to bring their own horses and their own rifles.

The provisional government had no money and no authority to raise any. The treasury of Oregon contained $43.72 and it had indebtedness of $4079.74.

A committee was appointed to obtain funds from citizens and another to approach the Hudson's Bay Company. The latter was unsuccessful but the citizens responded, merchants of Oregon City donated $1000, and farmers gave wheat which was then accepted as a medium of exchange.

The governor appointed Cornelius Gilliam as colonel to lead the volunteers to Cayuse country to capture the murderers and Joe Meek to go to Washington, D.C. to plead with his relative, President James Knox Polk, for territorial status and soldiers to protect the settlement. Gilliam and Meek traveled together and on February 27, 1848 they left The Dalles. There were but a few of them, although forces under command of Major H. A. G. Lee joined them there.

They met the Cayuses at Wells Spring or a little east of there. The Indians were under Chiefs Gray Eagle and Five Crows (who had had the first pick of the women captured in the Whitman massacre and had chosen Miss Lorinda Bewley). Both were more than a little arrogant. Five Crows boasted that he was immune to white man's bullets and Gray Eagle said he could eat them. Neither boast was justified for when Gray Eagle rode close to the volunteer lines and shouted that he would kill Tom McKay, that soldier shot him dead and Charley McKay shot Five Crows (Hezekiah) in the arm, shattering it.

The white men marched on to the Walla Walla valley where their intent was to arrest the murderers and bring them to trial. They did not want to start an Indian war, not having the resources to win it. But Gilliam's forces did fight a few skirmishes.

Colonel Gilliam decided to return to Oregon City to confer with Governor Abernethy and see if more troops could be provided. With about half of his force (which probably never exceeded 100 men) he camped at Wells Spring. While dragging a lead rope from a wagon he was instantly killed because a soldier had laid a cocked rifle in the wagon and the rope caught on the trigger. Gilliam was 49 on that fateful day of March 20, 1848, a native of North Carolina, a lay Baptist preacher, brave and forceful, holding more prejudices against Catholics than against Indians.

In any event the white men and the settlement headed by a weak government based at Oregon

City, were not to capture the killers of Marcus Whitman. The guilty ones were known and they fled to the Snake River country. But a few months later, when Oregon had achieved territorial status and some soldiers were sent to support it, it was able to keep the Cayuses from their land and to make it so uncomfortable for the Indians that the tribal chiefs persuaded five of their number, Tilouyaikt, Tamahas, Klokamas, Isaiachalakis and Kiamasumkin to surrender to officers at The Dalles and stand trial. They were found guilty and hanged June 3, 1849 at Oregon City.

Thus Morrow County had a part in the history of one of Oregon's early Indian wars, although a small part. Indians did not frequent the northern part of Morrow County, for the quality of grass was not to be relied on for horse feed. The trail across Morrow County made by the emigrants was the only one known; the Indians preferred the better grassed and better watered country nearer the mountains.

THE CAYUSE WAR

If the Whitman massacre is to be considered a victory for the Cayuse tribe it was the last one it ever had for the repressions put upon them by the whites and the execution of five prominent members of the tribe reduced their standing among the Indians of the area between the Rocky Mountains and the Cascades until they were no longer of military importance. In fact, the Cayuses were never a large tribe, their natural pugnacity not making them attractive to more peaceable Indians.

The territory of Oregon, now with some taxing power and a workable government, even though its chief officers were appointed from Washington, was interested in preventing any other outbreaks. The Whitman massacre, scared the boots off the residents of the Willamette Valley, every one of whom had some reason to fear Indians, most having been scared at least once in crossing the plains or having trapped and hunted among them. There were probably no more than 12,000 inhabitants scattered among the trees between the Columbia River and the Rogue and a determined band of Indians could have massacred a sizeable number of the residents of Jacksonville, Salem or even Portland, where the bewhiskered citizens were still arguing about what to call their little settlement among the big trees.

That was a reason for Oregon to become involved when Kamiakin, the most important chief the Yakimas produced, began making trouble in 1855.

When Territorial Governor and Indian Agent for Washington, Isaac I. Stevens, was negotiating a treaty to put the Indians on reservations there was a big argument going. The whites had built a sort of road from the juncture of the Snake and Columbia Rivers to Steilacoom on Puget Sound and emigrants passed over it during the fall, which irritated Kamiakin, who didn't want anyone crossing the land of the Yakima "nation" without his consent.

Federal troops were stationed at a rather elegant army post at The Dalles and a portion of them were dispatched to Yakima to build Fort Simcoe, which in architectural splendor rivalled the base in The Dalles, both sets of buildings having been designed by Louis Scholl. Fort Simcoe proved rather useless, Kamiakin having been killed shortly after it was built and Father Wilbur arrived to talk the remainder of the tribe out of their combativeness.

The Oregon Mounted Volunteers was a rather fancy name for a group of citizens who volunteered to fight for a few months and who generally furnished their own horses and guns. The officers were nearly all politicians, the custom being that if a man recruited enough men for a company, he could be a captain, and if enough for a regiment, he could be a colonel.

Colonel James A. Nesmith was the leader getting his appointment from Governor George L. Currey. James K. Kelly was Lieutenant Colonel and also a politician.

The Oregon Mounted Volunteers were sent in the winter of 1855 to establish a camp along the Umatilla River as a sort of warning to Peu-Peu-Mox-Mox that he should not join his little band of Walla Wallas with Kamiakin's powerful Yakimas.

The scattered conflict was called the Cayuse War, although it was a series of skirmishes with no major battle. The Walla Walla River and the Umatilla River reach the Columbia a comparatively short distance apart and the two valleys are divided by low ridges, making it possible for troops stationed on the Umatilla to watch Indians on the Walla Walla without much difficulty.

The Oregon Mounted Volunteers reached the

15

Umatilla at what is now Echo and established a camp, naming it Henrietta in honor of Mrs. Granville O. Haller of the U. S. Army, a popular officer, husband of a more popular wife it seems. It wasn't much of a fort, being constructed by erecting split cottonwoods about nine feet long and tamping them into a two-foot trench dug in a square. Buildings were erected within this enclosure for officers' quarters and to protect the men. It was never much of a fort, but did serve as headquarters for troops that raided Indian villages beyond Wallula (Fort Walla Walla) and did capture Peu-Peu-Mox-Mox on the Touchet River and killed him when he attempted to escape some time later. His death is one of the most disputed stories of Indian warfare. The fact was that Peu-Peu-Mox-Mox had sufficient reason to dislike all whites and was really a rather conciliatory chief. He was killed while a prisoner and at least partially bound and the whites added nothing to their boast of superior civilization by cutting off his ears for souvenirs.

Fort Henrietta's value was that it kept the weak territory in an aggressive posture toward the Indians and provided a base for watching them. The soldiers got about the country, hunting horses (which the Indians continually stole) or chasing deer or just riding around on what soldiers in that day called a "scout", which meant that they went out looking, not especially for trouble but equipped to handle it if accosted. The men at Fort Henrietta were interested in the Walla Walla valley and paid small attention to Morrow County other than to ride out Butter and Birch Creeks with regularity.

In 1859 W. D. Ponder, 1st Lieutenant of the 1st Dragoons, Washington Territorial Volunteers, stationed at Fort Walla Walla, made several rides as far west as Rock Creek and close to the mountains to spy out the terrain and discover Indian trails. It was the custom of the Indians to go into the mountains hunting in the fall, just as white brethren do today and Ponder accosted them, although picking no quarrel. The Indians told him that white men had a bunch of cattle on little Butter Creek which substantiates the story that drovers, probably from Texas, had moved cattle onto the tall grass of Morrow County well before 1860.

The country would have been settled anyway even if another occurrence had not put speed into the operation.

Morrow County residents have always enjoyed the Blue Mountains right at their back door. In earliest times citizens went out on the creeks for fish and hardly an able bodied man lets the hunting season go by without one weekend spent in search of deer. Winter sports are getting into stride in recent years and this cabin at Cutsforth Park on upper Willow Creek is a permanent cabin to house hunters and skiers. (Courtesy Orville Cutsforth)

GOLD

Gold was discovered in Idaho in the late fifties and all of northern California was still in a sort of hysteria over gold in that state. The earliest emigrants to Oregon had been under the trees on their donation land claims in the Willamette Valley for almost twenty years, long enough to build up some sizeable herds of cattle, bands of sheep and most important of all, some young men anxious to start out for themselves. Pioneers, it must be recognized, could raise a son to the age of self-responsibility in fifteen years instead of the twenty-five it takes now. They were at an excitable age.

Parties of gold seekers began walking across the mountains on the trails discovered by trappers and hunters and one such party on June 7, 1862, found gold in Canyon Creek, a tributary of the main stream of the John Day River. When the news reached the rather staid setttlements in the Willamette Valley other parties set out to hunt for gold. There were some who went alone, bold ones with no fear of marauding Snakes or those with sufficient confidence to presume enough discretion to evade them.

The Canyon Creek gold had been found in black sand and a creek with black sand was looked for, a shovel was the tool used instead of a pick. The prospectors, whether in a party or alone, often came up the Columbia River to The Dalles on the little river steamers. From there they knew they had to turn south off the emigrant road to reach the gold fields of the John Day.

There were no roads, nor even trails, leading to that Golconda. Army explorers had marked a trail diagonally across present Sherman County to reach the John Day River near Bridge Creek and some took this route. Others crossed the John Day at the Emigrant crossing at the mouth of Grass Valley canyon and went up Rock Creek, by which route they reached the top of the divide around Hardman as a way to the north fork of the John Day. Some went east to Willow Creek and if they took the right hand stream at the juncture of Rhea Creek and Willow Creek, found themselves on the same trail as if they had gone up Rock Creek, but an easier one. Some went all the way to the moun-

tains on Willow Creek and had a steep climb to reach the summit. Some went all the way to Butter Creek before turning south and they, too, found the going pretty rugged before they reached the top of the Blue Mountains that divides present day Morrow County. Those who went on to Umatilla Landing were probably bound for the Idaho mines, for Umatilla Landing was the taking-off point for the diggings there.

These were the northern entrances to the John Day country in the early sixties. Men didn't often strike off across country; nearly all had a map of some sort, the location of water was often marked on them and water was something they had to have. They stayed on the creeks. These prospectors often walked and led a pack animal and both required frequent water to survive. There were no roads for wheeled vehicles until venturesome packers took wagons from The Dalles to Canyon City over a route that eventually became The Dalles Military Road by official dedication in June of 1869.

The road from The Dalles to the Canyon City gold diggings was traveled by pack trains as soon as there was demand for supplies by the miners who were working there. Merchants hired pack train owners and men who owned a string of mules bought goods on their own and set off for the settlements to peddle their goods at a neat profit. The presence of Indians—unhindered by soldiers who were off fighting the Civil War—made packing a risky occupation, but there were scores of pack train operators who were not afraid.

The men who came to the mines were true pioneers and they did the early exploring in eastern Oregon. When they returned to their homes in the Willamette Valley after a few months of gold seeking, they told of the tall grass on the hills, the narrow and fertile creek bottoms and the absence of heavy timber. Some of the young men did not return to the valley but settled on some likely looking creek to start a new life.

Early Oregon emigrants were originally from the prairie states and had difficulty getting used to the tall trees of the wetter parts of their new state, so in the early sixties some of them drove their herds

Left: On a cold day a man approaches the old Heppner Flouring mill and poses beneath the spillway. Water to power the mill came along the hill from Willow Creek. (Courtesy Mrs. Frank Barclay)

Below: W. J. Leezer came up from Umatilla Landing to start a tin shop and hardware store and this picture would indicate that it was on the southwest corner of Main and Willow. This would have been in the 1880s. (Courtesy Morrow County Museum)

of cattle and sheep across the mountains in search of a drier and more grassy range. Word of grass spread as quickly as did word of gold.

A. S. Wells, who made a trip through present Morrow County in 1858 and came again in 1864 with a pack train, reported that John Jordan had a cabin at the forks of Rhea and Willow Creeks. He stayed long enough to have the location named for him and an early name for Rhea Creek was Jordan. T. W. Ayres and his brother were located on Butter Creek, A. J. Breden was on Willow Creek a little above the mouth of Clark's canyon where Oscar Clark had settled. William Y. Cecil was at the emigrant crossing of Willow Creek. Some of these men undoubtedly had cattle, although the horse business was a better one in the 1860s because there wasn't much demand for cattle. They could be driven to California where there was a growing population in need of meat, but in Oregon nearly everyone raised his own. There was a better demand for horses, especially if broken to ride or pack. And then a horse would take care of himself better in the winter, could range farther for grass or water. Another way to make money was to feed miners who were traveling all over the country.

Generally the men who were in Eastern Oregon in the early sixties had no intention of settling on land. They came for gold or grass. The gold seekers panned the sand along every creek and moved on to the next sandy bar, keeping out of sight of Indians, searching for treasure; the herdsmen moved less frequently but did drive their horses or cattle to different grass as soon as an area began to show the effects of grazing. Both gold and grass were free, that is, belonged to the government, which put no restrictions on their use or appropriation.

After the Civil War the government began to do something about the Indians who had been raiding the camps of prospectors and burning the homes of settlers without federal opposition. Army camps were established in favorable meadows and the excuse given for construction of The Dalles Military Road was to service these camps. A few battles were fought between Indians and soldiers, but no sizable forces were involved. Indians did not like to fight in large numbers, lacking organization, and there were never many soldiers. The Indians were gradually put on reservations, the Warm Springs reservation in Wasco County shortly after the treaty of 1855 between Joel Palmer and the tribes in that area, and by 1868, General George Crook had the Snakes and Paiutes corralled on reser-

vations in Harney and Malheur Counties, the latter on a reservation at another Warm Springs on the upper Malheur River.

A few men had already brought women to Eastern Oregon, but it was mostly a man's land. The federal government, in accordance with the wishes of Abraham Lincoln, had passed the homestead act which made it possible for the head of a household to get a quarter section of land by merely living on it for five years and doing some fencing and house-building. This made the grass lands attractive to a different class of people: farmers, men who wanted to use the land for different crops than the native grass. There were really few men of this class until after the railroad came in 1883.

By that time the grass of Morrow County was being harvested by cattle and sheep. A Texan named Menefee brought cattle from that state and established a camp on Birch Creek sometime in the sixties and G. W. Shippey had some Shorthorns on Willow Creek. Dol Reed and James Robinson were the names of other early stockmen with cattle or horses. There were undoubtedly others whose names are not recorded because they did not stay long enough. Early stockmen were rovers.

Among those who came in the sixties and remained to make an impression were Amanuel Pettys who came in 1868 and C. A. Rhea, who settled on the creek that still bears his name, in 1864. George Vinson settled on little Butter Creek in that decade and a couple of other men came to Big Butter Creek. They were John Vinson, who ran a store and sometimes a postoffice at the place named for him and John H. French, who came from California to settle just above Vinson in 1869. Neither were technically residents of Morrow County but each had an influence on it.

Albert Wright came in the 1870s and established himself on upper Rhea Creek and raised a family of boys and girls that are still represented in affairs of Morrow County. Benjamin Parker, eventually the owner of Parker's mill, came in 1876, early enough to saw the lumber for the homestead cabins of the Eightmile and Gooseberry section as well as many buildings in Heppner.

Thomas Morgan was an ex-stage coach driver who settled on Rhea Creek and married a Rhea girl. He filled many public offices, being one in whom the people reposed confidence. Ellis Minor was a butcher, hotel keeper, livery stable owner and father of a distinguished brood.

Ed Day was an early sheepman who was interested in improving the native strains by importing

Early day riders were—or appeared to be—a part of the horse as does Art Minor when settled into his deep saddle on a favorite horse. In 1922 Minor wrote a few lines expressing his appreciation of the old timers of the consolidated picture:

"These pioneers who left their fathers' homes; their native sod, from man had lived apart.
They blazed the way to a land untrod and there with nature lived heart to heart,
In a little cabin built of logs, chinked in, and with sod and dirt covered o'er.
A fireplace for a stove, one sliding window, and oft they used the earth for a floor.

Oh, how these pioneers they would weep; the life blood quickens in their veins,
Could they see these bleak and barren hillsides.
Oh, these grainless barren, barren plains.

Weep not for things past and gone, but bid the cowboy and things of his day adieu,
For when the latchstring it was severed the west and the spirit of the west went too."

Delaine bucks to cross with the Merino ewes. For years he had a ready sale of purebred sheep. Joe Mason settled on Rhea Creek in 1871 and went to raising wheat and alfalfa. His origin was in Portugal and he was the father of the well-known Bert Mason, merchant of Ione. Peter Borg came from Sweden and learned the jewelry trade which he practiced successfully in the frontier town of Heppner until he retired and left the business to his youngest son, Oscar.

George Noble was a German who left his native land to venture into a new one. He finished his apprenticeship as harness maker in time to serve in the Civil War, then came west. He took land in Morrow County in 1872 and bought cattle but soon went to making saddles and serving in public office. Black Horse James G. Doherty was a native of County Donegal who preferred to raise wheat rather than sheep as did most of his countrymen.

J. Crockett Kirk settled in Sanford Canyon in 1870 and in his elder years became a resident of Heppner where he was in business. Henry C. Gay was a Rhea Creek sheepman who was the first state representative from the then new Morrow County, succeeding Jackson Morrow in 1886.

Mike Kenny was from County Leitrim as were many of the Morrow County Irish and Mike was both sheepman and wheat farmer who helped many young micks get a start.

Sterling P. Florence ran his stock from upper Willow Creek to the Columbia River in the days before fences. William Y. Cecil was a kindly Englishman who lived on the Oregon Trail early enough to see covered wagons pass his door. The Hynd family was close by—and over in Sand Hollow as well—natives of Scotland who had long lived in England. There was a great brood of them, William, Thomas, Annie, Charley, Jennie, Jack, David, Margaret, to say nothing of Cousin Bob who was the original partner of W. B. Barrett, another Englishman in lower Sand Hollow.

Orin E. Farnsworth came from New Hampshire in 1874 and hauled his wool to The Dalles before the railroad came. David Hardman settled just a little east of the town that, after long experiment with less conservative names, was finally named for him.

There were many more who came early and stayed to be planted on the hill above town: Frank Gilliam, Thomas Matlock, Julius Keithly, Henry Padberg, a German who settled in Rhea Creek on land still owned by the family. And mention should be made of Charles Cunningham, an Irishman whose residence was mainly Umatilla County but who was a factor in Morrow County life.

If one wants to debate about who was the first sheepman in the county he will find plenty of adherants of several men. William Penland was near Lexington in 1870 with sheep and John Davis, Milton Hale, K. Lemons and Joseph Crook had some. In real early days sheep were poisoned around Eightmile, probably by a weed.

TRANSPORTATION — COMMUNICATION

The transportation and communication routes in Eastern Oregon were few in the early sixties, even after gold was discovered in Idaho, Baker and Grant Counties in Oregon. The Oregon Trail was still used by a decreasing number of emigrants, there were river boats on the Columbia plying from Si Smith's boat landing just below the mouth of the Deschutes River to Umatilla Landing. This was the principal shipping point to Idaho and Baker County and packers daily loaded strings of horses and mules for the Idaho and Baker County mines. The prices were too high for any but the enthusiastic to pay and some preferred to go overland at the cost of time.

The Canyon City mining settlement was served by the road from The Dalles to that place which, after 1869, had an official designation, although the idea for it emanated from a group of enterprising men in The Dalles who obtained every alternate section of land of a six-mile strip from that city on the Columbia to a point on the Snake River opposite Fort Boise, almost 600,000 acres.

There were similar military roads from Albany and Eugene ending at the same place and there was a well-used pack trail from Red Bluff, California to the Idaho mines.

A postoffice had been established at Oregon City in 1847 and in 1849 both Salem and Portland obtained a postoffice. There had been a postoffice on the Oregon Trail at Umatilla as early as 1851 but only for a few months. By 1863 it was at Umatilla Landing. Wascopum (The Dalles) had a postoffice in 1853.

In 1867 Daniel G. Leonard obtained a postoffice for Scotts, his stopping place on the east side of the John Day River on the Oregon Trail and that year also, James Rast had a postoffice at Cecils, or more appropriately Cecil, for it was the home of William Y. Cecil, who had lived there since 1862. There was, of course, a postoffice at Canyon City in 1864, to serve the miners of that camp. The progression of settlement can be traced by postoffices as well as by the roads but the record of postoffices has been better kept.

The young men who had gone to the mines began drifting back to their homes in the Willamette Valley, some afoot and bedraggled and some with a saddle horse and maybe a pack mule and a buckskin sack of gold around their middles. They were farm boys (who wasn't in 1860?), farmers at heart and when they found an attractive bit of meadow they were tempted to stay right there and squat on it. If they had heard of the homestead act which Abraham Lincoln had advocated in his campaign and had gotten passed in 1862, they could look forward to permanent ownership.

Because settlers, mostly from the valley, were coming to claim a home in the meadows, the lines of communication were changed to accommodate their needs. They didn't settle along the Oregon Trail in Morrow County; there was nothing there to attract a settler, not then, not now.

By 1872 Amanuel Pettys, who had settled near John Jordan at the confluence of Willow and Rhea Creeks, obtained a postoffice which he named Willow Forks. The date was June 3. Pettys often had to ride a horse to Scotts to get his packet of mail. The route from Willow Forks east was first to Acton on Butter Creek, but soon there were enough settlers to cause the mail carriers, whether pack train operators, as at first, or stages, which came later, to go on up to Willow Creek, thence up Hinton Creek to Vinson on Big Butter Creek, which had been designated as a postoffice on the same day as Pettys had been so honored. From Vinson the trail led to Pilot Rock which had had a postoffice since late in 1868 and from there north to Pendleton (earlier called Marshall) where a postoffice had been established in 1865.

The government land office, responsive to the evidences of settlement had surveyed the township at

Amanuel Pettys settled at the juncture of Willow Creek and Rhea Creek and obtained a postoffice called Willow Forks. He often rode to the stage crossing on the John Day for his packet of mail. (Courtesy of his daughter, Mrs. Edith Nichoson)

the juncture of Willow and Rhea Creeks in June, 1859, and in October of 1860, had surveyed the township where big and little Butter Creeks join. By 1867, eight years later, the flat where Hinton Creek comes into Willow was surveyed. By that time surveying had become general, not only the bottoms where men were living, but out on the bunchgrass hills.

The nation was recovering from the Civil War, Southerners were moving from their war-torn country to the promising West and men of the North were paying attention to the attractions presented in letters from relatives who had gone West over the Oregon Trail. As for Morrow County it had attracted families from the Willamette Valley who had been unimpressed with the desert they had crossed a generation before. Cattle and horses dotted the hills of Morrow and families could be found beside nearly every creek.

WHY STANSBURY FLAT?

With postoffices established at Willow Forks and at Vinson on Butter Creek one of these seemed certain to become the metropolis of the new territory. Each had advantages, although Vinson was in a narrow part of Butter Creek. Willow Forks had many advantages as a townsite. Something other than nature must have intervened to make the flat at Hinton and Willow Creeks the most populous place in Morrow County.

George H. Stansbury was designated as postmaster at Vinson when that office was established on that June, 1872, the same day Amanuel Pettys became postmaster at Willow Forks. On February 3, 1873, Stansbury was reappointed postmaster and the location of the office was given as Stansbury Flat.

Stansbury had obtained the claim of a squatter named David Estes who had a cabin south of present May street and just west of Willow Creek in Heppner and had filed a declaration of intent to purchase the W½NW¼ and the NW¼SW¼ of Section 35 and the SW¼SW¼ of Section 26 in Township 2 South, Range 26 East Willamette Meridian. He filed that declaration on April 24, 1870. That was almost two years before he had been appointed postmaster at Butter Creek.

Somebody had a hand in all this. It may have been Tom or Mike Quaid, two Irish boys who had a ranch on Balm Fork where August Mallory, himself a possible manipulator, had also settled. Mike Quaid was killed by a horse in 1874, so his abilities as a mover of public affairs has never been appraised. Stansbury displayed no inclinations as a mover and shaper of events. However there was a human mind involved. It could have been Frank Maddock's.

Before Stansbury moved "his" postoffice, with or without knowledge or consent of the federal government, someone had persuaded Henry Heppner and Jackson Lee Morrow to move down to Stansbury Flat and build a store building. The few stockmen settled on Willow Creek, Balm Fork and Rhea Creek were probably not more than twenty-five in number but their wants were extensive. They had to haul their supplies from Umatilla Landing or from Castle Rock, a location on the Columbia above the mouth of Six Mile Canyon, where river boats would stop and unload freight. These men wanted a store to take over the job of bringing in supplies and distributing them.

Henry Heppner was born at Pleschen in Posen province in German into a Jewish family. In America he had worked for merchants in California and

For almost half a century sheep provided the economic lifeblood of Morrow County, sheep scattered and grazing; sheep being separated in corrals; sheep being driven to the mountains by the thousands; and a more modern version after the feed was thinned. (Courtesy Shirley Rugg)

had at one time operated a pack train of mules out of The Dalles and out of Umatilla Landing. Tom Quaid had also packed out of Umatilla Landing as had probably another and older brother, who signed his name frequently on the register of the City Hotel in Heppner as Patt Quaid. Mike Quaid was listed as a mule packer in the 1870 census. Heppner had a contract making sacks for a flour mill in LaGrande and Jackson Morrow was running a store there when accosted by the promoter of Stansbury Flat.

After Morrow had looked over the site at Stansbury Flat he went back to LaGrande and with Heppner decided to speculate on a store in the new location. Heppner went off to buy goods and Morrow came to put up a building. It was on the northeast corner of what became Main and May Streets. Lumber was hauled from Van Armen's mill at the head of Butter Creek. There was a big celebration on August 10, 1872, when the store was finished, with stockmen from the surrounding creeks dancing, shouting and perhaps drinking to the success of the new venture.

Jackson Lee Morrow was an excellent man to operate a pioneer store. He was born in Kentucky and married to a girl from Indiana. They had crossed the plains in 1853, going to Olympia, Washington, where they had entered the mercantile business. He was a lieutenant-colonel on the territorial governor's staff in the Indian disturbances of 1855-56. Then in 1863 he moved to LaGrande, Oregon, still a merchant. Here he was elected county treasurer; Morrow never had any trouble getting elected to office. He was a pleasant and popular man, ever obliging, always helpful.

Henry Heppner was different. He was 5′ 6″, a 150-pound bundle of mental energy, always planning the next move. More than anyone else he shaped the destinies of Heppner and the unknown manipulators of his coming could not have done better. People loved Jackson Morrow; they respected Henry Heppner.

Who were these celebrants who christened the new store on Stansbury Flat? The census of Umatilla County for 1870 was brief, there being but four precincts in the entire county and what is now Morrow County had few pages of that. Noted was Thomas Scott, 50, who lived on the John Day River; John H. French, 36, and wife Annie, 19, and two children living on Butter Creek; Joseph Vey, 21, listed as a farmer; George H. Stansbury, 37, who called himself a farmer, being owner of $300 in real property and $1800 in personal effects, with his wife, Elizabeth, 24, and two daughters; David Anderson, who had homesteaded the southeast quarter of Section 35, just south of present day Heppner; Hugh Fields, 44, who claimed $12,000 in stock; Frank Maddock, 34, who was listed as owner of $2500 in land and $10,000 in stock with his wife, Lucy, 24, and four children; Peter Saling, 39, William Penland, 31, who had settled at Lexington with his wife, Jane, 27, and said he was a farmer, although he later was the biggest sheep man in the county; Amanuel Pettys, 36, farmer; John Shipley, 42, who told the census taker he was a saddletree maker; John Jordan, 39, a farmer; John S. Vinson, 61, a farmer.

The fact is there wasn't a farmer in the lot. Probably every head of a household raised a few crops on his land, but grass grew on the creek bottoms by nature's hand and the income was from stock, and there wasn't much of that nor much of a market for what there was. It was not until 1874 that Joseph Glidden obtained a patent on the manufacture of barbed wire. Before that land was fenced with poles or with rock. Cattle and sheep ran at large and tilling the soil—the occupation of a farmer—was difficult without the possibility of enclosures more convenient than poles or rocks. There were others in the vicinity, the Rheas on the creek named for them, William and Thomas Ayres, Thomas Matlock, Elisha Sperry, David Herren, Ellis Minor, William Cecil, down the creek, George Noble and S. P. Florence may have been there for the celebration.

From then on the settlement on Stansbury Flat grew rapidly. Before the year was out it had been named for Henry Heppner, a suggestion, it is said, that came from Jackson Morrow. An old history says that Stansbury would have called it Willow Creek or Willows; a bibulous few would have named it IXL, that being from the label of a popular elixer found on the shelves at Heppner & Morrow's store and Perry Oller liked New Chicago in anticipation of a future as a livestock and commercial center.

The postoffice was established after its move without benefit of legality from Butter Creek. Tay-

lor Spencer came in from Rhea Creek to open a store and that fall Allan J. Shobe, a physician, with an inclination to do almost anything else, moved in to promptly have the canyon running into town from the southwest named for him. He was induced to start a drug store and Heppner & Morrow let him have their stock of drugs, including, presumably the bottles of IXL.

O. H. Hallock had started to do blacksmith work, that necessity of all pioneer communities, and Bishop Chase and George Stewart set up a similar shop. Things were booming for it was a long way to Umatilla Landing or Castle Rock and enterprising merchants and tradesmen were trying to furnish the stockmen with their wants.

By 1875 there were enough children to make a school desirable. Henry Heppner rode around the community on a cayuse to solicit funds and Nelson Jones contributed the remainder so that Henry Johnson, carpenter, could go to work. The building was put up on Gale Street, barely a block from the store. Henry Heppner furnished the bell.

Dishaway and Sanford opened a saloon in a building erected with lumber hauled from Umatilla Landing and Henry Heppner and Frank Maddock bought the stock of goods left by Taylor Spencer when he died. Thus Heppner was in competition with the original store. Actually the partnership of Heppner & Morrow lasted a comparatively short time. Morrow was a shopkeeper, having done that nearly all his life. Heppner was a trader, a dealer, who preferred to handle money rather than goods. He did not care for ownership of property; he liked to get commissions for the handling of other people's property. Thus he became a dealer in wool, hides, the equipment necessary to the sheep business, the warehouseman. Well-liked Jackson Morrow could deal with the general public.

Since the town of Heppner was growing and there was evidence that it might be permanent it seemed to the citizens that some order might be advisable. Stansbury was willing. Although the land had been surveyed in 1867 the surveyor's marks were not discovered by the town planners with the result that Main Street runs a little east of true north. But whoever was responsible, Heppner citizens to this day may be happy that Main Street was made 100 feet wide. Other streets are 60 feet wide. Blocks are 330 by 264 feet and each of the ten lots in a block are 66 by 132. The town doesn't exactly fit the map in another regard: the line between Sections 26 and 35 is about midway between Baltimore and

Church Streets. But these things are disturbing to few but the title men.

A Declaration of Intent to purchase gave considerable leeway to the declarer. As early as October 23, 1875 Stansbury deeded the west half of Block 5 to Dr. Shobe which gave the doctor control of the mouth of the canyon named for him. He paid $100 and in the next January deeded a 50 x 150 foot plot to A. J. Breeding for $200 indicating that the price of real estate in the new town was booming or that George Stansbury was a little of touch with affairs. Even by the next March he sold Lot 1 in Block 6 (where the Chevrolet Garage now is) for $25, this to J. D. Dishaway when he was fixing to put in his saloon.

From then on Mr. Stansbury furnished steady business to O. H. Hallock and Frank Maddock, the town's notaries public, by selling lots. Henry Heppner and Frank Maddock had bought Lot 5 in Block 3 (the bank corner), and Frank Goble and Perry Oller bought land on which to erect a hotel. Issac H. Chase, Dave Herren, John Gilmore, Abraham A. Wells bought business or residence lots. Then Mr. Stansbury decided to end it all by selling the remainder of his claim to Thomas W. Ayres who moved in from lower Butter Creek and with the Ayers money in his pocket Stansbury deposited the money in the land office to settle his Declaration of Intent. This on March 20, 1878.

The 1870s were years of growth for Umatilla County which included Morrow. The population increased from 2916 to 9614. The value of products had risen from $514,816 to $958,965. Number of horses from 13,712 to 16,905 and by 1880 there were 28,588 head of cattle in Umatilla County. Sheep had increased from 29,960 to 291,477 and in 1880 30,937 acres of wheat was grown, not much of it in Morrow County. The market was strictly local and it was used for feed and seed.

By 1880 Heppner counted 318 persons in the town, unofficially, the boundaries being just what the census taker wanted to include. From census figures and information in a directory printed by George Himes and distributed by J. K. Gill it is possible to know something about the town.

There was a Baptist Church which held meetings once a month and oftener if preachers came by. Rev. Roscoe Oglesby was often pastor. There was a Masonic Lodge that met once a month. Thomas Ayres had a livery stable, J. P. Bushee, the Western Hotel and probably by that time he was the Wells-Fargo agent, succeeding Jackson Morrow. There was a flouring mill that had been started by a man named Beagle who had built a mill race from Willow Creek above town alongside the east hill to a point west of the present hospital, and down the hill to give power to turn a mill wheel. Stansbury granted him the right-of-way in payment for the right to irrigate. Dennis & Hewison were the operators. This mill was later owned by Elijah Sperry. J. G. Gilmore owned the City Hotel, Hall Brothers were blacksmiths. O. H. Hallock was postmaster and druggist, J. D. Locknane was constable and operator of a variety store and Minor and Theodore also has a variety store. Kirk and Basey were harness makers. General merchandise stores were run by Henry Heppner, Dave Herren, Maddock & Bishop, Morrow & Son. C. W. Mallory had a drug store and McKinnon & Co. were blacksmiths. W. J. Leezer had moved up from Umatilla Landing to open a store where he sold stoves and tinware. Mrs. William Warren, the stone mason's wife, sold millinery and Dr. Shobe ran a livery stable. P. O. Borg had arrived from Sweden to start a jewelry store late in 1880. There were four saloons with Hawker & Munkers, William Kathan, Matlock Brothers and G. W. Swaggart as proprietors. S. Parker Garrigues and Julius Keithly were sawing lumber in a little mill. Matthew Lichtenthal was making boots and shoes. Andrew J. Stevenson owned a producing brewery, Ellis Minor was listed as a butcher. Of physicians there were Eugene R. Swinburne, Alfred Kinney and Lewis Shipley. James Roberts, a young man of 25, listed his occupation as "gaming" and there may have been enough gambling in early Heppner to provide a professional with an income. Chinese natives cooked in the hotels and operated laundries.

An oddity in this day is that nearly all of these men moved from one occupation to another as opportunity presented; stockraisers became merchants, Thomas Ayres made some money on Butter Creek raising cows, bought the townsite of Heppner and ran a livery stable. J. D. Locknane had a variety store, a grocery before starting the Belvedere Saloon, which literally means "beautiful view" and we wonder if Mr. Locknane intended the interpretation.

The 1880 census shows conclusively that the occupation of the producers of the county was stock raising and certainly sheep were the predominating stock. Columbus Rhea, Albert Wright, O. T. Douglas, William Penland, who already had extensive bands, John Alex Thompson and Daniel Boone Mulkey were sheep men of consequence. One of the stimulants to the sheep industry was that Mon-

Sheep in the mountains corralled in a flat. Sheep were Morrow County life blood in the 1880s and 90s.

tana was getting into the production of wool and the practice of trailing sheep east from Oregon was getting started. It lasted for over 15 years and provided a market for sheep not otherwise possible.

Crews were working along the Columbia River for Henry Villard and his company, constructing the railroad grade for the steam train, the Oregon Short Line, that would be connected to Portland in 1884 by completion of the Huntington section.

It was quite a town and the stockmen who had arranged to get it started must have been elated. By modern standards the income from livestock and what little farming could be done was grossly insufficient to support so many tradesmen and retailers. But many of the residents had brought money with them and there was an abundance of hope. Hope may not do much for the stomach but it is wonderful to inspire the spirit. It was not until 1880 that John Royse began claiming that he grew the first wheat in Morrow County on a homestead west of Hardman.

26

THE BIG SCARE

The year 1878 is memorable in Heppner and Morrow County history because it was the year of the big scare. The Bannack Indians in southern Idaho were a part of the Shoshone tribe; they were adept at plunder. On their reservation they had a flat or prairie where camas grew plentifully and the Indians went there annually to dig it for a sort of bread, but the white men, probably with the connivance of the agent were using the prairie for hogs that dug the camas root. The Bannacks protested without avail.

It was a similar situation to that which prevailed the year before when the Nez Perce Indians objected to white men moving into the Wallowa Valley against the provisions of the treaty some of them had duly signed with the government.

Maybe it was these reasons, maybe it was one of those things not calculated by man's time clocks, like the sprouting of seeds, the rebellion of wives, the changing of voters registration, the warpath time of Indians. Buffalo Horn was chief of the Bannacks, having succeeded Pokatello some years previously. He had been scout for General O. O. Howard during the Nez Perce campaign and the next spring thought it was time for a little action.

The Bannacks had murdered one Alex Rhoden in November of 1877 and when the murderer, Tambiago, was executed the tribesmen were nervous and a little trigger happy—and worst of all they had triggers, having obtained them by some of several means possible to them. There is a story about all of them.

At Battle Creek, near Silver City, Idaho, the Bannacks met a party under Captain J. B. Harper and PiUte Joe, a scout, said he killed Buffalo Horn. However, the Bannacks moved on across the Oregon border stealing and marauding in pretty fair order for Indians, which causes this writer to think that PiUte Joe was boasting and the braves had the leadership of Buffalo Horn.

The Paiutes were on the Warm Springs reservation on the Malheur River and were getting along pretty well until Samuel Parrish, the agent, was replaced by W. V. Rinehart. The Indians didn't like him. Leader of the Warm Spring Paiutes was Ehegante (Egan) a Cayuse who had been adopted by the Paiute chief. He was thus a brother-in-law

of Lee Winnemucca, son of the big chief of the Paiutes. He had won his position by marriage, not by demonstrated ability. Nevertheless several writers credit Egan with being a pretty good Indian on a hunting party and he was probably shamed into going to war by being called the Indian equivalent of "chicken."

He led the young Paiute braves into the Steens Mountain country where they stole many cattle and horses, burned the Smyth home with two men in it, raided the Pete French ranch at Diamond swamp and killed a Chinaman and some white men who were alone.

The theory that northwest Indians were in collusion to start a big general war and wipe out the whites once and for all had often been advanced, but the Bannack-Paiute war of 1878 was really an uprising in the Indian fashion, without preparation, without supplies, a spur of the moment uprising fitting no sensible timetable.

Captain Reuben Frank Bernard of the First Cavalry, together with Orlando (Rube) Robbins and his scouts (mostly from Arizona) caught up with the Indians at Silver Creek between Camp Curry and Harney Lake on Sunday morning, June 23 and fought the first serious battle of the war. Both claimed victory but it was the Indians that moved, going up Silver Creek to present Izee and on north across a wide pass in the Blue Mountains to come down into the main bed of the John Day River between Dayville and Canyon City. This was the main body of Indians; little bands broke off right and left to burn and destroy at will as they moved through the mountains and encountered sheepherders and isolated stockmen.

The settlers from the John Day to Wild Horse were scared; some left forthwith for The Dalles, some went to Pendleton. Men came home from looking after stock and found the home place deserted and appearing as if the Indians had already been there.

The apparent plan of General Howard was to drive the Indians toward the Columbia River and get them into some open country where they could be defeated. This did not suit the settlers. Howard did catch up with the Indians on Birch Creek, after a party of volunteers from Pendleton had fought

27

and retreated from Willow Springs after suffering several casualties. Bernard had a Gatling gun which fired more rapidly than did the muskets and he maneuvered this into position on the slopes of Battle Mountain and drove the Indians back south over the hill with serious losses. Howard then decided that the hostiles would move on northeast and cross the Snake River. He did not want to pursue them over the trail made by the Nez Perce the year before so moved with a few companies of infantry and some artillery to the mouth of the Grande Ronde where he awaited them.

The Indians, instead, raided the agency, five miles above Pendleton and burned many of the buildings. One account said they found a barrel of whiskey in a freighter's wagon and had a big celebration. In a day or so the soldiers under Captain Evan Miles fought the Indians near the Agency and drove them on farther east.

The role of the Umatillas (Cayuses) was important and completely dishonest. Umapine was chief of the Cayuse scouts; he tried to deal with Miles as a possible ally and at the same time was dickering with Egan about joining the Indians against the whites. Buffalo Horn was undoubtedly dead at this time, having either been killed by PiUte Joe or in the battle at Silver Creek. Umapine had done something for which the whites were going to punish him which was another reason he was playing the middle against both ends. By July 15 he had made his decision, having decided that the soldiers would win.

Therefore, according to an account in The Oregonian of July 20, 1878, he went with about 40 of his tribe to the Paiute-Bannack camp near Meacham and called Egan out beyond rifle fire for another parley. Here the chief was seized and told he would be taken to the Bostons (whites). He resisted and was killed along with four others of the Malheur Paiutes. They took his scalp to Captain Miles who found it insufficient evidence on which to believe Umapine so they went back and brought Egan's head and right arm that had been wounded at Silver Creek. That was apparently enough and Umapine was forgiven and allowed to return to his reservation and his position.

But when the Indians were scouting around Birch Creek the excitement was great in Heppner for Birch Creek was but a few miles from the Butter Creek postoffice (which had been re-established) and isolated sheep and cattlemen had been killed in the mountains closer to Heppner.

On the north side of May Street and west of Willow Creek the citizens dug a pit and erected a sort of fort, covering the roof with the excavated dirt to prevent firing by brands. Portholes were provided. Frank Maddock was chosen captain and J. L. Morrow, lieutenant and A. S. Wells, second lieutenant. Some Indians did come to town and were held in a vacant lot for a few days but allowed to go on to the Columbia when they seemed peaceable.

The ferry at the mouth of Rock Creek on the John Day did a big business for a few weeks and excited settlers came tearing down the grade as if pursued by shouting savages. Generally it was the women and children who left home; the men stayed to look after their stock and possessions. Some who left never did come back, preferring life not so close to the frontier. For years those who did not flee felt a silent superiority to those who did.

PEOPLE ARE COMING

Communication in the 1870s was much less extensive than it is now, but much more personal. When a man living on a Morrow County creek wrote to his brother in the Willamettte Valley to say that a man up around Rawdog had grown a good crop of wheat on a few acres it was taken as gospel. It wasn't a feature story in a newspaper nor a build-up for a promotion campaign. And if the writer also said that there was a good looking quarter section that could be had by some of the provisions the government had to give away the public domain the valley relative might be on his way east as soon as he could catch up his horses and load his belongings onto the high-wheeled wagon.

That was the process by which many of the early settlers came to Morrow County. They were the first generation descendants of Oregon Trail emigrants, already tired of the big trees and stumps and rain of the country west of the Cascades and anxious to get a piece of land that didn't have to be cleared before it could be farmed. There were others. Villard's (Union Pacific's) Oregon Short

The Heppner Hills often smelled like sheep; they were every place,
almost half a million of them.

Line was buiding into Oregon from Utah and land-hungry men could get within a few hundred miles of the free lands of the Columbia River basin by railroad cars. They could walk the rest of the way. Iowa, Illinois, Missouri and others of the middle border states sent interested emigrants and adventurous young men from Maine and New York came to see what opportunities the west offered.

These first settlers on the grazing lands of Morrow County bore English names with few exceptions and the witnesses who swore to the observance of the homestead laws were also of English descent. And the descriptions of their homesteads place them in the uplands around Dairyville, Eightmile, Gooseberry and on the creek leading into Butter Creek on the eastern boundary of the county, or on Willow Creek. They came fast around 1880 and the bunchgrass hills were scarred by their walking plows and the trails barred by their fragile fences to the great annoyance of the stockmen. Down in the draws, away from the wind and near a hopeful source of water, their little cabins nestled. candlelight dotting the landscape for a short time at dusk.

These were ambitious men and they had most durable wives. The men could walk all day behind a three horse, 12″ plow and the wives could carry water, cook, bear children, raise gardens and find time to grow a few bright flowers to enliven the drab surroundings. They came to stay and stay they did. They multiplied like the children of the old lady who lived in a shoe and by 1890 when the first official census of Morrow County as a political unit was taken there was almost as many inhabitants as there are today.

They demanded services from their government in addition to the land and there was a postoffice at Ella in the spring of 1882 although the country around Ella was never the most productive. But there were settlers everywhere. And Eightmile had a postoffice in 1883 to take some business away from Midway where there had been a postoffce since 1874. In 1884 postoffices blossomed all over the Heppner hills with one at Adamsville, far to the south, Alpine in lower Sand Hollow, at Atwood in late 1883, Castle Rock, the shipping port for the county in 1883, Gooseberry, Salineville also. Hardman had had a postoffice since 1881, Lena since 1873. In the early eighties, so complete was the settlement, Morrow County had far more postoffices than it does today—and it wasn't even a county yet.

A prospective homesteader had first to find a piece of land that he liked and relatives or prospective neighbors could be helpful in that; then he had to file on the land after checking the surveys and finding the official stakes. At Heppner O. H. Hallock and Augustus Mallory would locate homesteaders for a few dollars and make a nice piece of change for the service. If the settler had some money he might file a declaration of intent to purchase, if he wanted to plant trees he could file on a timber culture, if he was a veteran of the Civil War he could obtain a soldier's additional homestead. And, if he decided to locate on the north end of the county he could buy Northern Pacific script for $1.25 per acre. There were numerous methods of obtaining land for the government was anxious to get rid of it, to get it into the hands of homeowning citizens

29

who would produce from it and pay taxes on it. The government, in those days, was helpful.

The homesteader had to have horses; they were the only source of power. Some of the horsemen of the county could provide. If he had driven in from the valley he had horses; if he had come by stage or train he had to buy. There were dealers who would sell him a plow and a wooden framed harrow with which to break up the tough sod after it was turned over and this was a process not done in one year even if a right-lap or a single disc was used. He could seed his crop by broadcasting or he could get a neighbor to help and sow with a tailgate seeder which wasn't much better. Inasmuch as wheat produced but one crop a year the homesteader had to raise something else to have income between harvests. There were few who would lend so homesteaders saw both sides of the coin called independence.

His wife could grow a garden, he could acquire a few head of cattle or sheep and nearly every homesteader had a few hogs for meat and market. There were no jobs nearby to be had except herding sheep which required that much time be spent away from his property. There were many lean months for homesteaders. But most of them stuck it out until they could get title to their land. Then the evolution of consolidation began; it is not yet ended.

When it was time for harvest the equipment was as crude as the tillage tools. A reaper was often used to cut hay and while it was the first implement invented by Cyrus McCormick to get the farmer away from the back-breaking work of swinging a heavy cradle, it was an awkward piece of machinery resembling something in a Rube Goldberg cartoon.

Headers were in use as soon as there was much grain to cut in Morrow County. They were a push machine powered by six horses with a 12′ or 14′ sickle in front of them and a draper that moved the cut grain to the left where it was elevated into a big wagon box by a spout with two drapers and hauled away to a stack. There was a tiller wheel in the rear of a header by which the driver, with the aid of the team, could steer it around corners in a manner not much dissimilar to the modern push combine. If the "header puncher," as the operator was universally called, was watchful and attentive he could do a very good job of saving the grain, but handling it so many times was wasteful.

A heading crew usually consisted of a puncher, two or three header box drivers (depending on the quality of the crop), a loader to manage the grain as it came out of the header spout so as to get as much as possible in the box, a stacker and a spike pitcher to help the box drivers throw their loads onto the stack. Farmers soon invented nets by which the entire loads were rolled onto the stack in one operation and the spike pitcher became a net puller and spent his spare time cleaning up around the stack, for the nets were never very tidy.

Farmers had the idea that grain should go through a "sweat" before it was threshed and they liked to wait for two or three weeks before the thresher came. The combine pretty well disabused farmer minds about the necessity of the sweat but it

This is how they headed the grain, box driver with three horses, indicating level land; loader sitting on the top of the spout, header puncher astride the tiller wheel driving his team of six "donks" and another box driver awaiting his turn. (Courtesy Erling Thompson)

was once a prevailing theory. Stacks were up to eighty feet long and often twenty feet wide and as high as the stacker could make them although the header puncher and the stacker had to decide how large part of the field would be put back into a stack to maintain some sort of symmetry.

The first threshers were horse power, another awkward piece of machinery. Ten or twelve horses were hooked to a series of sweeps in teams of two. The sweeps were fastened to an iron stand that was securely staked down. Inside it was an upright shaft that was turned by the sweeps as the horses pulled around and around. At ground level there was a set of bevel gears to direct the power at right angles toward the thresher cylinder. A driver stood on the stand with a whip and kept the team moving at as steady a pace as possible. It was necessary to change teams at frequent intervals for some of the horses became dizzy and all of them became tired if the grain was heavy.

A. M. Flory and H. B. McMillen had such a one near Lexington that burned July 25, 1889.

The separator itself was not much different from the modern thresher in design although better bearings have been invented than the old soft babbit of early days. Grain is still separated from chaff by a process of beating by a cylinder thence by shaking and blowing the chaff off the grain with fans. Rubbing and winnowing were inventions of ancient people.

After the horse power threshers came the steam engines, the first ones were not self-propelled and had to be hauled by horses. These were an impressive bit of equipment with their pistons shuttling back and forth in the dust and their shrill whistle announcing welcome mealtime or blatantly calling the crew out of the blankets. The separator was driven by a heavy canvas belt 120 feet long, 8 inches wide from the engine drive wheel to the cylinder shaft and power was more certain and much steadier than from a horse-power, for the engine never got tired. The elimination of fatigue as an element in production has been a major accomplishment of machinery.

At first the straw and chaff was run out the back end of the separator and stacked but before long man invented a blower that blew it onto a high stack and made a whining noise that could be heard for miles. It sounded like something was really being done. Steam threshing engines were fired by straw and a grimy fireman was kept busy stoking the thing throughout the long day until he banked his fire after the machine was silenced, and laid his weary body down for a few hours sleep, before he had to arise earlier than anybody to get up steam for the next day's run.

The crew consisted of an engineer to boss the fireman, a separator man who bossed the whole operation and kept the machinery going, two forkers who moved the grain off the stacks to the derrick table by "Jackson" forks, a huge hand of steel and wood with four or five teeth set into a solid piece of wood. It was a huge claw and was pulled toward the table by a team of horses guided by a derrick driver at the other end of a cable that ran through several pulleys. The forker directed the derrick driver by signals and they had to work as a team to be efficient.

Once on the derrick table the grain was in charge of two hoedowns who were armed with hoedown forks (a pitchfork with bent teeth). They fed the loose grain onto a long feeder (a continuous draper) with a hoeing motion, preferably at an even pace. It was fed directly into the cylinder by the short feeder. Alongside the separator sat two sacksewers, each on a couple of filled sacks and between them worked the sack jig who hung empty sacks onto a pair of spouts through which threshed grain came, and sat them in front of the sewers full, for sewing. The sack sewers laced the top of the bag with twine and a four or five-inch needle, straight and sharp, taking from nine to fifteen stitches—the more the better—and pulled the sack onto his knees and strode with it to the pile a few steps away where it was piled five high in an invariable design that made them easy to count.

In addition to two forkers and two derrick drivers and four hoedowns—two at a time, they changed every fifteen minutes—the engine crew of two, two sacksewers and the jig, there had to be someone to take care of the straw and someone to bring some of it around to the engine so the fireman could get to it easily, a roustabout to do the things no one else had time to do, and usually two men with teams (four or six) to haul water because the threshing machine was out in the middle of the fields and there were a lot of thirsty horses involved and the engine had to have water or would produce no steam. Water bucks pulled tanks containing up to 600 gallons on their wagons and made as many trips as necessary.

All this was basically powered by a cook and often a helper who spent the long days in a cookwagon set at some short distance from the machine, preferably on the lee side. These faithful females baked bread for about twenty men, roasted or boiled

meat for them, cooked bushels of potatoes, boiled buckets of beans, made gallons of gravy and occassionaly had time to bake a few cakes to satisfy the appetites of dusty, grimy men who were working close to sixteen hours a day. The women had to wash the dishes after that, and start breakfast before.

The era of the big commercial threshing machine lasted from about 1890 when the steam engine came in, to about 1916, when the little combines made them obsolete. Not many men are alive who worked on them, and they have become old and boastful. Surely as to durability and energy expended per day, they earned the right to boast.

The comparatively big crews generated a high degree of loyalty and when the crew went to town on Saturday nights, there was boasting around the bars and maybe some fighting, for among so many robust men, some were always combative. Such delights were not for the engineer and the fireman, who stayed with the machine to clean the flues, or the separator man, who always had repair work to do.

Pay was good, five dollars a day and board for forkers, $3.50 to $4.00 for sacksewers, and as much as $6 or $7 for the engine and separator men, and $2.00 and $2.50 for the lesser members of the crew. A waterbuck might get $3.00 a day if he had to move the separator from setting to setting in addition to hauling water.

When the threshing crew had sounded its last whistle the farmer had his crop in two piles at each setting, one of threshed grain in sacks and one of straw in a tall cone that would resist rain for a whole winter. The next job was to haul the sacked grain away to the warehouse for sale. This he did by wagon, loading as much as fifty of the 140-pound sacks onto each wagon and pulling them, preferably coupled two in one outfit, with six or eight horses over the long and always dusty roads. The iron shod wagon wheels made dust out of the dirt roads in a few trips.

Sacks were loaded nine in the bulkhead, three

by three on edge; three on edge in the wagon bed, two lengthwise on top and then as many as the wagon would haul crosswise.

The first combined harvester-threshers as they were called, came in just before the century and they were huge, wooden-framed machines pulled by thirty or more horses working in strings of six, with two or three leaders. A special hitch was used — the "shanandonah" — that permitted each horse to be bucked back so he could not run away if the leaders were stopped. A combine driver crawled to his seat far over his team and steered them around the field at an even speed of two miles an hour as the huge bull wheel turned the sprocket that drove the cylinder. Gasoline engines had not yet come to the farm.

The driver controlled his team with two lines, nearly always of white cotton rope. They had to be extra long, for when the combine topped a hill and the long team was below the driver on his high seat, the leaders were far away. When the machine went into a deep draw, the driver found himself down among the horses reeling in lines by the handfulls.

In the middle teens McCormick and Deering each invented a small combine cutting eight foot, and pulled by a mere eight horses, that could be sold for $1600, and these "stubble bugs" made every farmer his own thresherman.

So far in the past is the machinery described, that this generation has not seen a sample of it. Scrap drives for war have removed every discarded header from the fence corners and every old thresher from the farmstead. The age is gone and the men are gone, leaving little trace except a few reminiscent words in history books.

Settlers in the area that was to become Morrow County, did not have it so easy as did those farther east or west. After the railroad came along the Columbia in 1884, Umatilla County farmers could haul wheat a comparatively short distance; it wasn't so far down Alkali canyon for the Gilliam County

Here is an excellent view of a horse drawn combine, driven by a huge bull wheel, geared to the cylinder for power. The photographer was above the team which was on a slope permitting a view of every horse. There were 30 of them, driven by two lines in the hands of a man with a loud voice and preferably a sense of speed so as to keep the machinery running with little variation. The old time combine drivers considered their work an art.
(Courtesy Mrs. Elaine S. George)

wheat growers, and Sherman County homesteaders were even closer. But it was a long haul from the Eightmile country to railheads on the Columbia, with the result that very little grain was hauled to market outside the county during the 1880s. But wheat growing went on just the same, for on September 9, 1885, the Riverside Enterprise, a newspaper published at Alkali, noted that three threshers were out in the Eightmile country. Incidentally, it was also news that there was a new schoolhouse at Eightmile near the Andrew Rood place, the only such project to be successful at that date, although a school was planned at Gooseberry. M. C. Harris was editor of the short-lived Enterprise.

New farm machinery was being developed fast, and Minor, Dodson & Co., at Heppner advertised John Deere plows, Buckeye shoe press drills, Vorbin disc harrows and seeder and Schuttler farm wagons, also barbed wire. Gilliam & Coffee were selling pumps, gaspipe, Fish Bros. wagons, Champion mowers, reapers, headers and threshers. The little flouring mill at Heppner could take care of small amounts of wheat, but until the railroad came into Heppner in 1888, the market was very limited.

Water was the bane of the homesteader's existence in Morrow County. Except for the few who lived along the many creeks, water was scarce and for the settlers whose land was in the southwest part of the county, Eightmile, Gooseberry, there was seldom any water but that which was hauled by wagon. Nearly every homestead had a water-wagon and the housewife could get a bucketful by dropping the hose at the back end to fill her container. Even that was an improvement over hauling water in barrels mounted on a sled, which was the start for many.

There were few roads down into the creeks, and such as there were, were steep. Farmers not too far from the Jake Young place, high on Hale ridge, could haul from his spring and have a downhill pull. Others had to find roads down into Rhea Creek or Clark canyon or even find water in the few waterholes in Eightmile canyon, which was a seasonal search. There was no need to find a road into Dry Fork.

The houses the homesteaders built were small, because both lumber and money were scarce. Families were often small, for many of the home-

steaders were young people. Often single men built the first cabins and waited until the school district hired a suitable school ma'am for them to court (and the competition was strong). Water came from the waterwagon, or later, from a cistern, and there was never enough of it; dishwater and wash water was saved to nourish a few flowers or stimulate the garden vegetables, and many a family cow had to get used to the flavor of dirty overalls in her drinking water. Whenever possible, water was used twice.

There wasn't much in the homestead cabins in the way of equipment. There was a stove, for fireplaces were too wasteful of hard-to-get wood, and there was a table, likely homemade, and some chairs that might also be of home manufacture. There might be a few of the wonderfully comfortable rawhide chairs, and if the homesteader was handy with hammer and saw, or impressed by his wife's need, he could put together some shelves and cabinets for the storage of dishes. And there were barrels for flour and a canister of some sort for sugar and coffee. There would be wash tubs and a washboard and a clothesline in the backyard. A bed was necessary for sleep and women were handy about using the old clothes to make quilts to cover the beds.

Light was from coal oil lamps, often a little glass bowl with a wick and a chimney, later increased in power by a reflector and eventually developed into a fanciful object of art with painted bowl and brass decoration. Before electricity reached the farm a gas lamp was invented that gave more light in exchange for greater care.

"Not much," would say the modern women who have more convenience in a hunting camp. "Enough" would say the grand dame who presided over the pioneer home. She knew that a home is a product of the spirit and that convenience or ease is only an adjunct to it—not a necessity.

In the fall of 1888 the Heppner *Gazette* published the assessor's statement showing 110,770 acres of land assessed in private hands (that is less than ten percent of the land in the county). It was valued at $388,118. The value of lots was $102,834 and the improvements on lots at $154,542, merchandise and implements $204,532. Thus the valuation put on the towns, mostly Heppner, was greater than all the farming land. It should be noted, however, that homesteaders did not make final proof on their land until it was necessary, for when they did so it became taxable. Perhaps, therefore, there was more than the above figures indicate in private ownership.

The same set of figures shows 8,042 horses and 7,304 cattle and 136,951 sheep. The gross value was $1,968,436 but it was the custom in that period to subtract the indebtedness from the gross assessment, so with debts and exemptions the taxable property of the county was $1,009,794.

The big taxpayers of the county were all livestock owners or business men. William Penland paid on $40,000, Joe Vey on $11,575, Charles Cunningham on $10,700, C. A. Rhea on $13,490, Rush Bros. on $13,625, Tom Quaid on $9,095, Heppner & Blackman on $15,000, T. W. Ayres on $15,523, Wm. Hughes on $6,240, J. G. Maddock on $25,000, Mike Kenny on $1,648 and J. L. Morrow & Son on $6,848. It was customary to publish the names of owners of property in excess of $1,000.

But if wheat growers were not listed among the wealthier men of the new county they were still trying. J. I. Benefield came into Heppner from Lexington to report that he was putting in 310 acres of wheat and said that B. M. Booher would have 200 acres, D. C. Crow 150, Andrew Reaney 300, J. & M. Evans 300, J. F. McAllister 300 and others were expanding their wheat acreages. The railroad had just come through to Heppner to create an aura of optimism.

Farmsteads were bleak. Here started Harry Duvall and wife Amanda. Eventually trees grew, and more buildings, and better fences, but the start was dismal enough to test the strength of a soul. (Courtesy Morrow County Museum)

Some notes indicating the trend of agriculture appear in the early *Gazettes*. The cayuse stock was being increased and diluted by the use of Clydesdale, Cleveland Bay and English Draft stallions. E. L. Matlock had a band of 200 horses for sale at $37.50 per head.

When a business in town is sold it is news to the local publisher for it is an indication of a change that will be felt by many subscribers. When one homesteader arranges to buy out his neighbor it was seldom recorded in the public prints which probably didn't care to note that another citizen had departed the county. Not all newspapers published reports on the success of crops unless exceptionally good. Crops grow slowly and there is no drama in the process unless it is spectacularly good or bad.

THE COUNTY OF MORROW

Early in 1885 ambition was stirring in the western part of Umatilla County as the influx of homesteaders increased the population at a tremendous rate. The population of Oregon almost doubled in that decade and in the mid-Columbia region the rate was much greater.

A young and ambitious people were anxious to control their own destiny and thought, naturally, of having their own county government. It will seem something of an oddity that the formation of new counties in early Oregon seldom, if ever, aroused opposition from the parent county. It was like a mother watching her daughter get married. Wasco let Umatilla depart in 1862 and gave its blessing and when citizens around Heppner started agitation for a new county Umatilla's representative in the house introduced the bill, Morrow County HB 4. The representative was L. B. Cox, a Pendleton lawyer, of the firm of Cox & Minor. Jackson Morrow of Heppner was the other Umatilla County representative. He had served in 1876 and had a little experience, more, in fact than had Cox who was a first termer.

The story is that the decision to form a new county was made before a name had been chosen and that legislators, liking Jackson Morrow, appended his name to the bill creating the new county. There was no struggle and during the same legislative session Gilliam County was formed from the eastern part of Wasco County. C. N. Cartwright, a state senator representing Wasco, Crook, Klamath and Lake was author of the Gilliam County Bill. Although Umatilla County did not oppose the division the Pendleton *East Oregonian*, then under the editorship of C. S. Jackson, commented in a brief news item about the formation of Gilliam County: "More counties, more officers, more taxes. How the dear people love to be taxed."

It is apparent to moderns that not much planning was done before the boundaries of the new county were drawn. Eightmile Canyon starts in Morrow, runs into Gilliam which also gets the lower end of Willow Creek. Morrow County runs to six south of the base line. Had it continued another row of townships to seven south, as was proposed in 1889

E. B. McFarland opened a store in Lexington in 1885, as soon as the town had a name.
(Courtesy LaVerne Henderson)

by T. E. Fell, when he represented Morrow County in the legislature, it would have been much easier to construct and maintain the Monument road which would have been all in Morrow County. Grant County was never much interested in a road that took produce out of the county. The eastern boundary leaves most of lower Butter Creek in Umatilla County and leaves an awkward division in upper Big Butter Creek, leaving Vinson in Umatilla County. The pioneers were interested in getting their own county as a political unit and not sufficiently concerned with the geographical features.

It immediately became the duty of Governor Zenas F. Moody, who had incidentally done much of the surveying of the south end of the new Morrow County, to appoint the temporary officers to serve. He named Augustus Mallory to be county judge;

George W. Harrington to be sheriff; S. Parker Garrigues, clerk; W. J. Leezer, treasurer; W. R. Ellis, school superintendent; J. L. Fuller and Frank Gilliam, county commissioners; Julius Keithly, surveyor and T. R. Howard, county assessor. These men were to serve until 1886, a little over a year later when permanent officers were to be chosen at the general election. Of much more importance to Morrow County was that the location of the county seat was to be determined at the June election of that year.

Heppner citizens donated money for a courthouse which was a wooden structure on the location of the present stone building. This act of generosity or statesmanship did not go without notice.

William Penland, who had settled at the mouth of Black Horse Canyon about nine miles below Heppner, decided that he had an excellent location for a county seat, which he did; it consisting of many acres of fairly level land along the east side of Willow Creek. It had many more acres of reasonably level terrain than Heppner. Penland didn't have much for municipal facilities, wasn't incorporated, didn't even have a postoffice, but Lexington did have a certain amount of stability having been a sheep camp when David Estes was alone with his beaver traps on the flat known later as Stansbury. Lexington was no Johnny-come-lately as a competitor. Penland set out to capitalize on all this, aided by as enthusiastic a bunch of citizens as could be rallied in any frontier community and backed by homesteaders in the fertile Black Horse country, the Social Ridge settlers and even farther south to Eightmile and Gooseberry the newly arrived citizens supported Lexington's claim. Maybe it was because Heppner had a sort of monopoly on business and monopolies are always resented.

Penland had come in the sixties and was established as a stockraiser by 1870. He had built a big house for his headquarters, hired lots of herders, was on the way to acquiring land in such quantities as to require page after page in the assessment records. He came from Kentucky and his wife from Iowa although of Kentucky parentage. That is the reason the town was called Lexington.

Bill Penland started late but he moved fast. Mary Bedefield had a postoffice at Salineville on Willow Creek which had been established in January of 1884. It was discontinued in April of 1886 and the mail sent to Lexington. Nathaniel Yeats was named postmaster for Lexington November 11, 1885, just in time to get the Salineville mail. It was also several months after Morrow County had been established in the previous February.

These early settlers around Lexington declared a sort of vendetta against Heppner, an opposition that lasted into succeeding generations and was expressed in many ways. They were a vigorous bunch of patriots. They came from all over the nation. McFarland had an early store, T. W. Halley was a hardware man, Andrew Reaney had the livery stable and the Reaneys were concerned in many of the activities around Lexington in the eighties and nineties. Henry Padberg, a native of Germany, had settled on Rhea Creek and soon allied himself and his numerous family with the fortunes of Lexington. W. B. McAllister had a grocery store and often the postoffice, and William Blair had another grocery. These citizens, as a counter to Heppner's court house, pledged $3,000 for the construction of one if they should defeated Heppner at the election to be held June 7, 1886 .

The paper that carried the campaign of printed propaganda was the *Bunchgrass Blade*, a sheet that perished with the hopes of Lexington, unfortunately, for the title was indicative of imagination and aggressiveness.

The influx of homesteaders onto the bunchgrass hills had given political power to Lexington and it was closer to the center of population than Heppner, nestled close to the mountains. Penland was a sheep man and in 1885 had been increasing his flocks for over fifteen years and was a competitor worthy of attention to the little coterie of men who ran the town of Heppner. The campaign was bitter and Heppner only won by the support of Lena and Dairy. The vote was:

	Heppner	*Lexington*
Lena	78	5
Alpine	8	78
Wells Springs	4	59
Cecil	4	61
Ione	7	82
Dairy	75	33
Heppner	463	82
Lexington	3	149
Eightmile	19	71
Pine City	12	16
Castle Rock	7	5
Dry Fork	11	17
TOTAL	691	658

It was said at the time that the factor that determined the election was the existing courthouse that Heppnerites had donated to the county, Lexington contested the election but lost out in the court. County seat elections in early Oregon were nearly always contested, were always bitter and fraud was always charged.

An intimation of the effort made in the campaign is contained in a report from the Hepper *Gazette* for June 15, 1886 and reprinted in the Pendleton *East Oregonian*: "A dashing troop of well mounted boys rode out of Heppner last Saturday, commanded by S. R. Reeves. They were deeply interested in the county seat question and having no vote to cast as yet they volunteered to go way out into the fastness of the Blue Mountains where the bell wethers roameth, and take the place of Heppner herders who desired to come to town to vote. Some of the boys in the outfit were but ten or twelve years old and some went to mountain camps full fifty miles from Heppner and singly and individually took charge of 2000 sheep for several days, cooking their own meals and sleeping in the tent or little bough shelter near the corrals with one ear open to detect the growl of the midnight bear or the cry of the cougar who watches the sheep camp with a mouth for mutton and a desire to get wool in his teeth. The boys were mostly mounted on their favorite cayuses and they presented an animated appearance as they proceeded out of town."

Another bill in the 1885 legislature, and one that reflects on the change being made, was the passage of Jackson Morrow's legal fence bill. He had help from other Eastern Oregon legislators but the bill defined a legal fence in every county but Union to be one consisting of "substantial posts, six feet long and in the ground 18 inches, not more than 30 feet apart, three wires with false posts four and a half feet long every eight feet with three furrows plowed on each side." Such a fence was lawful against horses and cattle after it went into effect on October 1, 1885.

Barbed wire had not been accepted by the public at that time and the legislature evaded the term by alluding to "wires of the kind in common use." Previously a legal fence had to contain some wood.

Stockmen, used to ranging their animals all over the country without restraint or herding, were disdainful of farmers who plowed up the grass. It was their contention that if their cattle or horses entered a farmer's field and devoured his growing grain it was the farmer's responsibility for not having a better fence. What was a legal fence had to be defined to give farmers a defense against stockmen and that was the intent of the bill. Farmers could afford barbed wire and making it legal helped them. There were many fights over fences as farmers tried to keep stock from their crops. Some sheepmen were adept at herding flocks near cultivated land and careless about letting them graze under the fences and into growing grain. Farmers were sure some of it was intentional—and it was.

THE ELEMENTS OF GROWTH

Heppner was lucky in the 1880s and like other lucky towns or people because of good planning. Heppner planned it that way, not only the town, but the man; the growth of Heppner, the town, is clearly traceable to the ambitions of Heppner, the man. Henry Heppner was a trader, a commission merchant whose success depended on transportation into his warehouses from as wide an area as possible.

That is why William Sidney Shiach, the historian who wrote the history of Morrow County for W. H. Lever of Spokane, publisher of histories of many eastern Oregon and Washington counties in the early 1900s, was impelled to say: "The business men of Heppner have ever been characterized by a broad-minded and enlightened public spirit, and their liberality and business acumen have enabled them to command the trade of the interior country to the south and in every direction, in spite of the machinations of rivals. How extensive that trade is may be readily imagined when we glance at the map, at the same time bearing in mind that all that section shown by it to be naturally tributary to Heppner is rich in the products of flock and herd. It was long ago stated that "all roads lead to Rome." A road map with Heppner as a center reminds one of a spider's web. Though not quite as complex as the epicure may, without violence to truth, be compared to it. By a road from the northwest it is connected with Ella, Ione and Lexington, and of course with the country surrounding these; one leading in from the northeast makes it accessible from Echo and Atwood in Umatilla County and Acton in Morrow County, the Heppner-Acton road being joined by one from Alpine. From the east comes a road from Pilot Rock and Vinson in Umatilla County and Lena in Morrow. From the southeast come two roads, one from Ritter in Grant County, and one from the Monument road as it is called, giving connection by itself and its numerous branches from the east, southeast, southwest and west, with Prairie City, Canyon City, John Day, Mount Vernon, Long Creek, Dayville, Hamilton, Monument, Rudio, Wagner and Waldron in Grant County, Mitchell in Crook County, Fossil, Lost Valley and Lone Rock in Gilliam County, and Parker's Mill, Hardman, Eightmile and Gooseberry in Morrow County. It has cost Heppner no little effort and expense to retain all this trade. Its business men frequently had to go down into their pockets for money with which to repair these roads, but whatever sacrifice was necessary has been freely made and as a reward Heppner has the reputation among commercial travelers of being the best town of its size in the northwest. With this large sheep country tributary to it, it is not surprising that the town ranks second as a wool exporter in the state of Oregon."

About 1900 a photographer caught some prominent citizens of Morrow county who were willing to pose in front of the bank. From the left they were Otis Patterson, who was editor of the Gazette, and soon to become the registrar at The Dalles Land Office; Gene Freeland was a banker albeit the striped overalls; the slim man is E. M. Shutt, sheriff, who packed his gun in a holster in front where it was handy instead of on the hip (Shutt came to a strange end. He had a son who grew gradually blind even with the best medical treatment Mr. Shutt could obtain. While living in Los Angeles, about out of funds, Shutt shot the boy and then himself in what has been called cowardice and bravery, but was certainly realism). Next is George Conser the bank cashier, a man who gives the impression of being able to strut sitting down; in the rear is Alton Bacey the town marshal, only accidently flouting his star; Frank Gilliam was often mayor, was partner in a hardware and implement store, a man of substance and character; Henry Blackman, who ran a store, was state senator and a nephew of Henry Heppner; J. A. Woolery, a visitor from Ione, a man with a knack for making money and acquiring land; and only partially shown is Henry Heppner, himself, a man who wouldn't try to crowd into a picture. Note the vests: Grandpa knew the utility of the vest, a portable rolltop desk, a comfort against the wind and a garment of infinite variation. (Courtesy Garnet Barratt)

It will be remembered that the John Day valley was the lodestone that was sought by most of the business men of the northern part of eastern Oregon. Everyone wanted an entry into the John Day valley for that is where the money was made because it was a successful producer of sheep and cattle, livestock that could be trailed out over necessarily primitive roads. Partly because of the discovery of gold at Canyon City in 1862 the early settlement of eastern Oregon was concentrated in the John Day country. Canyon City had a postoffice before Pendleton and a mere fifteen years after Portland and eleven years after Wascopum (The Dalles).

In the early sixties, when miners were digging for gold on Canyon Creek, there was a trail and later a wagon road down the John Day River to The Dalles, which was the distributing point for all the interior. It was later designated as The Dalles Military Road with a federal grant to 592,557.89 acres for its building and maintenance. The Dalles lost the business it had won at first because it permitted poor upkeep of the road. Baker built a road over high Dooley Mountain to reach the John Day town of Prairie City. There was once a road from La-Grande to the south over which Peter French hauled lumber and supplies to his Blitzen Valley ranch. Pendleton built a road to Long Creek and eventually on to Canyon City and Heppner built a road to Monument on the north fork of the John Day River and encouraged the road to Ritter although the sheep industry at Ritter was not so thriving as it was farther down the river.

In the late eighties the Heppner *Gazette* often carried letters from citizens asking for small appropriations to complete or repair the road from Hep-

pner to Monument, as little as $500, it was said, would make the road better and preserve the trade. On May 2, 1889 the comparative freight rates were published from Monument wool markets. It showed a rate of 3/4 cent to Heppner, one cent to Baker and two cents to The Dalles. It was conceded that Heppner got the major part of the business.

Arlington, where Henry Heppner maintained a wool warehouse for years, was restricted by geography and competed with Heppner only in the Lone Rock and Fossil areas. It was not until 1920 when the John Day highway was built that Condon could tap the John Day stock country. Before that the gorges of that river thwarted trade down the river. In 1888 Henry Blackman, Henry Heppner's brother-in-law, was elected to the state senate from Morrow and Grant Counties and obtained an appropriation of $10,000 to build a bridge across the north fork of the John Day at Monument which permitted the sheepmen of that fertile valley to cross the river in safety and haul their wool to Heppner.

And geography helped Heppner too. The first homesteaders in the Eightmile and Gooseberry country could not haul downhill to Lexington and Ione. There were roads, or at least water grades, down Clark Canyon and Rhea Creek, but the first

This was a threshing machine in the days before the combine. The derrick drivers have been brought around the stack to be pictured, the sack sewers wait to start a five sack high pile and the inevitable clowns gesture for notice. This would have been typical of the 1890s. (Courtesy Morrow County Museum)

settlers had no way to get down onto them. There were no roads. When Morrow County was established in 1885 the temporarily appointed county court had no money and because of the county seat fight had no desire to levy a big tax, even if it had been collectable. Umatilla County officials, understandably, were not about to spend their meager road funds on a departing daughter.

Homesteaders had to wait until the county court could lay out roads which required some force to obtain rights-of-way and some funds for road construction. Road building wasn't so very difficult as there were few long stretches of rock to be blown out, a dirt road could usually be planned to evade them. But roads down into Rhea Creek and Clark Canyon are necessarily steep. Eightmile Canyon is rocky and no county road had ever been built down it. It wouldn't go anywhere anyway.

So settlers in the Eightmile and Gooseberry country had to pull their wagons up the hills to the south until they could cross the many forks of Eightmile canyon at about the same places as does the present Heppner-Condon road. From there they went east and crossed Rhea Creek at Midway (now Ruggs), pulled up Cason Canyon and down into Clark Canyon, out on the flat again before braking their wagons down Donaldson Canyon, across Shobe Canyon to the long Heppner hill. That was the only road. Much of the wheat that was grown in the higher land of Morrow County in the early days was hauled into Heppner because the roads to Ione or Lexington hadn't been built and the routes presented serious difficulties.

Also lumber was being hauled into Heppner from above Lena and Vinson to be sawed at the Garrigues mill and the lumber from Parker & Gleason's mill southeast of Hardman was coming into Heppner over crude but passable roads that all spring felt the iron tires of heavily laden wool wagons from the north fork of the John Day at Monument and Ritter. No wonder Heppner grew.

In 1880 it was credited with 318 inhabitants although the count was an estimate, no incorporation being accomplished and no boundaries established. By 1890 the official census gave it 675, more than doubling its population and by 1900 Heppner had 1146, not quite doubling again. Morrow County's population was 4215 in 1890 and 4151 in 1900. The growth since that time has been in industry and service population. The farming population has steadily declined.

In 1885 Columbus A. Rhea moved in from the creek named for him and started a bank in Heppner, the First National, and J. G. Maddock, Louis Maddock and Hugh Fields also had a bank. There were churches and lodges and all the organizations of modern existence including saloons of which four were recognized by the first county court at the very first meeting. There were nine by the turn of the century for Heppner wasn't a good town from the point of view of strict morality. In the old papers there are frequent references such as "Miss May Bond was pulled last Saturday night for keeping a bawdy house and dug up $13.50 to patch up injured justice in Heppner town." And there was mention of the forays of inebriated cowmen and sheepmen and their payment for their delinquencies in the matter of conduct.

After the county seat fight was over and Heppner finally declared the base of county government it seemed appropriate that the town be incorporated. This was done by legislative enactment and the bill signed by Governor Sylvester Pennoyer on February 9, 1887. First officers elected were Henry Blackman, mayor; E. R. Swinburne, Ellis Minor, Thomas Morgan, J. B. Sperry, S. Parker Garrigues and George Noble, councilmen; M. C. McDougall, treasurer and O. H. Hallock, recorder.

Incorporation made possible some civic improvements not hitherto feasible, such as the building of a wide sidewalk (some say ten and some say twelve feet wide) down the length of the business part of Main Street. And Heppner began to be interested in some central water system. This took years of doing.

Incorporation had little to do with the building of the railroad into Heppner, that project being in the hands of citizens interested in furthering trade. Heppner had so proven itself as a center for the collection of wool and wheat and a likely shipping point for cattle, that the Oregon Railroad & Navigation Company was glad to build up Willow Creek from the Columbia River to haul out the freight. The warehouses were full of it. All the railroad asked was the right-of-way and ground for a depot. The depot and warehouses in Heppner have always been at the north end of town, well removed from the business part of town and at times there has been agitation to move them a few blocks south, but the cost of competing for land with commercial business has always deterred the move. There are advantages to having the shipping business removed from the retail. When the first train arrived in late November, 1888, a little more than appropriate celebration was held. Henry Heppner and Jackson Morrow drove the last spike; Henry Blackman made a speech laudatory of Heppner and the railroad company; Company E of the Oregon National Guard saluted with a volley and at seven p.m. bonfires were lighted, anvils roared and the engine whistled to create a noise that bounced off the bunchgrass hills with a resounding and satisfying echo. It was a grand night and citizens danced until dawn at Garrigues and Rogers opera house. Austin Wells was injured by powder burns while firing anvils.

The winter of 1888-89 was a very bad one for all of Eastern Oregon, it being long and cold. Many thousands of head of stock died. This offset to some extent the fortunate arrival of the railroad and changed the method of stock management by making it more careful. Stock could not be wintered in the open without danger.

It was 1889 before Heppner got around to considering its lack of central water supply and the danger of fire. It was late in the year before the city council contracted with a firm in Ithica, New York, to drill a well 500 feet deep, if need be, to try to get sufficient water. There wasn't enough, so the high insurance rates continued. In 1891 the Garrigues sawmill burned, forcing another effort to get water for the town. The city did buy a hook and ladder outfit but without enough water, the expenditure was of doubtful value. Finally H. V. Gates of Hillsboro, Oregon came to the council with a proposal to drill a well and put in a pump and electric light system. Before long the Heppner Light & Water Company was formed to take the plant from Gates, but it was several years before it had complete ownership and Mr. Gates was an interested creditor for a long time. But by 1893 Heppner had a limited central supply of water, instead of individual wells on every residence lot and also water mains to carry water all over town. And there was a fire department of sorts. The details of the installation were of great interest to the editor of the Gazette who wrote about it fully.

Although there were several small hotels in the town including the City Hotel, operated sometime by Ellis Minor, and the Mountain House on south Main Street up Shobe Canyon and some smaller ones, citizens felt that a big, ornate hotel was necessary to uphold the dignity of the town. The Palace Hotel Company was formed in October, 1889, with Tom Quaid, J. W. (Billy) Morrow, C. A. Rhea, Henry Blackman and J. B. Natter as incorporators. It was some time before the building was to be completed, 1891 in fact. It was on the northeast corner of Main and May Streets, was three stories and built in the Victorian style. Will VanCadow had the first lease, although Mrs. VanCadow was generally in charge. Phil Metschan, son of Phil Metschan, the state treasurer, came over from Canyon City to manage it for a time later until he went to Portland as manager of a famed city hostelry.

In 1889 Coffin & McFarland, general merchants, came up from Arlington and put up a big brick building on the corner of Center and Main, The Fair, that was a landmark for years.

THE LOST BOY

This story in various forms has been often told. It came to light again when a typewritten copy was found in the papers of Josie Jones when she died in June of 1970 at the age of 96. She was born Josephine Ursula Rhea, daughter of Mr. and Mrs. Columbus A. Rhea at the family home on Rhea Creek. She married Newt Jones. The story was apparently written by several persons, but is well told nevertheless, and is descriptive of the life in Morrow County in the early nineties.

"One day in the long ago year of 1893 several of us town boys, including Len Gilliam, Ralph Thompson and others decided we would go over to Dutton's Canyon to drown out some squirrels. Sometimes we would snare them with a long string looped over their holes. But this time we decided to get our victims by the use of water, which we would pour down their holes. Out would come little Mr. or Mrs. Squirrel like a drowned rat. This was late in August. We were all about 12 or 13 years old at that time, but we always had to take the little Gilliam boy, Earl, along with us and he was only three years old and always in the way. Along about four o'clock we decided to send him home after a pail of water to get rid of him. We thought we would play for a little while yet and would beat him home.

"When we got back over the hill to the Gilliam home, Mrs. Gilliam asked us where Earl was and we said we had sent him home hours ago. It was beginning to get dark by this time and Earl's folks began to be very much worried about him. They spread the word around that Earl was lost over the hills west of Heppner and maybe was eaten up by the coyotes by this time. I remember so well the flashes of the old coal oil lanterns and torches as the men of the town searched the hills and canyons back of town. They searched all night long but did not find him, so they knew the coyotes had got him.

"Here is the story of what really happened in the western hills that night, as told me by Mrs. Josie Jones of Heppner. "Newt and I were going home to the Cunningham ranch that evening after a day spent in town shopping. Unknown to me, Newt was breaking a very mean horse that day and didn't want me to know just how mean he was, so he was giving most of his attention to his driving. The other

horse was a good tame one. It was beginning to get dark by this time, but I happened to be looking out over the sagebrush and bunchgrass and told Newt that I saw a coyote about a quarter of a mile west of us. He stopped the horses and gave me the reins and got out of the buckboard and took his high powered rifle he always had with him. He took careful aim and was about to pull the trigger when I screamed and said it looked like a child of some sort. Good thing, too, as Newt was a dead shot with any kind of gun.

"He got back in the hack and circled around down to where he could get a good look at whatever it was. It was a little boy about three years old. Newt couldn't get very close on account of the horse began to rear and buck so he told me to go over and get the child. When I got there the child was almost frozen as the nights in this country get cool even when the days are hot. He was barefooted. He had on a little dress all torn and his little pants were hanging down in the back. I couldn't get him to say a word and we didn't know whose boy he was, or where or how he had got out there in the wild hills, miles from nowhere. I had on one of those old fashioned blue lined duster coats we used to wear in those far off days. I wrapped him in this coat and tied a bandana handkerchief over his head and took him back to the hack. We didn't know what to do with him, and then Newt told me about the mean horse he was using, so we decided to take him to the John Woodward ranch about half a mile away. Newt thought he might be one of the Woodward boys but he didn't know for sure. Newt asked Mr. Woodward if any of his kids were missing but he said they were all there when he went to bed. Just then Jack, their oldest boy came out and looked at the child and said: 'That is one of the Gilliam kids.' Mrs. Woodward wrapped a blanket around him and then put him to bed. She fed him before putting him to bed but he wouldn't even try to talk. She put him to bed with Fanny, their seven year old girl, as that was the only place for him. We went on home and decided to send our hired man, George Means right to town to tell the Gilliams their boy was safe and sound and the Woodwards would bring him home in the morning. But Mr. Means was not at home. Early the next morning Newt hitched up the team to the hack so we could go to town but the horse kicked the hack to pieces and our trip was off, but Newt saddled up his saddle horse and headed for town. Sometime during the night when the whole town was out looking for the boy, Frank Roberts found him at the Woodward home.

"Monday morning we came into town and about the first man I saw was George Conser, the banker, and he gave me the dickens for not bringing the boy in that night, but I told him we didn't know who the boy was and that the team was so vicious that Newt was afraid to drive it with the child along.

"This is the end of the story as told to me by Josie Jones, but Leslie Matlock told me that he and some other men were on Heppner flat looking for the boy when Frank Roberts came and told them that he had already found Earl and that he was safe and sound. Leslie said that they all raced their saddle horses all the way back, down the Fristo hill clean into town down Main Street.

"That small boy of three years, Earl Gilliam is still living in Heppner and is our master plumber and a partner of Gilliam and Bisbee Hardware Store. He is now a grandfather. The day they brought him to town the business men passed the hat around and took up a collection of about $10.00. Earl's wife told me last night that Earl's father invested that $10.00 in an insurance policy and they never drew any of the money until she and Earl were married and they used the money with accrued interest to make the down payment on their home on Baltimore Street where they still reside."

Their son, Jackson Earle Gilliam, is now the bishop of the Episcopal Church of the state of Montana.

IRISH & SWEDES

The first settlers in Morrow County were run-of-the-mill Americans to judge from the names appearing in early newspapers. In 1889 these names made news in copies of the Heppner Weekly *Gazette*: Sawyer, Jones, Leatherman, Hummison, Wren, McGrew, Locknane, Ayer, Mann, Bisbee, Johnson, Hager, Kramer, Penland, Taylor, Newman, Green, Dawson, Kirk, Shipley, Gilliam, Wallace, Wright. There were others, of course, but all representing the mixture that is America.

Sherman County had its German settlement, Gilliam County had its Scotch influence and Morrow County had two ethnic groups to season the native stock that came from the middle border or the Willamette valley to make first settlement on the bunchgrass hills of Morrow.

In addition to the Irish, Morrow County attracted scores of Swedes. Many of them were from a Swedish settlement in Kansas, attracted there, no doubt, by the news of passage of the homestead law that permitted any American citizen to acquire land for a small payment and stated improvements. Swedes began coming to Morrow County about 1885 when the county was established.

Not all of them could speak English which caused them to stay together. They took up land in the Eightmile and Gooseberry sections and closer to Ione and also north and east of that town.

The only work available was to herd sheep and many of the men went into the mountains with bands of sheep for the early stockmen, but they didn't like that. Harvesting of nature's bounty was not the role of the Swedes; they had no pattern of stock management on open ranges in their native country and few of them had been in America long enough to acquire the skills needed. They were farmers, used to digging in the soil to plant their crops, used to waiting with patience as the seed sprouted and emerged from the soil, grew leaf by leaf, waving joyfully in the wind, and headed out and matured. Patience was a part of the Swede's way of life.

These quiet, impassive people were strange to the first settlers who had come in the sixties and seventies with intent to harvest the grass although some went into the mountains to harvest timber. Both were crops already grown. Over much of Morrow County the several kinds of bunchgrass stood tall and their roots were deep in the soil so they could withstand the frequent droughts and floods of a violent climate. Those who came later in the eighties and nineties followed the same tactics and differed only that they went farther into the mountains for summer range. There was little feeding in winter.

The Swedes were nearly all devout Lutherans, so much so that by the spring of 1886 they attracted a pastor whom they met at Alkali and conveyed him to Eightmile to establish a congregation. Almost the

first thought was an arrangement for worship. They were that kind of Swedes. The early Swedes stayed by themselves and stayed away from towns as much as possible; they took no part in public affairs and in the eighties, when they were settling on the hills of Eightmile and Gooseberry or in the flatter lands north and east of Ione their names appeared in the local paper only when they proved up on their homesteads. In the nineties, a decade marked by a serious depression and consequent revival of business, Swedish names seldom appeared in the *Gazette* or the *Times*.

When the History of Umatilla and Morrow Counties was published in the first years of the new century no representative of the now well-known Swedish families had his biography entered. It cost $20. The Swedes took little part in the public life of Morrow County until they had attained some affluence and had their land paid for or were well along on that project.

They did, however, progress religiously. From the first organization of the congregation they continued to hold meetings with pastors who came in a few times a year for a Sunday or two of religious observances: sermons, christenings, confirmations. Pastor Eric Norelius, who had first come to the Swedish settlement, noted that there was land available and that it was very good land, and would make forty bushels per acre. That indicates a large supply of hope among the pastor's flock for the crops were much less than that. But there was wood to be had for the cutting in the mountains only a day or two away by horse team, water could be found at thirty feet or more for stock and a garden and the Swedes, not minding the work, made a way of life that was satisfying and they stayed.

By 1897 the Lutherans were sufficiently well off that they named a building committee and erected a little church, 24 x 36 feet and named it Valby (Shepard's Dell) although the location is on a windswept hill in the Eightmile country of semi-arid Morrow County.

Nearly every one of the Swedish population of Morrow County belonged to the little congregation, even the "northern" Swedes who had to come from below Ione for meetings and sermons. That was a long drive by team and wagon in early times. Pastor Norelius noted that "a peculiar, mixed language is spoken in this community" but as children grew up this changed and by the time the little church was dedicated the sermons were in English.

The Valby church stands alone as a remnant of rural culture in Morrow County, gaining in attendance steadily and attracting more adherents every year. The comparatively new Lutheran church in Heppner is a progeny of the mother church on the hills of Eightmile.

Probably the names of the first Swedish settlers can be heard more often in Morrow County than those of any other group, although the names of first settlers are common.

Now nearly every family in the county is allied in some matrimonial relationship to one or more of the Swede families and the Petersons, Bergstroms, Troedsons, Swansons, Carlsons, Lundells, Andersons are in every activity. Many are living on the original homesteads their ancestors took up eighty years ago; verily the Swedes came to stay.

There were some Irishmen living in Morrow County very early, perhaps the first being William Hughes, who arrived in time to be included in the 1870 census as a farmer aged 31, with a wife, Catherine, 28. William went into the stock business and branched out into other occupations which gave him enough money that he could finance young countrymen who might be interested in acquiring a band of sheep. He also wrote to Irish families to recruit young Irishmen for the sheep camps of Morrow County, getting many of them from County Leitrim or Donegal, a far piece from his native Tipperary. Charles Cunningham came in the early 1870's and took up a pre-emption claim on Butter Creek in 1876. He became one of the largest and most progressive of the sheep men of the area although he is most often identified with Umatilla County.

It was the sheep business that attracted the Irish and they were good at it. However some of the early immigrants went to wheat farming. Felix Johnson settled on upper Butter Creek on a creek that now bears his name. Jeremiah Brosnan settled nearby and raised stock. Mike Kenny came to settle in the central part of Morrow County in 1883 and raised both wheat and livestock, becoming affluent enough to help many other County Leitrim lads come to America. Also here early were the Dohertys, Pat, B. P. and James G. There are dozens of Dohertys in Morrow County and no one will promise to straighten out the relationships, although it appears that there were four non-related Dohertys who all came from County Donegal. James G. was called Black Horse Doherty because he owned a good share of Black Horse canyon where he was a successful wheat grower. Another early Irish family were the Quaids, Tom, Mike and Patt. Tom had a ranch on Balm Fork and is recorded as being one of those influential in getting Morrow and Heppner to start a store on Stansbury flat. Mike was killed in the seventies and his body was one of the first to be buried on the hill. Pat (he signed it Patt) was a citizen of prominence in early Heppner.

The great influx of Irish came about 1890 and they almost took over the county for a decade or two. Their story has been interestingly told by Judge John F. Kilkenny (now of the federal appeals bench at San Francisco), son of one of the most stimulating, John Kilkenny, who came with Jim Carty in 1890, direct from County Leitrim.

John Kilkenny was here but a few years when he borrowed some money from Bill Hughes and bought a band of sheep to take to the mountains. He was, from that day, off on an expanding business that brought him fame, wealth and a lot of fun until the depression of 1939, when he died, his fortune somewhat reduced. But it was enough.

The Irish sheepmen worked their sheep from Sand Hollow, where many of them wintered, south to the Blue Mountains and down to the north fork of the John Day, using the free grass. They were a jolly lot, hard working and attentive to their flocks when in the field and inclined to lusty brawling and fighting when the responsibility lessened in the winters. Accounts from the police court in Heppner during the nineties show many fines paid by John and Frank Kilkenny or Uzz and Lee French.

It was a hard day for the Heppner marshals when they came to town, although usually profitable for the city's funds. It was all in fun as Judge Kilkenny records: "In the Celtic community of my youth, it was a mark of cowardice to carry a six shooter. All controversy was settled by fists. The grudge, so frequently pictured in today's "Old West" was entirely unknown. The bloody adversaries of tonight were the laughing companions of tomorrow. Woe to him who might suggest a reference to the night before. To them, of course, a good rough and tumble fight was a delightful form of exercise and a test of physical prowess, rather than a violation of the law. With such a philosophy, it is quite understandable that a goodly number could never appreciate why these moments of pleasure were rudely interrupted by a town marshal or county sheriff under pretense of law enforcement." The record proves that.

The Irish added an exuberance to life in Morrow County and made Heppner distinctive. They were gay and generous; they were boisterous and brawling; they drank and they gambled. But they were also pious and penitent, hard working and dependable. When the Irish got together for a wake or a feast day, the hills rang with their laughter and sometimes yet, the third generation Irish can hear in memory the strains of "Dear Old Donegal" echoing in deserted Sand Hollow. They were fine seasoning for a new county.

Most of them have drifted away; their adventurous spirit leading them to different climes. They were excellent sheepmen for several reasons. Not many were married, the Irish immigration did not include many young women, and young Irishmen were without family worry when they went into the hills for a six-month stay with the sheep. They were a faithful and loyal lot of men and their escapades upon release from responsibility were few, although noteworthy at the time.

Some of the Irish of Morrow County built up considerable fortunes on the sheep business. Charles Cunningham's estate is retained in the Cunningham Sheep and Land Company of wide investment. Kilkenny ranches are found in many places in Morrow County despite depression losses. William Hughes, once the richest, left property. Mike Kenny, Jerry Brosnan and several Dohertys became affluent and independent of bankers.

The Irish influence was strong in Morrow County at the turn of the century and a decade or two afterwards. It helped give Heppner the reputation of a wild western town, which it hardly deserved, although there were Saturday nights when the sheep were home from the hills and the cattle in the feed lots, when it was wild enough to suit the dreams of a movie producer.

In the old days men slipped the wool off the backs and bellies of sheep with hand shears, developing strong wrists and strong arms for the blades were pushed as much as opened and closed. And what if some decided to grow some wool of his own? (Courtesy Oregon Historical Society)

GRASS IS GOING

The marvelous bunchgrass that grew in varying profusion from the Columbia River to the Heppner hills and beyond was barely touched by the few stockmen who came before 1870; it was still waving luxuriantly and impressive by 1880, although the stock had increased many fold; by 1890 stockmen were going farther south, across the first range of the Blues for summer range. The end was in sight for those who came to harvest the crop of agropyrum spicatum, poa ampla and the little fescues that had grown for centuries from bleak hilltop to fertile bottom.

The dross from years, yea centuries, of tall grass, was six inches deep on the ground, so deep that no drop of moisture could run off the land. Not until the thick pad of decaying grass was trampled into powder and the grass eaten that supplied it, was erosion made possible—and that was the beginning of the end. The livestock industry destroyed its own resource.

In 1870 Umatilla County had 2916 inhabitants, and maybe 500 lived in what is now Morrow County; by 1880 these had grown to 9607, and maybe 2000 lived in future Morrow. These are, of course, estimates. The eighteen eighties saw great growth of population in Oregon, which grew from 174,768 to 313,767, almost doubling. And Morrow, which became a county then, had 4205 for the census taker to enumerate in 1890, doubling also.

There were reasons. The railroad came to Oregon and the Northwest and the itchy-footed in the East could get to the new land by easy-riding passenger cars to join the more adventurous who had come by covered wagon. Morrow had its own railroad since 1888, and there was the glamour of new land, the expanding sheep business, the fun of starting new, in new and slightly dangerous surroundings.

The boom was, however, ending by 1890, the best land already occupied by homesteaders, the best grass eaten and trampled, a depression was brewing. Morrow County lost population in the nineties, dropping to 4151. Gilliam lost from 3600 to 3201, although Umatilla continued to grow and, rather strangely, Sherman almost doubled again.

On November 19, 1891, the Heppner *Gazette* noted that wheat sold in Heppner at a price unprecedented for the season. Little Club went for 82½ and Bluestem for 85. That must have encouraged farmers, who could also feel good that the government was buying cavalry horses, 1000 to 1200 pounds, black, brown or gray and would pay good prices. It was a good time to get rid of outlaws. E. G. Sperry at the Belvedere Saloon provided headquarters for the buyers.

The Morrow County Land & Trust Company was organized in 1888 with Nelson Jones as president; Ed R. Bishop, treasurer, and T. E. Fell, secretary. It advertised the highest price for wheat, sheep pelts, hides and a storage capacity in Heppner of 5000 bags of wool, 50,000 bushels of grain, and at Ione a grain capacity of 30,000 bushels and 25,000 bushels at Douglas. This company was to be an important factor in local business for many years. The Morrow County Record, a new newspaper with J. W. Coffey as publisher, reported in the spring of 1891 that the Portland market for Walla Walla wheat was $1.25, wool 17 cents, small white beans three and three-quarters cents a pound, dried pears 11 cents, live beef four cents, dressed seven to eight cents, with mutton and pork going for four cents or a little better.

In the spring of 1892, the *Gazette*, having some competition, sent a man into the country to interview farmers—and probably try to pick up some subscriptions. He found that the farmers of Eightmile were working on a new scheme this year in order to plow more acres. They fastened a number of walking plows together to form improvised gangs and found them as effective as the more expensive ones bought from a store. These, however, were available, as W. B. McAllister at Lexington, was advertising Flying Dutchman plows—an early favorite. He also sold Buffalo Pitts threshers, Hodge headers (the old wooden frame, no doubt), Monitor press drills and wagons, carriages and buggies, and when a homesteader could afford a buggy, he was out of the poverty class.

At Ione, the reporter asked farmers to estimate the cost of raising wheat. They average about four dollars per acre and the yields reported were about 14 bushels, although 1891 had been a good year,

After the thresherman had gone the farmer could survey what was left. The thresherman's horses had eaten a lot of hay (that was a constant complaint) and he had left two piles; one of straw which was useful for many things including feed in the winter, and even to stuff the straw ticks that softened many a bed, and then there was a pile of wheat in sacks that could be hauled to the warehouse along the railroad tracks for sale at a price always too little. The outfit above was hauling into Ione probably from the Gooseberry country for he has eight horses and/or mules on three wagons carrying about 100 140 pound sacks. He could make a trip a day and would be lucky to finish the job before snow flew.
(Courtesy Morrow County Museum)

and some grain had made 20 bushels. It was said that one man with three light horses could farm 160 acres of land. Land was selling at prices varying from $2 to $20 per acre. In that good year locally, there was a report that Umatilla had 87,210 acres in crop with an average of 20.7 bushels, Morrow County had 37,192 acres with an average of 24.4 bushels, Gilliam 13,474 acres that made 24.0 bushels and Sherman had 41,850 acres making 18.4 bushels. The experienced wheat farmer will not take the reported bushels seriously.

H. M. Thornton, below Ione, had a band of 3000 sheep, had lambed 110 percent, spent $400 for herders, $210 for camp tending, $100 for board, $200 for lambing expense, some for salt and wool sacks, eight cents a head for shearing 2250 for a total of $1258. His average clip was nine pounds and he got 12½ cents for the wool. That was encouraging.

Homesteaders didn't have all their land plowed. Around Eightmile, William Haguewood had 320 acres, 80 acres cultivated; W. K. Harrah had 480 acres, 110 cultivated; V. J. Coffey, 480 acres, 90 cultivated. Farmers were beginning to use the summerfallow method. At Gooseberry, O. Bergstrom had 320 acres and 100 in crop. N. R. McVay estimated the cost of raising wheat per acre at $5.71: plowing $1.50, harrowing 20 cents, seed 30 pounds 25 cents, seeding 10 cents, harrowing 40 cents, heading $1.50, threshing 22 bushels at 8 cents $1.76. At a cost of 30 cents there was some profit in hauling it to Heppner if the price was 68 cents, which was reported in March of that year. McVay had not figured sacks that cost 8½ cents to add about four cents to the expense per bushel.

Billie Morrow, the ebullient son of Jackson L. Morrow, had been elected county clerk and in his official capacity was paying 2½ cents for squirrel

scalps. Small boys with a piece of string could pick up a little change by snaring sage rats. These little pests multiplied rapidly on the wheat of the new residents.

The reason the early history of any region is important is that the patterns are set early and are not often changed unless there be industrialization. Patterns set by the pioneers still rule; their crops are our crops, their roads are our roads, changes are in degree, not design.

Most of the experimenting was tried before 1900. As early as 1892, the East Oregonian reported that Thomas, Andrew and Frank Reaney, owning land below Lexington on Willow Creek, contemplated going into hop raising. The Matteson coal mine was an experiment into mineral hunting. It was located up Willow Creek and once employed several men who sank a shaft some 700 feet below ground. It attracted some otherwise affluent investors and caused some bankruptcies. Some farmers tried to grow fruit and some succeeded, although the product was of poor quality and the frost ruined the crop in too many years.

It was still a country not completely rid of the native flora and fauna, for Newt Jones reported the killing of a 44-inch rattlesnake in his bedroom and with Waldon Rhea, Jones had turned a coyote loose with 300 yards head start of the hounds, and they soon caught the varmint. Running hounds after coyotes was a form of sport followed by stockmen.

By the fall of 1893 wheat was down to 35 cents and three-year-old steers were selling for $2.00 per hundred and the price of wool was down to six cents. The Cleveland depression was on. Max Lichtenthal made an assignment to creditors and, although he returned to the boot and shoe business later, his stock was liquidated by Tom Quaid as

Rudie and his father, Bill Bergstrom pose by the highway sign of Gooseberry, named, it is said for the big gooseberry bush that grew around the dripping spring on the Jake Young place a few miles away where the early settlers got their water. Once there was a post-office here and the foundations of the old school are across the fence. Film. (Courtesy Ann Bergstrom)

assignee. Cox Brothers at Hardman and C. W. VanDuyn were others who had to close their businesses. And many other stores advertised a strictly cash basis for trade and big discounts for cash. There wasn't any cash or almost none, and what there was went for food, clothes could be made to last, taxes could be neglected, equipment was repaired. You could buy Heppner flour for $2.50 a barrel of 196 pounds. Church people held donation parties for ministers.

The National Bank of Heppner, which was largely a stockman's bank, started having troubles in the depression, and while it lasted until the fall of 1897, it finally closed, Ed R. Bishop advertising note holders and others to present claims for payment.

But the 1894 crop was good, the heavy rains that had destroyed some of the 1893 wheat in the stacks had soaked the soil. Sheepmen were selling sheep to Sam Palmer, who was driving them east. George Wright went as far as Soda Spring, Idaho, with one of the Palmer bands and reported that it was hard herding. The price wasn't much but it was money. Jake Young of Eightmile reported a crop of 26½ bushels of wheat on summerfallow, but the price was a puny 25 cents a bushel. Felix

Johnson took Silas Wright's wool, advancing 11 cents a pound on it. There were signs that the depression was ending; the Elks Lodge was organized late in 1895 with A. W. Patterson as first Exalted Ruler and some local men, tired of being depressed, formed a group called the "neversweats" to rout despair.

Late in 1894 the forces of repression had charged the saloonmen, J. B. Natter, George Tedrowe, Bob Krick, E. L. Matlock, E. G. Sperry and probably Low Tillard (who called his establishment the Telephone because it was the only one with a phone in it), with failing to close on Sunday. They aimed to please and did so well at it that not a single saloon was put in the hands of creditors.

By 1898 sheep were selling for four dollars or more and wool brought from ten to sixteen cents, and the demand for sheep to drive east on well-used sheep trails was good. By the end of that year the assessor figured that Morrow County had 55,546 tillable acres worth $128,257 and non-tillable land 319,198 acres, worth $317,010. There were 3915 horses and mules worth $53,534, 3344 cattle worth $50,935 and 170,196 sheep worth $235,467. Total property, real and personal, was $1,445,404, an increase of fifty percent since 1888 despite the depression. The land office at LaGrande reported that Morrow County was 25 percent timbered mountain, 40 percent grazing, 20 percent arid and 14 percent farming land.

Heppner was still a wool center and there was a constant complaint about the conditon of the road to Monument, but they hauled over it. The Monument road was Heppner's lifeline, its contact with the great basin of the John Day, that was one of the most productive areas of the state with its flocks of sheep and herds of cattle providing certain wealth every year. The record doesn't show that Morrow County ever put as much money into the Monument road as the importance of the road demanded. It was a seasonal road and used mostly in April and May after the wool was clipped. Morrow County sheep were shorn at home or nearby, usually right after lambing and before the ewes and lambs were sent off to the mountains. Sheep men along the John Day followed a similar schedule, but they had to haul over the Monument road because it was the cheapest route to market. The Dalles-Canyon City road didn't hit the main fork of the John Day until west of Dayville; it had been built to serve the military detachment stationed at Camp Watson and the mining camp at Canyon City. To get to that road a Monument sheepman would probably have hauled over the mountains through Fox, which was a sizeable town in the 1880s, and down to Mount Vernon and thence to The Dalles. There was no road down the north fork to market.

In 1898 the county engaged Henry Scherzinger to improve the Monument road and he did, keeping within the appropriation and finishing on time. But the machinery at the turn of the century was inadequate for making a good road. Ed Rounds of Monument says that freighters on the road to Heppner used six to ten head of horses, and even so had to double up on some of the hills.

The following table shows the distances from Heppner and the elevations. From Parker's Mill to the summit of the Blue Mountains the road climbs 600 feet in 3½ miles:

	Miles	Elevation
Heppner	0	1916
Rhea Creek	11	1926
Dairyville	20	3226
Toll Rock	26	3396
Parker's Mill	30	2916
Summit Blue Mts.	33½	3545
Little Wall Creek	40½	2600
Summit between Wall Creeks	42	3050
Big Wall Creek	45	2884
John Day Hill	51	3016
John Day River	55	2076
Monument	58	2090

The trip took eight days, which meant camping out for the teamsters and the weather was not always the best for outdoor living. They took grain for their horses and depended on grass for bulkier feed, turning the horses loose at night and rounding them up in the morning, an art that was developed by necessity and has been lost along with many other pioneer skills. In Heppner the drivers put their horses in Tom Morgan's feed yard and slept in their wagon beds. They ate at one of the several Chinese restaurants of which Heppner always had a number. When ready for the return trip the men drove around to the stores and supply houses to load up if they were lucky enough to get a load to haul back. Even a fair load would be more profitable than hauling wool sacks 58 miles for ¾ cent per pound. There were two freight forwarding warehouses that loaded wool wagons for the trip back with food supplies, barbed wire by the carload and loads of farm machinery, wagons and fence staples and other necessities for a developing country.

The route wasn't only used for hauling by wagon. Stock was trailed over it, bands of wethers going

to market or to Montana or Colorado for a summer, before hitting Chicago to become mutton chops for the affluent and mutton stew for the poor. Cattle were trailed over the road, taking time to eat down the grass that grew on the south slopes between the summit of the Morrow County ridge of the Blue Mountains and the north fork of the John Day River. Heppner was a good shipping point; the price was as good as any and the delights of the town were equal to those of Pendleton or The Dalles. Whisky tastes about the same wherever bought.

Hauling wool in the spring and hauling supplies throughout the year, together with a tri-weekly stage to Monument and Long Creek made Hardman a sizeable town before 1900. There were several stores and many stables and feed yards, a good school and a Methodist church, where all denominations met at specified intervals. There were also four fraternal orders and three halls where dances were held. These were often exciting and on at least one occasion fatal for a participant.

Hardman once stretched out far from the highway to the south and west and the rotting sidewalks of a once prosperous town indicate that hundreds of people lived here, as those with long memories will attest. The original name was Rawdog, which must have been given in jest. A rival settlement was named Yallerdog and it thrived as a competitor for a few years until most of its citizens moved into the larger Rawdog. The agricultural land around Hardman is very good, although mostly above 3000 feet, precluding the growing of tender plants, so the natives milked cows. That gave it the name of Dairyville or Dairy, by which it was known for years. David Hardman, who had the postoffice on his ranch near town, moved the office onto the main street and eventually the name of the postoffice became the name of the town.

Parker's mill was not only a saw mill; it was also a stopping place for the freighters who brought the wool from the John Day country. (Courtesy Harold Peck)

The men who came through Hardman hauling wool or freight or moving the lumber from Parker's Mill to Heppner, or driving stock, were outdoor types of rugged constitution, used to making decisions quickly and positively. The town that attempted to serve them and entertain them, naturally had to adopt the same characteristics and Hardman was no place for the weak-willed or indecisive.

In the late 1890s there were several instances of sheep shooting in the hills behind Heppner. Cattlemen resented the intrusion of sheep. Asa Thompson had a band shot up on Indian Creek and lost 200 sheep and Mrs. H. Welsh lost 125 sheep in a similar attack. Judge Kilkenny reports that his father's camp was attacked by night riders on an occasion or two. But the sheep and cattle war was never so vicious or as destructive as it became in Crook and Grant Counties.

Soon the depression was over, wool was worth almost 20 cents and wheat was selling for almost 70. The country was young, the grass not yet all eaten, and there was no time for considering the sad things of life. As Elisha Green Sperry advertised in the *Gazette*:

"The crescent waves on Cretan shores
The cross of Christ goes down,
The Turks are helped by Christian powers,
Who bombard fort and town.
Columbia's eagle hears nor heeds
Poor Cuba's piercing cry,
Then let us drown these shameful deeds
In Sperry's "Lobwood Rye".

And the roisterers flocked to the Belvedere to shout and sing and perhaps plan to seek gold in the Klondike, where their spirits could find freer rein. Some did that very thing.

MORROW COUNTY PRESS

This may seem to the reader a peculiar time to introduce the history of the press of Morrow County. The reason is that it has been a peculiarly good press, almost always in tune with the local power structure and helpful to the development of the county. There is always a power structure, of course. Sometimes it is the elected officials, most often not; it may be the bankers and businessmen; it may be the saloon keepers. It is always the people who count, who make the decisions—sometimes it is the women. A town or county must have a decisive power structure if it is to progress in any direction. When the power structure is weak or vacillating, as it occasionally becomes, it can often be stimulated by a newspaper that has the public eye.

Morrow County's newspapers have served in that capacity many times; they have almost always been edited by responsible men with a serious interest in the county beyond its availability as a place to make some money. Any history of newspapers in a pioneer country naturally revolves around the papers that have survived. In Morrow County, that is the *Gazette*, although the *Times* is represented on the masthead.

The history of Morrow County newspapers begins long before Morrow County was hatched—on September 12, 1851, to be exact. That was the birthdate of John W. (probably for William) Redington and the place was Cambridge, Massachusetts,

where he was born to Patrick and Mary Redington. At school he played with some lads who became well-known writers and at the age of twelve he went to work for the *Cambridge University Press* as printers' devil, running errands for the thirty-two printers employed there. Contributors were Longfellow, Lowell, Oliver Wendell Holmes, Charles E. Norton and Dean Howells, who was then editor of the *Atlantic Monthly*. It was a heady experience for a bright and attentive lad.

When he was twenty-one he went to New York as a printer and joined the militia where he rose to sergeant. When he tried to join the regular army he was refused because he was too small, so he enlisted as a musician. He was sent to Fort Vancouver, Washington, in 1874, but didn't like barracks life, so was given his discharge, on which it was recorded that he was 5' 5½" tall, fair complexioned, with gray eyes, brown hair that was almost always thereafter described as red.

Redington went up to Salem where he got a job working for the *Statesman*, with the title of city editor, which was a fictitious title, for the *Statesman* had a circulation of 500 and printed but four pages. After a few months he went into partnership with a friend in a job printing business. Redington boarded with Mrs. A. B. Meacham, whose husband had been commissioner for the Indians, and was a survivor of the peace party that met with the Modocs at the lava beds when General E. R. S. Canby was killed. Meacham filled Redington's head full of Indian tales.

With some other young men he planned a foray by horseback into Eastern Oregon, but the others backed out, so Redington saddled up and struck out alone in March of 1877. He came to The Dalles and rode south to Antelope following the general route of The Dalles Military Road. On the Warm Springs Indian Agency out of Burns he met Egan (Ehegante) and went hunting with him and a party of braves, beginning a long friendship with that unfortunate chief. The little redhead rode on to Boise and met Governor Mason Brayman and from there down to Salt Lake, where he worked in a print shop. It was the year of the Nez Perce war and General Oliver Otis Howard was chasing that wily chieftain, Joseph, across Idaho and into Montana. Redington couldn't enlist, so he rode up to Silver Bow, Montana, to join the volunteer scouts.

His experience as a scout determined the pattern of his life. A scout moved alone, riding often at night, creeping close enough to Indian camps to determine the strength of their army, taking care of himself without hope of protection from soldiers. It was a lonely, solitary existence and Redington loved it. It was wild and free but it entailed detailed responsibilities that could be performed independently. Daring was required, nerve, bravery, inventiveness, endurance. A scout was a slasher like a timber wolf; he fought savagely and quickly and fled the scene before the enemy summoned assistance. As for him, no assistance was available.

In 1878 he rode by Heppner to join General O. O. Howard in his fight against his old friend, Egan. Umapine, the Umatilla chief, according to Redington, had stolen a band of horses in Fox Valley, and went off to join the Bannacks. He wanted to return home, so planned to do some favor for the whites to regain his standing. He plotted against Egan to achieve forgiveness and delivered Egan's head in a sack to the white general, which is a version that agrees generally with history already recounted.

Western scouts were not often enlisted men or officers. They were more often hired on a contract basis and received pretty good pay. Many wrote about their experiences for the papers and this Redington was equipped to do.

In the spring of 1883, Redington again came riding up Willow Creek for another visit to the Heppner that he was to write about so eloquently. By that time J. H. Stine, an itinerant newspaper man, whose practice it was to go into a new town and collect a sum of money from the businessmen to start a newspaper. He ordered some type and a George Washington handpress and other equipment. He published a paper until he could sell it to the first one to come along. If there is speculation about what Stine did with the money it is natural; it is not on record that he saved it. The first issue of the *Heppner Gazette* was published March 30, 1883, and that is about the time Redington hit town to register at Ellis Minor's City Hotel with less than a dollar in money, a fair saddle horse and a background of thirty-one varied years.

To start the paper Henry Heppner and brother-in-law, Henry Blackman, had given $50 apiece; S. P. Florence, J. L. Morrow, T. W. Ayres, Frank Maddock, Tom Morgan, J. B. Sperry, G. W. Swaggert, J. B. Natter, W. J. Leezer, W. B. Cunningham, A. M. Gunn, Charles Hinton, W. E. Theodore and Ed R. Bishop added to the pot with about $25 each. They were a small part of the estimated 370 persons in the little town, some were merchants, two were saloon keepers, one a brewer and a few were stockmen.

Stine soon left town to venture in other fields and Redington had the *Gazette* to himself. He was never completely popular in Heppner; he always stimulated opposition. By February, 1884, there was another paper projected under the editorship of Homer Hallock, son of O. H. Hallock, a local man of repute. The men behind the new *Times* were responsible. The fight, truly in the spirit of an Indian scout, was quick and vicious. Redington turned loose all his power of invective and libel, accused Hallock and Augustus Mallory, two notaries public, with charging homesteaders too much to locate land, inferred that Mallory had stolen a hog. The *Gazette* offered to locate settlers for nothing. The *Times* lasted but a few weeks; the attack was too overwhelming. It made Redington feared more than respected. From it, however, he derived the slogan that he painted on barns all over the country: "Heppner Gazette (sometimes Gazet) Hell on Hog Thieves and Hypocrites." His slashing style of writing together with his combativeness won him a reputation in the state for western journalism and he enhanced that reputation by exchanging papers with any editor who would mail him a copy.

As an editor Redington was spicy and readable. He had little formal education but read a great deal and was well informed. He did not indulge in the social customs of the frontier. The county seat fight was over in June of 1886 with Heppner the victor by a small margin, and in November of that year

Redington sold his paper to Rev. Henry Rasmus, and went to Walla Walla, Washington, where he married Nellie Meacham, daughter of his one-time landlady. He tried several jobs that were not successful before going to Puyallup, Washington, as editor of a paper called the *Commerce*.

Rasmus soon told the *Gazette* to Otis Patterson, who came down from Waitsburg, Washington, and it was he who set the pattern of Morrow County newspapers as much as anyone. He was a conscientious man who worked well with the citizens of the community, prodding them about the Monument road, the lack of water in town, the absence of a fire department. He got things done and antagonized few. He did not get entangled in politics, although he did support the candidacy of Henry Blackman in 1888 for state senator, although Blackman was a Jew and a Democrat, and Patterson was a Protestant and a Republican.

He did not have the town to himself for long. *The Farmers' Alliance* started the *Morrow County Record*, edited by John Coffey. *The Farmers' Alliance* was based in Lexington and it is likely that it was printed with the same type that had been used in the short-lived *Bunchgrass Blade* that perished with the defeat of Lexington in the county seat fight. There had been the *Lexington Budget* at one time also. Vawter Crawford had been editor of the *Record* along with A. H. Hicks and Thomas Nelson. It was taken over by the Pattersons, Otis and Alva, during the depression of 1895.

The demise of the *Record* brought little solace for Patterson and the *Gazette*, for in 1897, E. M. Shutt moved in to start another paper called the *Times*. Mr. Shutt had started several newspapers in Oregon, but not as many as had his brother, Sloan P. Shutt. E. M. moved over from Antelope, where he had been publishing the *Herald*.

Otis Patterson received the appointment as receiver at The Dalles Land Office and departed from Heppner in 1898, selling the *Gazette* to Corleis Merritt.

In 1889 Jackson L. Morrow died after several months of illness and John W. Redington came up from Portland where he was living to attend the funeral of his old friend. Before he left he had bought the *Gazette* from Merritt. He moved his family including wife, Nellie and three daughters, into a comfortable house across the street from the office, near the Mountain House, and picked up the duties of editorship.

Redington was a great letter writer, one who liked to advertise himself, maybe a bit flamboyantly. He sent his paper to anyone who wrote for a copy and so entertaining was his style that he sold papers over a wide area, although never in any sizeable number. Thus, it was that on August 20, 1900, Owen Wister, who in 1905 was to publish *"The Virginian,"* came to Heppner and took up residence in the Palace Hotel. He rode about the country and visited at the Redington home nearly every night. Redington hoped to interest the young writer and lawyer in the Bannack campaign and perhaps in himself and his undoubtedly exciting experiences as an Indian scout. But Wister centered his interest in Wyoming as a scene for his major writing and never got around to using the Redington material.

The contest between Shutt and Redington was bitter, and Redington resorted to much the same tactics as he had used to demolish the first *Times* back in 1884. Both papers resorted to libel, but one day in February, 1901, the little redhead published a story that cast some aspersions on Shutt and a young woman who was working in the *Times* office. It was barely on the street and Redington was taking an armful of papers to the postoffice when he met Shutt and a first-rate fist fight took place. Redington was no match for Shutt, who was bigger and madder, and before anyone could interfere the *Gazette* editor was laid out on the sidewalk needing the assistance of someone to take him home. He remained in bed several days.

True to his scout's training, Redington retreated in the face of superior forces. He was not a bulldog. On May 16 he published his last *Gazette*, selling out to Fred Warnock and Ed Michell and departed his beloved Heppner hills.

His was not a quick and witty humor and quotation from his writing requires space, but he was a master of the quiet spoof (if that word has not lost its meaning in the intervening 70 years). He reported that Henry Heppner had lost some 39 mules in an Indian attack along the John Day River and that later Egan told him that he had put them on a mountain meadow to fatten, butchered them and sold them to the whites for venison.

He did not drink, which set him apart from other residents of Heppner, but he was a delightful companion, although too different, perhaps too learned, to be popular with the local population, who were a fairly rough lot. He loved his daughters dearly and probably started to sign himself John Watermelon Redington for their amusement. He died in a veteran's home in Sawtelle, California, in 1935.

Vawtor Crawford came down from Waitsburg to work for Patterson whom he had known there. He became county clerk in 1899 and served until 1906, when he went back to the newspaper business. E. M. Shutt became sheriff in 1903, selling the *Times* to A. J. Hicks. Crawford bought out Warnock, who had taken over Michell's interest in 1910, and in 1912 bought the *Times* to end the competition and establish a paper that has been a solid country newspaper for sixty years. The Crawfords ran it for over forty years, first Vawter, then sons, Arthur, Spencer and Jasper, and then Vawter's younger brother, Otheo G. The Crawfords weren't mad at anyone and were excellent printers, good writers and strong enough to not be swayed by temporary waves of public sentiment. And they worked for Morrow County and Heppner, observed it carefully and reported it respectfully.

Vawter, the pater familias, and Spencer, who was the manager, both died in the 1930s and young Jasper took over soon, to be followed by Otheo. He ended the Crawford regime by selling to Bob Penland. Wesley Sherman succeeded him but his untimely death in 1969 brought the Charles Heards to the management.

Ione had a newspaper for many years, sometimes two at once, but none of them achieved more than local importance. Miss Virginia Deaton was the first editor. She called her six-column paper with patent insides, *The Post*. W. W. Head, a minister, was editor of the *Ione Independent* some years later.

Addison Bennett was another editor who brought fame to a section of Morrow County. He was past middle age when he came to Oregon from Kansas, where he had worked on newspapers and had written the ballad: "The Little Old Sod Shanty on the Claim". Remember:

"The hinges are of leather
And the windows have no glass,
And the board roof lets the howling bliz-
    zard in.
I can hear the hungry coyote
As he sneaks up in the grass,
In my little old sod shanty on the claim."

Bennett became the first postmaster of Irrigon when the Oregon Land & Water Company was organizing the irrigation project along the Columbia above Boardman.

Bennett started a little newspaper called at first the *Oregon Irrigator* which he later changed to the *Irrigon Irrigator*. He had created the name *Irrigon* all by himself and the paper was distinctively his, full of a droll wit, some homespun philosophy, but not much advertising.

After Bennett had gone off to be roving correspondent for the *Oregonian*, the paper gradually died, its final issue being in 1912. Bennett lived until 1924, his native wit unhampered by age.

Boardman had a paper for a few years in the 1920s but it was undistinguished.

EARLY SCHOOLS

The children of Morrow were fortunate; they learned their morals from the church, their rules of daily conduct from their parents, their arithmetic from counting the number of pigs, their biology from the barnyard, their geography from running or riding across the hills, their sense of beauty from the sunrise. Parents were anxious to add the ability to read and write as a sort of frosting on the educational cake, and hired grade school graduates, itinerant males and some normal school graduates to instruct.

School houses were generally within walking distance of the patrons to be served and the children developed some muscle getting to school and back, or if they rode horseback, they learned how to treat a horse.

Children begin to learn at birth and the process never stops for long during life. Some thought might well be taken about what branch of learning to specialize in, but there is always learning, more to the alert, less to the lethargic, but learning pours into the brain through every organ of sense, except the mouth. The eyes, the ears, the skin, the fingers, and when and if a child learns to read all the learning of mankind is available in the printed word. Nowdays, through mechanization, some of that knowledge is available through the ears and eyes. Discipline is necessary, and attention. One who has the desire to learn can do so and those with curiosity about the most things, will become the best educated. There is no mystery or magic about it, mainly desire and effort.

The Heppner school was started in 1873 and it was the first in the county. Soon there was one at Lena. It was not until the eighties after settlers had begun to take up some of the hill land, that

schools were started in other parts of the county. The Ione school started in 1885 and for a year after Mr. Sperry built the schoolhouse, there were no pupils, or not enough, to make the hiring of a teacher worthwhile.

By the fall of 1888 there was a high school at Heppner, although not the full four years. According to the *Gazette*, in the morning, Vocal Music, Reading, Elocution, Grammar, Algebra and Penmanship were taught. After recess there were classes in Mental Arithmetic, English Literature, Ancient History, Drawing, Practical Drills. In the afternoon there was Natural Philosophy, Arithmetic, Geometry, U. S. History and after recess, the final periods included instruction in Grammar, Arithmetic, Bookkeeping, Physiology, Chemistry, Spelling, and the day ended with more Vocal Music. The curriculum indicates that it was mainly elementary.

An Eightmile correspondent announced January 3, 1889, that the first term of public school was concluded December 15, the schoolhouse was the best in the county with good desks and large enough for all pupils. A writing school had been held two evenings a week. A party was given to mark the closing of school, a party that attracted the Beckets, Vaughans, Munkers, Carters, Gays, Robinsons and others.

There was a schoolhouse at Ella by 1888, and the Swedes around Fairview had built one in about 1887. Gooseberry citizens claimed a school by 1886, whether projected or in operation. The Saddle schoolhouse was built in the middle eighties. There was a school at Pettysville which was probably the reason the first Ione school was unattended.

When homesteaders came to take up land, they built schools all over the hills. These were usually little buildings, maybe 16x20 feet and were nearly always cooperatively built by parents of children. Some who had teams and a wagon hauled the lumber from Parker & Gleason's mill or from Van Ormen's mill on Butter Creek; there was always at least one man who had some experience as a builder, and everyone helped with the labor and the cost. Furniture could be made out of plain lumber, a stove installed if the school was to be held after frost, which was uncommon. Most of the early schools were in session but three or four months of the year; later there were two periods, one in the spring and another in the fall. Attendance was not steady as boys were often kept at home to drive a plow

team or do some other farm work when they reached the age of ten or twelve.

There were not many books, almost no maps, never any teaching aids, but there was pretty good discipline, although occasionally some of the older boys took it in their heads to disrupt school. This was frowned upon by the elders who had sacrificed to start the school and insisted that attending be considered a privilege. If a boy didn't behave himself he could stay home and plow or pitch hay.

Some of these little schools bore strange names, some indicative of high hope, many descriptive and some beautiful in concept. There was Willow Way on upper Rhea Creek and Golden West down the creek a few miles. Strawberry, Blackhorse, Juniper, Missouri Ridge, Democrat Gulch, Alpine (in lower Sand Hollow where there was nothing alpine), Pleasant Vale, Rocky Bluff, Sand Hollow, Twin

Pines, Green Cottage, were surely descriptive and named to enhance attractiveness.

In April of 1889 the *Gazette* noted that the school census of children between the ages of four and twenty years were 749 males and 768 females, and of these 978 were in school. There were 29 teachers and the total disbursement was $11,892.00.

By the spring of 1892, the number of pupils had declined to 1486, but 1026 were in school. The value of schools and grounds was $16,700, and of apparatus was $3197. The average salary for male teachers was $48.46 and for female teachers was $43.38. The county school superintendent got $40 per month. There were 58 districts and 53 reported that there was an average of 4 4/5 months taught and twelve schools had a Webster's dictionary.

Everything, nearly, has changed except the idea that it is possible to raise the status or ease of living by going to school.

IONE

Even when Umatilla Landing was the shipping point for packers to the Idaho mines the river boats would stop at Castle Rock where there was a landing place a mile and a half above the mouth of Sixmile Canyon. The pioneers didn't need much but what they did need was important to them. Stock salt was a necessity for salt licks were too few; few white men learned to like moccasins, they wanted shoes; flour was a commodity in demand

until the mill was built in Heppner and even though there was game in the hills some salt pork was handy to have around the cabin. Other things that were hauled in from the outside were powder and ball and later ammunition, sugar, beans, glass, and nails. Of course, the process of making necessities out of luxuries was going on then as now to create demand.

The Ella school, taken in 1898, is typical of the country schools the settlers built to have their offspring taught the three Rs. And to hold church in and entertainments and speakings and even protest meetings. (Courtesy Carl Troedson)

By 1898 Ione decided to compete and built this solid and impressive school with its prominent bell and bell wheel to call youth to "come and learn, come and learn." (Courtesy Oregon Historical Society)

The road to Castle Rock led straight south across the desert and it was so sandy that small loads were all that could be hauled on a wagon; a pack string was more efficient. The road followed Fourmile Canyon up to Ella where Frank Oviatt had a post-office as early as 1882 and from there it is almost straight south to Reitmann Canyon that leads down to the flat along Willow Creek at Ione. There was traffic along this road even before Heppner and Morrow started their store and there was also some traveling up and down the creek for early day stockmen were there with their herds.

Ed Cluff, a sheepman, owned the eastern part of the townsite-to-be of Ione and he had been there since 1872. George Emerick owned the western part farther down the creek which runs east and west there. By 1883 Elisha Green Sperry, a pioneer in many things, acquired the Emerick land. Sperry thought that someplace along the creek there would be a town and the land here was level and it was only a few feet down to water; the high hills to the south sheltered the site. He went ahead, undaunted.

There was a little girl living in the flat with her parents by the name of Ione Arthurs and she was pretty and cute so Mr. Sperry, who had a good sized family of his own, named the town for her.

The name seemed to fit for Ione has never been a town that had delusions of grandeur; few have ever proclaimed to city council or chamber of commerce that Ione was to be a second Chicago. No, Ione was content to be a little country town with what merchants were necessary to sell what was demanded by the stout Swedes who settled south and north on the bunchgrass hills.

The first business in the town is sometimes said to have been a saloon which Charles McFarland opened with the aid of Mr. Sperry, who was enamored with the saloon business and conducted one in Heppner for many a year although he came from a family of preachers. The saloon business had no disagreeable connotations until the Women's Christian Temperance Union became powerful.

Aaron Royse opened a store and George Loutrelle started a blacksmith shop. Mr. Royse had a post-office, established in 1884, getting the business from Pettysville, a mile or so up the creek. Sperry built

a schoolhouse in 1885 but there were too few pupils, his own being too old for school—his eldest, Phoebe, already married to Robert Wills, who was running a store.

When the railroad was completed late in 1888 there was no longer use for Castle Rock, so the warehouses where goods were stored until they could be hauled inland were torn down or moved away bodily. Some of these came to Ione, it being the closest town although a good twenty-five miles away. T. E. Fell, wool dealer, moved his warehouse to Ione and it was there that Mr. Wills had his store. When the railroad was being built T. J. Carle had a small hotel and by 1891 Joseph A. Woolery moved down from Dairyville to start a store. He was a pusher who kept things moving. Mat Halvorsen opened another store and before long took in Bert Mason whose Portuguese father had a ranch on Rhea Creek. Halvorsen went to farming and Mason spent a lifetime selling supplies to Ione citizens.

Paul Balsiger was one of a numerous family of Swiss and he started a blacksmith shop which grew into a hardware store, sold later and operated for another lifetime by Omar Reitmann, one of a big family of Germans who stayed near the ancestral acres and in their youths were marvelous baseball players. Paul O'Meara, an Irishman, ran a blacksmith shop until his death.

In the late nineties there were several stores, the hotel, a saloon or two, a photograph gallery, a newspaper (the Post), the Blake butcher shop—almost every convenience any little town could wish. But the country north of Ione had its periods of failures and one of them came along about 1905 and the settlers moved away in droves. Bert Mason recalls that five country school houses were moved into town to become residences and the town lost population from the 600 it had boasted a few years earlier. Its population was 439 in 1920. It had been incorporated in 1899 with E. G. Sperry as mayor and M. S. Maxwell, recorder.

As roads were built into the Eightmile and Gooseberry country more of the wheat from farms there was hauled to Ione and made it a center with huge warehouses that turned to elevators as harvesting methods changed.

LEXINGTON

Lexington was started with an entirely different concept than Ione. It did have delusions of grandeur. In 1885, although Bill Penland had made the level land at the mouth of Black Horse Canyon his headquarters since he had arrived from Kentucky in the late sixties, it was still pretty much a sheep camp, but there was a blacksmith shop with Jack McVey at the forge, an eating house and a warehouse for the Penland wool. The business was mostly self-engendered.

There is no available evidence that Penland held any malice toward Heppner; he did business with its merchants and apparently patronized its banks. But he decided to get the county seat and William Penland had a whim of iron.

He operated from his ornate dwelling just south of Black Horse Canyon, a house described as a two and a half story house with a wide porch along the front and on the south side. The front door opened to a wide hall and doors from that led to a parlor on one side and a sitting room on the other, both with bay windows. The huge dining room occupied the center of the house and it is probable that many of the Penland employees were fed there for behind it was a large kitchen and the store rooms for supplies and a convenient woodshed were facilities sufficient for that purpose. It was the home of a nabob. After his death in 1901 it fell into less careful hands and was eventually torn down and a newer house built on the spot, not so grand but still a fine house.

Lexington has had several large and well-known stores, the one owned by Homer McFarland perhaps being the first. There was also Davis and Wormman. W. B. McAllister had a store for years and briefly a bank and Barnetts had a store for years.

Karl Beach was prominent in many ways in Lexington life, being an early implement dealer. Elsie Beach taught the first school, actually before there was a school house.

Lexington has had many events that can be ascribed to hard luck. In 1886 fire destroyed the Reaney livery stable and some fine horses belonging to that numerous family. Some stores were burned also. A jury decided that the fire was incendiary and sent two men to the penitentiary for setting it. The three blocks of business houses had to be rebuilt. Fire was the bane of the small wooden towns of the pioneers who lived with open flames for light and heat.

On June 14, 1888 a cyclone hit Lexington, an oddity in the county. Mrs. G. W. Brock was killed in the wreckage of the Brock barn and the wind went on northeast demolishing homesteaders' cabins and school houses that were in its path. The trees in the well-used Lexington grove were beheaded as if cut with a sickle.

Lexington, although started as a sheep camp, early began to be a center for the wheat business aided by the good soil of the Black Horse country and north of there and after a road was built down Clark Canyon by the wheat of the Social Ridge area.

Lexington became the headquarters for the Morrow County Grain Growers with its numerous agencies and it is the center of the wheat business of the county and the supplies needed therefore. Many dollars are exchanged in the wheat business but not many people are needed for operation. Lexington's population remains small although its business is large. It once had an airport that is still the best landing field in the county.

THE HEPPNER FLOOD

June 14, 1903 was a hot Sunday and the 1146 citizens of Heppner were lethargically doing only what was necessary in the sultry heat. Small boys played in ankle deep Willow Creek, businessmen lounged in comfortable chairs on lawns or in shaded rooms; in the saloons the gamblers mechanically shuffled the cards and bet without enthusiasm; women bustled about in kitchens for the afternoon was ending and families must be fed.

There had been some rain the previous Thursday but not enough to do much good for the crops and the community hoped for more. About five o'clock

This is Heppner before the flood, taken before 1902 when the new, stone courthouse was built. The courthouse is the white building in right in the site of the present courthouse. The channel for the mill runs behind it and turns squarely west downhill to turn the mill wheel in the white building almost in the center of the picture; the old Heppner school, then less than ten years old stands beyond. Other reference points are the Catholic church in left foreground and the old Palace hotel. (Courtesy Morrow County Museum)

it began to rain, slowly at first, almost apologetically, but enough to break a desultory conversation. Citizens who looked to the south saw a dark cloud drift northeast, growing blacker as it neared and the rain became heavier, sending adults inside and the small boys scurrying homeward. And then hail fell, normal hail at first, but soon as large as chestnuts and some said it was like a blanket before the windows. It made a tremendous roar, muffling other sounds, and it lasted for over an hour until an estimated two or more feet had fallen.

When over Balm Fork three or four miles above Heppner the black cloud released tons and tons— and tons—of water; water in such amounts that great gashes were cut in the rocky north side of that canyon so deep that they may be seen after sixty years. The water rushed down them to the floor of the creek in quantities that moved rocks weighing hundreds of pounds and shoved or rolled them ahead of the wall of rushing, muddy water that also cleaned the drying hay from the meadows as another prize of conquest.

The storm went on northeast and dropped additional tons of water on Willow Creek, losing little of its intensity. Rocks were moved, houses and barns destroyed, fences swept along with the hay crop they were protecting. The flood struck Hinton Creek several miles above Heppner and dropped

more water but it had lost the greatest quantity in Balm Fork and Willow Creek that had to discharge through Heppner. Black Horse Canyon and Sand Hollow were also flooded.

When the waters of the fork and the creek came together at the upper edge of Heppner they were at least twenty feet high, that being the lesser of many estimates made by those who saw it and lived. The first building in its path was Fred Krug's laundry built across the creek at the upper crossing in the town; it held for a minute or two while the waters heightened and then it was crushed to add its debris to the floating lumber and trees and hay. It was not a flowing flood; it was a rolling flood that crushed with power.

Before it reached Court Street it demolished the home of A. Abrahamsick, killing her and fatally injuring him, and the William B. Barratt house where lived county commissioner Ed Ashbaugh. He was in Portland and safe but his entire family was drowned. West of Court Street and east of the creek lived Perry Dawson, J. L. Barnett, J. W. Waltrenburger, A. W. Rasmus, B. F. Vaughn and just above May Street were some houses occupied by Chinese and the home of Mrs. Kirk. James Fritz was also east of the creek.

West of the creek were the homes of W. L. Saling, E. M. Shutt, and T. R. Howard all of which were

61

This is Heppner the day after the flood. The mill shows up more plainly although the new blue stone courthouse barely shows at all. From Court street west to Chase and below clear to Gale nothing stood but a few of the most hardy trees. (Courtesy Morrow County Museum)

lost with family members who were home. This above August Street. Alfred Ayres and T. W. Ayres lived on the west side of the creek and had some protection from a row of poplar trees that grew on the bank, nevertheless both Ayres houses were floated away.

The May Creek bridge offered some resistance to the flood but only enough to make it higher and increase its destructive roll. On the east side of the creek were houses occupied by the French and Gurdane families and some small outbuildings. All were demolished and those at home drowned.

On the west side of the creek were the more ornate, the more expensive residences of the town. First below May was the home of C. A. Rhea, the banker, then in line that of Dr. P. B. McSwords, next being a house occupied by A. C. Giger, then the home of George Conser, W. O. Minor, Judge Julius Keithly and that of A. J. Wells all up the creek from the Episcopal church and all were swept away in little more time than it takes to recount it. Across Chase Street were the homes of George Swaggart, just north of Gilliam & Bisbee's machine shed, then the homes of the Mallorys, Augustus and W. L. Below Willow Street lived William Wells, James and T. J. Matlock at the corner of Chase and Center.

Across Center Street was the home of J. W. Morrow, living in the home of his late father who had founded the town, and on Main Street lived Mrs. Lloyd Elder, a widow who kept a cow. North of her was the residence of Phil Cohn and Mrs. Dawson, the elder. Below Baltimore Street on Main were the residences of George Kintzley, H. W. Bartholomew, C. E. Redfield, William Walton and James Roberts.

The creek bed became a little wider but the power of the flood was not appreciably lessened as it swept on to engulf the homes of A. M. Gunn, Ben Patterson, George Noble, Mrs. Welsh, E. J. Slocum, Dan Stalter, E. E. Morrison, W. W. Lippset, John Patterson and G. W. Phelps who lived near the ordinarily peaceful waters of Willow Creek. Robert F. Hynd's house below Water Street, split in two and he escaped although Mrs. Hynd and their daughter died.

Houses had been built with little or no foundation and such houses were raised and floated away and even those with stone or brick foundations were soon crushed by the force of the debris hurled against them. Residents were caught in the trap of their own homes or were drowned when trying to flee, few who were in the path of the flood escaped and those only after terrifying experiences. It lasted not more than twenty minutes and by that time over 250 of the town's residents were drowned or killed by flood driven timbers.

George Conser and wife were at home with Dr. P. B. McSwords and J. L. Ayres, enjoying a warm evening on the lawn. When it began to rain the Consers retreated inside and then upstairs as the water rose. The house was carried off its foundations and floated for some yards before reaching a bank allowing the Consers to be saved. McSwords and Ayres were lost.

Phil Cohn was asleep alone in his home, his family being away. The house floated down to W. O. Minor's alfalfa field a mile below town and Mr. Cohn crawled out unharmed, but badly shaken.

Julius Keithly, 70, who had an extensive garden along the creek, had his house wash away while he was upstairs. He found himself on a part of the roof tearing downstream on the flood. He saw his wife in the water on some floating lumber near him and he put out his hand to her but her feet were held fast and she could not be saved.

The wooden Heppner Hotel was on the southwest corner of Main and Church Streets and was then operated by Pearl Jones and Mose Ashbaugh. All of those families were drowned and a large number of the guests when the Pole Thompson livery stable washed against the hotel, crushing it.

Women, garbed in the long and heavy skirts of that era, found it impossible to wade in water a foot deep so could not flee to the hills fast enough. Modesty prevented discarding the skirts although one did. Mrs. James Willis and husband and children started for safety but the husband and most of the children were caught. She reached the railroad tracks and crawled under a freight car which protected her from floating timber until she could discard her clothing; then she broke open the door of a wool warehouse and wrapped herself in wool sacks. A freak of the flood deposited her smallest child on a rick of wool sacks where it was found, little hurt. Mrs. Willis was seriously injured and later died.

A. M. Gunn and wife sent their four children toward the hills but by the time they reached the Methodist church the water was all around them and they stayed. The elders both drowned.

Almost every family had a miraculous story to tell of rescue or all were silent because there was no miracle.

The managers and guests of the Palace Hotel saved several persons who came floating by on wrecked houses or debris and one of the Japanese houseboys of the hotel lost his life in attempting to rescue others.

When Mike Galloway awakened the morning of June 15, 1903 this is what he saw from his studio window at the southwest corner of Main and May Streets. People were already about not having stayed up all night as had Galloway. The sign for Garrigues was an old one when he operated on a smaller scale. His store stood and the roof may be seen over the top of the saloon building in the middle of Main Street. Already the search for the dead had begun. (Courtesy Morrow County Museum)

These pictures were taken by Galloway and developed by Sigsbee. Here the camera is pointed on the alley between Main and Chase Streets, looking south. The flood had cleared the town to the left and the piles of lumber held the remains of former citizens. (Courtesy Morrow County Museum)

May Street was full of buildings and disengaged lumber from houses that were destroyed upstream; every building on the east side of Main Street in the block just north of May Street was destroyed or moved except the Palace Hotel, which was a solid brick structure. On the west side of Main Street the buildings were of more durable material and were not moved; in fact there was comparatively little water in them, the buildings across the street giving them protection by holding the flood into the main stream.

But along Willow Creek, from far above the town to the alfalfa field below, there was almost complete destruction and few buildings were left standing, except the well built churches.

As soon as the flood was reduced in intensity two young men, Bruce Kelley, 31, and Leslie Matlock, 30, thought they could do something to warn the towns below Heppner. Kelley went to Stewart & Kirk's livery stable to saddle some horses and Matlock broke into Gilliam & Bisbee's hardware store for wire clippers and they were off, going down the west side of the canyon on the old stock road at the start. It was still raining and growing dark; the

going was rough and muddy and the stops frequent to open the many fences. They reached Lexington after the flood had hit that town destroying several houses, driving the inhabitants to the hills. The riders decided that they could beat the flood to Ione so they set off again always on a dead run. They came to Ione in the summer dusk and shouted the citizens into activity. Mayor J. A. Woolery, who had a knack for taking charge, called his flock together and ordered them to the hills below the rimrocks and sent young men to carrying bedding for them to sleep on for the night. Little damage occurred in Ione, with one small house being washed away, according to Bert Mason, an eye witness. Mason and William Adkins, another young man, accompanied Kelley and Matlock back to Heppner, arriving in the early dawn.

Word was sent to Echo and Pendleton and to Arlington and the names of couriers have been lost in dispute. Word was sent out from these towns by telegraph to the soon shocked world. Help was needed, men to dig away debris and hunt for bodies, women to wash and care for the dead, carpenters to build coffins, officers to keep order and prevent

64

looting, cooks to feed the hungry. Beds, blankets, food were in demand. Not for long. Oregon responded with money and men; the money totaling $61,297.47 when finally the official record was announced.

An eating counter was set up in the Palace Hotel, then managed by Phil Metschan Jr., and a morgue was opened in the opera house and the dance hall above the Belvedere saloon in the new, stone Roberts building.

Here were brought the bodies, bruised and dirty, for hasty identification if possible. For the first day or two there was no water with which to wash them except that which was carried, but soon the city pump, which was above the deepest flood, was put into operation and the pipes repaired. Many of the dead were children and as whole families had been drowned it was hard to identify all of them or even know to which family they had belonged. There was hysteria and bereavement in that room above the Belvedere, which in accordance with official edict, was closed.

The *Oregonian* sent Leslie M. Scott to Heppner and his first dispatches were published in the Wednesday issue and they were accurate and detailed. On that day he wrote this description: "An army of men and horses is sifting great wastes of debris. An army of women take charge of the bodies as they are borne out of the wreckage by straining arms of men, an arm, a leg, a finger, a lock of hair, a tuft of clothing—these are harbingers of horror beneath the mud. Babies and little children lie there buried, many with gashes or bruises on their tender bodies. Forms of women frequently come to light bereft of all clothing save where a corset shields them from the gaze of anxious searchers. Clothing of men is less frequently torn away. The bodies are borne to the Roberts hall to be washed and dressed by women, to be shrouded in coarse white cloth, to be laid in rough wooden boxes. There is no time for ceremony. It is the grim reality of death. And women, who would faint at scenes one-thousandth part as awful obey the mandate of necessity without flinch. The floor swims with the half-diluted mud that drips from the victims, but the living patter through it or sweep it out when it gets too deep. The rough boxes go to the cemetery not singly in hearses, but many at a time, piled high on wagons."

Fred Lockley was there from the Pendleton *East Oregonian* and reported the scene in the Roberts building: "One little girl was lying in a crude box, the light from a smokey lantern falling upon the satiny smoothness of her bare shoulder. It lit up her clustered ringlets of golden hair till they looked like finespun gold. Her lips were partially closed. Her expression had nothing of fright or pain, rather one of utter peace and content." "She is one of our unidentified dead," said the woman in charge.

Women of all classes of society worked in the improvised morgue. The ladies of the town who frequented the parlors where five hundred was played amidst the finest surroundings Heppner afforded, worked alongside women whose residence was the "Maison de Joie" just behind the Roberts building.

Monday was hot and Tuesday was hot and Wednesday brought no relief, making it all the more necessary to find the bodies although some were found packed in the hail that had fallen along with the rain. And to complicate matters, Heppner had been a little town of agricultural background in which many families kept a cow or a saddle horse or even a few pigs and these animals were dead in the same piles of debris as their owners.

Frank Gilliam was mayor of Heppner and he and E. M. Shutt, the sheriff, took charge, appointing George Conser, a banker, as a third member of the committee. They directed the rescue work. Matt Lichtenthal was put in charge of donations that were coming in as soon as communications were established.

The railroad had been washed out in places clear to Ione and the roads were damaged so a great deal of work had to be done before supplies could be brought to the stricken town. Handling relief were Dr. A. K. Higgs, Thomas Quaid and A. C. Bartholemew. J. A. Woolery came up from Ione to manage the supplies and promptly put Bert Mason in charge of the stocks of food and clothing that came in. The job of cleaning the streets so they were usable was given to Dee Matlock, Frank Roberts, Arthur Minor, Dave McAtee and Lee Cantwell. In charge of police were Al Roberts, John Rasmus and Frank Natter. There was little looting.

For the remainder of the living population the job was to attack the piles of lumber and hay and barbed wire in search of bodies of man or beast. Teams were used to move the larger piles. It was necessary to look through the partly demolished houses to see whose remains might be there. The days were long, the heat oppressive, the urge ever growing. The strong scent of formaldehyde permeated the air to constantly remind the workers of the necessity for haste.

A crew of men was kept busy digging graves atop the hill at the end of Chase street where the

This is lower Main Street just above The Fair which is the two story brick building on the right. Art Smith's little jewelry store seems pretty well gutted and hardly a wooden building could be salvaged for further use. (Courtesy Morrow County Museum)

cemetery gates swung ever open, and teams went back and forth bearing the dead wrapped in available cloth in hastily made coffins of plain boards. One of Ora M. Yeager's memories is that as a youth of seventeen he worked with his father, J. A. Yeager, the town undertaker and carpenter, hammering coffins together for what seemed days on end.

The Pendleton paper reported: "Rev. C. H. Lake will stand as he has stood all day and all night saying burial services over the dead as they are laid away in crude coffins."

Heppner's spirit in the face of disaster was the subject of comment by several observers. Leslie Scott wrote, "The beauty of Heppner is gone, but not its pride. No community could rise more bravely under adversity."

The story of the Heppner flood has been written many times and was well reported at the time. It can be accurately written so as to be read in less time than the flood lasted, but words, no matter how put together, cannot recall the horror of a city so suddenly destroyed, of 250 persons killed in an angry moment of nature.

At Lexington no lives were lost but houses were wrecked and those in the flat were flooded. One of the town's churches was washed into the other one with damage to both. The road in 1903 followed along the hill a block east of the present highway and when it reached Black Horse turned westerly through the business section of the town. Stores with the names of once prominent families still on them are along that street. The canyon proper is north of what was the main street, kept there partly by a ditch which it sometimes overflows at the eastern edge of town. The Heppner flood was temporarily halted by the railroad bridge above town and citizens could hear it and see it in the dim light and through the falling rain, so they took to the hills.

Mayor Samuel E. Notson, who was also school principal, and his family lived near the creek. With their four children they started to escape. Mr. Notson started north which would have taken them across Black Horse but Mrs. Notson, perhaps with "feminine intuition" insisted on going up the main street to reach higher ground. The footbridge across Black Horse went down.

Mike Galloway was undoubtedly Irish but he was not one of the Morrow County Irish who came direct from the ould sod, he having been brought to the area on April 6, 1884, by his parents, being then a few days short of nineteen years old. An oddity of his life was that in the winter of 1887-88 he went to school in Echo when he must have been 22 years of age.

After trying the carpenter trade he drifted into photography through connection with G. W. Foor and working at that occupation in Pendleton. He bought out Dave Herren, a well known photographer later in The Dalles and set up shop at the corner of Main and May streets, upstairs over what was often a pool hall.

Mike Galloway never married which gave him much time to ramble about Heppner and investigate whatever was going on. On the day of the flood he and Fred Warnock, publisher of the Gazette, returned from a walk down to the depot and dropped into Chris Borcher's saloon to play billiards. We quote from Galloway: "We were playing on the second game when I looked out the window and saw huge drops of water striking on the roof on Noble's harness shop. I said to Fred, 'look what huge drops of water.' It came faster. We quit the game, went to the front and stood out under the awning. In those days all the buildings, except the Palace Hotel and the bank, had awnings made of wood which extended out over the sidewalk.

"Will Smith came by with his umbrella and asked me to go to the bridge on May Street to see the water rise. I replied: 'Wait until the shower is over or slackens.'

"It grew in intensity and soon water was running down Main Street covering the entire surface. Bolts of lightning began flashing and rolls of thunder such as I never have heard equalled. It grew darker. We three were silent except I exclaimed: 'There goes one of Conser's trees.' He had planted three locust trees alongside the bank and the water had uprooted one, ten or twelve feet tall. The water kept rising in the street now about a foot deep.

"We looked up the street past the Palace Hotel to the building where my first gallery was, and a woman, Mrs. William Brant, came out on the porch

screaming and throwing her hands in the air." The men thought there must be a fire and started for their fire carts but Galloway turned back at the Palace Hotel corner where a lot of trees were being pushed into the street by Thomas Ayres' house that crossed Main Street almost to the bank. "Will and Fred jumped into the water and across Main Street. I turned back down the street." Galloway wrote: "I had a new suit on for the first time that Abraham-sick, the tailor, had just finished and I didn't want to get it soiled, but I did. As I passed the door of the hotel Lilly Cohn came out and said, 'Mike, have you seen Gladys?' 'No,' I replied. 'Come in here Lilly, it's the only safe place along the street.' She threw up her hands and screamed as she ran down the street a few doors and was caught between the awning and the sidewalk with two waitresses and rescued later on a back street.

"I went into Swaggert & McAtee's saloon. George Swaggert was just coming in the back door, crying, and left it open. (Editor's note, he lived just back of the saloon.) I raced back to shut it, and before I got back to the front Shutt's house slammed against the rear, knocking a window out and busted a panel out of the door.

"I got on a platform where the piano was, next to the north window. I looked out and saw two wooden buildings between the Palace and the saloon moving across the street. The one next the hotel moved clean across the street, the other one settled half way across. Then very soon another wave hit and it drove it into the awning on the other side. Then Gilliam & Bisbee's machine shed moved by. I saw a 3½" wagon wheel that got fastened at right angles to the current, half the hub shoved out as though it was only placed there temporarily. Plows, wagons, mowers, weeders, etc., were coming by. Then the sidewalk and the awning went. The water began receding. It was almost up to the top of the platform on which I stood in the saloon.

"At this time I looked down at my feet, and on the outside of the building there was a man feeling his way and trying to get a finger hold on the wall. I jumped down into the water and tried to open the door, but the pressure was too heavy for me and I called for help. Lou Keeny (the bartender) came and we finally got the door open and pulled Eugene

This picture was taken farther down on Main Street, below Church and the wrecks are of Pole Thompson's Livery stable and the Heppner Hotel where many lost their lives.
(Courtesy Morrow County Museum)

Gilliam and another man into the building. They remained a short time, not to exceed ten minutes, then jumped out and I followed. I saw a woman floundering at the rear of the Palace Hotel. I started to rescue them but my progress was very slow through the hay, barbed wire, boards and hail four feet thick that would not support my weight. I got about half way to them when the Jap boys of the hotel came out and rescued them. I think there were two women and a girl of fourteen or fifteen and a baby.

"I retraced my steps or trail and went to my sister's apartment on the second floor of Borg's jewelry store. It was vacant. When I came down the stairs there were two men (one I remember was Mike Roberts (trying to get Tom Ayres and wife off the roof of their house. There was groaning in the lower part of the building. We investigated and found Abe Abrahamsick suffering from a crushed pelvis. We took him to bed in his own building just a few steps away. He later was moved to the Palace Hotel where he died the next morning about three o'clock, I was told.

"I then went to a crowd of people on the hill above the head or west of May Street. There I saw the lake on the alfalfa field (the old race track). Waves were rolling like the waves of the ocean. I then went to seek out Elmer Morrison and wife. Their homes were gone but not far. On my way I met Frank Spalding and we moved together. The first people we encountered were George Conser and wife. Some men were helping them out of what remained of their house. They were mud and water from head to foot. Frank and I proceeded on. We came to the top of the Opera house where Mrs. Herbert Bartholmew lay groaning. Herb, Dr. Kistner and their girl, Elise, and a boy were there. We could give no aid. At this time Park Garrigues came running across the roof (which was flat), jumped into three feet of water and waded across to his porch where his wife was standing with outstretched arms. We went on down and as we neared a bend in the creek we saw people trying to fish someone out who was floating. We got there in time to assist a little. It was Mrs. George Noble (Gene's mother). Tom Driscoll and wife took her to their home.

68

"We went on down and came to the John Jenkins home just beyond a twelve or fourteen foot bank of the creek. The children were in the house, a boy and a girl around fourteen or fifteen years old came to the door next to us (we were on the opposite side of the creek). We motioned for them to go back and finally made them understand. The elements were roaring. It was hard to understand a person fifty feet away. We went on till we were behind Oscar Minor's stock shed where we met Bill Estes coming back from an orchard. He (Estes) said: 'It's no use going any further. They are all okay but Phil Cohn. He has three or four gashes on his head and is crazy, going the wrong direction for home.' Besides Phil and Bill there were Dan Stalter and his daughter (I believe Elizabeth), Bob Hynd, Lee Matlock and others I have forgotten.

"We hastened back to town. When we got to the bank Les and Bruce were leaving, or rather were on their way. Someone suggested news should be taken to Arlington. Dave McAtee said, 'If someone will go with me, I'll go.' Frank Spalding said: 'I will go.' So horses were secured and in a few minutes they were on their way. Then came Harry Bartholemew to go to Echo to send telegrams to relatives and friends. It was just getting dark when Harry rode off with our telegrams.

"About this time someone reported Conser's Jap had been recovered lying in the middle of the street. Also A. C. Giger's body was wrapped around the same tree the Jap had lodged in. Next day two more bodies (Nora Adkins and Mrs. Lum Rhea's little girl) were uncovered at the root or base of this tree, covered with a rug.

"I was with a gang exploring in the vicinity of the old Jack Morrow house when someone yelled: 'Run for the hills, another flood is coming down Willow Creek.' Our lights were torches, candles, two lanterns and it was dark between flashes of lightning and we all started on the run for the hill. The ground was muck, the basements and out-house holes were full of water. Bob Creek, Chris Borcher's bartender, fell in one of the out-house holes and couldn't get out. We could hear the yells he was tolling out for help. We got him out, the word came that it was only a three or four foot swell in Willow Creek.

"At 4 a.m., I gave out and went to bed. Got up at 8 a.m., got a cup of coffee and started to look over the situation. I got to the Methodist church where I met Oscar Minor. After a brief confab he said: 'The farmers will be coming in and no hay for their horses. I think I will save some of the hay lodged against my house.' (His house had lodged across the street from the church). I said I'd help so we started in. It was just like baled hay. It was cutting our hands so he said: 'I will go to the remains of the Thompson and Binns stable and see if I can get some pitchforks.' He did, and after working awhile he said: 'I stuck my fork into a body.' So we removed the hay carefully and were glad when we found it was a horse with four others there. I went to try to find a team to pull them out and never

Down the valley in what was Oscar Minor's Mountain Valley stock farm workers attacked this drift and found eleven bodies before it was scattered and burned. (Courtesy Morrow County Museum)

69

The home of T. W. Ayres that had stood next Willow Creek at the corner of Chase and May once proudly carried the cupola of the old courthouse that Ayres thought was a proper and fitting decoration for his residence. The white building is the Park Garrigues hardware store. (Courtesy Morrow County Museum)

The Alfred Ayres residence stood just south of the T. W. Ayres house on Chase Street. It was wrecked but not moved far.

returned. I went to the gallery and soon began to make pictures. They had most of the trees cleared out of Main Street before I got that picture."

Mr. Galloway had sold his gallery to Bert Sigsbee May 15 with the delivery date set for June 15, the day after the flood. For several days Galloway took pictures and Sigsbee developed them.

In its Thursday, June 25, issue the Heppner *Gazette* listed the following names of bodies recovered, not entirely in alphabetical order:

Clara Andrews
Cecil Ashbaugh
Mrs. Ed Ashbaugh
Gladys Ashbaugh
Erma Ashbaugh
Nora Adkins
Moses Ashbaugh baby
Iva Ashbaugh
Wm. Ayres child
Vastie Andrews
Wm. Ayres boy
Margaret Abrahamsick
Winnie Ayres
John L. Ayres
Eunice Briggs
Helen Boyd
Leon Banks
Mrs. R. Beard
Baby
Baby
Mrs. Guy Boyd
    and child
Chinaman
Chinaman
Chinaman
Mrs. Ada Curtis
Chinaman
Chinaman
Chinaman
J. H. E. Dennie
Carl Dennis
Chinaman
Mrs. Dawson
Mrs. Percy Dawson
Percy Dawson's boy
Percy Dawson
J. R. Dawson
Lloyd Estes
Blanch Estes
Mrs. Wm. Estes
Maud Elliott
Florence French
Nora Floreon
------------- Farmer
Bertha Fristoe
------------- Fray
W. A. Fisher
Gertrude Ford
A. M. Gunn
Mrs. A. M. Gunn
A. C. Giger
Mrs. C. D. Gurdane
Mrs. Frank Harryman
Clara Hamilton
Mrs. Lillie Hamilton
Jerry Hamby
J. L. Hockett

Hazel Haynes
Mrs. Hanson Hart
    (or Ranson)
Mrs. Hamby
R. F. Hynd little girl
Bert Hynd
Mrs. Robert Hynd
Mabel Howard
Mrs. M. B. Haines
J. J. Harris
Nellie Howard
T. R. Howard
Mrs. Thomas Howard
Jeanette Hodgkin
Frank Harryman
T. B. Harryman
J. L. Hockett's child
J. L. Hockett's child
Jas. Jones
Two Pearl Jones children
Mrs. Pearl Jones
Pearl Jones
Amanda Jones
John Jenkins
Mrs. John Jenkins
Zelma Jones
Jap
Mrs. Jesse Kirk
George Keithly
Keithly grandson
Mrs. Maud Keithly
Mrs. Hattie Kintzley
Fred Krug boy
Mrs. Fred Krug
George Krug
Fred Krug girl
Fred Krug
Fred Krug's little girl
Mrs. J. M. Kernan
Ray Long
W. W. Lipset
Pres Looney
Jas. Long
Mrs. Jas. Long
Clara Long
Jas. Long's girl
Maud Liffler
Mrs. Susan Liffler
Mrs. S. McBride
Mabel Mallory
Mrs. S. M. Morgan
Mr. Robert Morgan
Wilford McBride
Mr. McBride
Anna McBride
Dr. P. B. McSwords
Zassa McDowell

J. W. Matlock
Robert Morgan
Mrs. Thos. Matlock
Frank Oxley
Mrs. H. Padbry
Andrew Peterson
J. J. Roberts
Ora Roberts
Mrs. Jas. Roberts
Ed Rood's girl
Mrs. C. A. Rhea
Mrs. C. E. Redfield
Blanche Redfield
Amy Stalter
Robert Stalter
Bonnie Stalter
W. L. Saling
Mrs. Mattie Saling
China Sullivan
Mrs. D. B. Stalter
Louis Stalter
Leah Stalter
Fern Stalter
Doris Thornton
George Thornton
Mrs. George Thornton
Dr. Vaughn
Mrs. B. F. Vaughn
Wm. Walton
Mrs. Wm. Walton
Mrs. Clara Woodard
Mrs. A. Wells
Abe Wells
Geo. Wells
Harry Wells
Jas. Willis
Fred Willis
Mrs. Eliza Willis
Grover Wright
Stewart Wyland
Unknown
Body Unknown
Unknown, man
    of 30 years old
Unknown man
Small boy
Woman
Woman unknown
Small boy
Little girl unknown
Baby unknown
Two small boys and
    little girl unknown
Woman unidentified
A. Abrahamsick,
    rescued, but died.

This was Heppner in the first years of the century a near as can be recalled by O. G. Crawford and Ar. Crawford who trod the streets daily in search of news and advertising. Businesses changed often. But it was much like this at time of the flood.

1. Frederick's Bakery
2. Abrahamsick's Tailor Shop
3. P. O. Borg's Jewelry Store
4. Two small offices used by lawyers or shoe repair
5. Mrs. Morrison's Restaurant
6. Wells & Son Furniture Store
7. Three small buildings owned by Henry Heppner. He lived here.
8. Heppner Times
9. Will Stewart and John Kirk's Livery Barn
10. Heppner Gazette
11. M. B. Galloway's photograph gallery upstairs, later Bert Sigsbee's, Pool room or saloon beneath.
12. Pap Simmons Blacksmith shop
13. Law office of Gilbert W. Phelps
14. Gid Hatt's Barber shop
15. Bode, the tailor
16. First National Bank
17. Rhea & Welsh Grocery
18. Gilliam & Bisbee, hardware
19. Hemphrey Drug Store
20. Matt Lichtenstal's Boots & Shoes
21. T. R. Howard, Grocery
22. Wood's Confectionery
23. Art Clark's Jewelry
24. J. E. Gibson, barber shop
25. Patterson's Drug Store, Dr. Kistner office in rear
26. Masonic Bldg., with postoffice and stairs in alley in rear
27. Heppner-Canyon City Stage barn
28. Frank Hatton, blacksmith shop
29. Mollie Reid's two story "Chateau de Joie"
30. M & M Saloon
31. Chinese Restaurant
32. Jack Wherry's Meat Market
33. Wm. Schrivener, blacksmith shop
34. Next a little place where Mr. Tyler sold peanuts and candy
35. Art Smith's Jewelry & Repair shop
36. Durkheimer's Grocery
37. E. J. Slocum's Drug Store
   Across Center St. was the FAIR, a big general store and then Tommie Brennan, a Boston Irishman, shod horses. On the corner of Main and Baltimore was the Elisha Sperry house even then

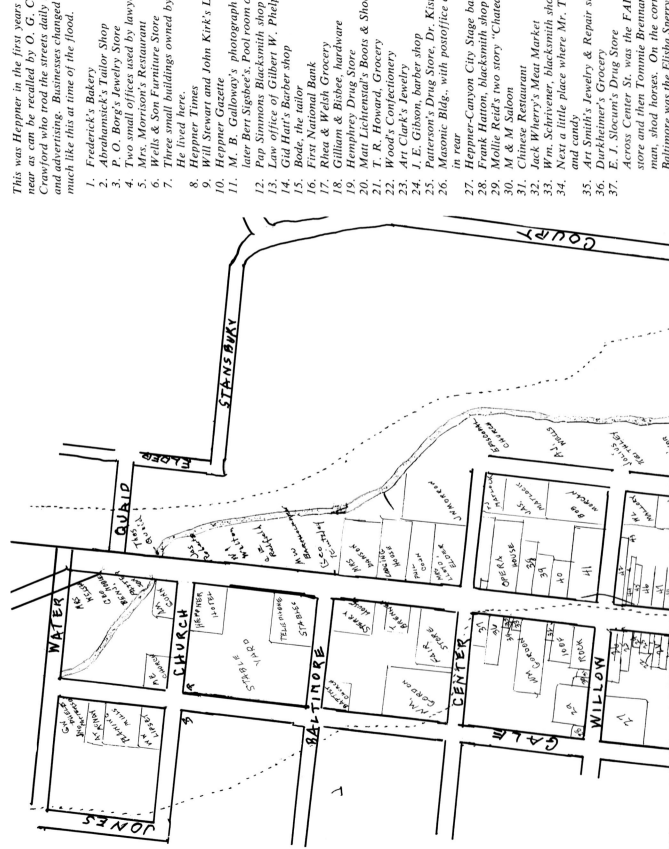

and yard and on the corner of Main and Church was the Heppner Hotel. A. M. Gunn's blacksmith shop was across Church.

Across Main it was all residences except for a small lodging house between Phil Cohn's and Mrs. Dawson.

On the corner of Main and Center on the east side was a hitching rack and Lee Cantwell had a bicycle shop next the Opera House.

38. Mrs. Estes or Foster W. Adams had a lodging house
39. Adjoining restaurant
40. J. L. Yeagers funeral parlor
41. Garrugues & Son lumber yard. They also owned Opera House.
42. Grocery Store owned by Thomson & Thomas or Matlock & Hart
43. Chinese Restaurant
44. Noble's Saddlery
45. Chris Borchers's saloon
46. Matlock's Gem saloon
47. McAtee & Swaggert's saloon
48. Lilly Cohn's Millinery store
49. George Aiken's Saloon
50. Gentry's Barber Shop
51. Small building used by patrons of the Palace as display room

East of the Palace was the warehouse of farm machinery of Gilliam & Bisbee and north the residences of Geo. Swaggert and Mallorys.

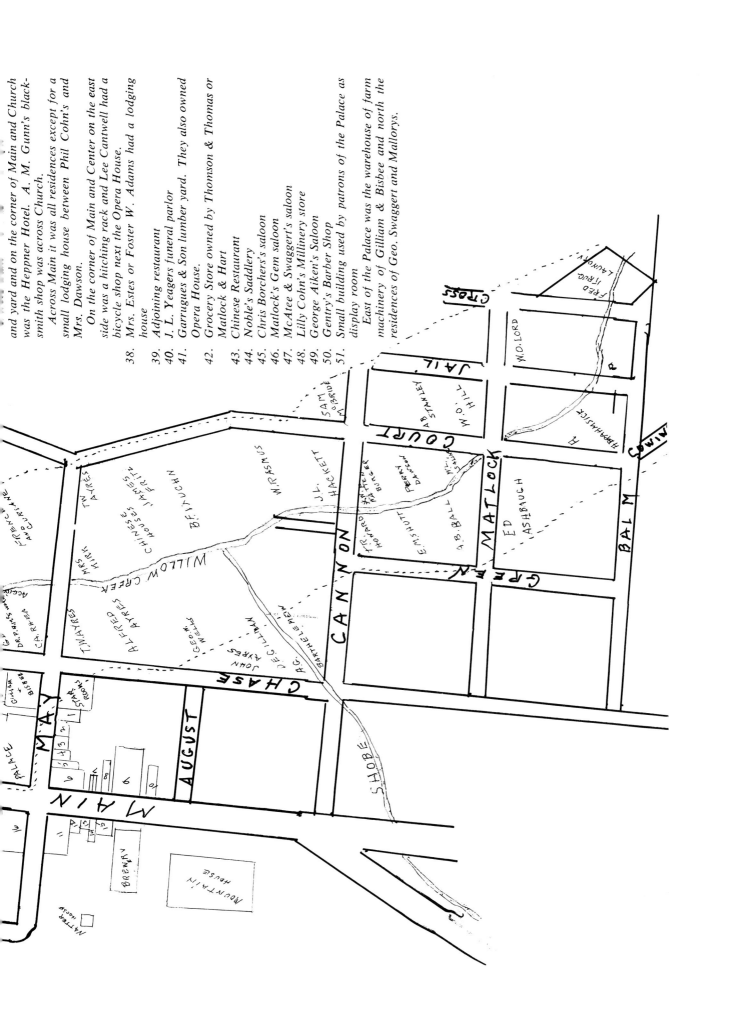

Here was the tent camp of the Portland Relief committee set up as soon as roads could be cleared. It was located west of the present Christian church and here was fed many of the men and women who worked at the jobs immediately at hand. (Courtesy Morrow County Museum)

The Union Pacific station stood although assailed by many tons of debris. Mr. and Mrs. J. M. Kernan lived here as station agent and became alarmed at the flood and started for the hills to the right and neither made it. Had they remained in the station they would have lived. (Courtesy Morrow County Museum)

The same paper noted that later information was that the bodies of Elsie Jones, Mrs. Clyde Wells, Ora Kelly and J. H. Stine had been recovered.

Still listed as missing were Lois Hamilton, Ralph McBride, James Beard, Boyd girl, Ed. Ashbaugh's baby, J. K. Carr's baby, Hockett's baby, Oxley's baby and Mrs. Andrews.

In the issue of July 2, 1903 the *Gazette* announced the finding of the body of Mrs. Ida Andrews and of a boy about eight years old. Identifiication was impossible except from clothing, jewelry or dentistry.

The only body found below Lexington was that of Mrs. J. L. Keithly and that was found on the Reaney place a mile below that town.

The relief committee with Mayor Frank Gilliam, Sheriff E. M. Shutt, and banker George Conser kept a careful record of receipts and disbursements, a record that was published in detail August 27, 1903. At that time receipts of $61,016.95 were accounted for. They came from all over the nation, from individuals, from lodges, from churches, from governments large and small.

The funds were expended as such funds are to-day—to give relief where and in such amounts as it was considered would do the most good. Men who worked (and presented a bill) got $2.00 per day, a team was worth $3.00 per day and women's wages were one dollar. Cash was doled out to the needy, to send the body of A. C. Giger back to Kansas, to send the four children of the drowned A. M. Gunns back to her parents in Michigan, to help remaining members of residents to start living again in some sort of shelter.

The property damage was soon listed at $600,000 but that was added to each week and in these days is meaningless.

HEPPNER IN THE NEW CENTURY

Many newspapermen were impressed with the opportunity for boasting that came with the change of centuries and issued pamphlets about their areas telling of the opportunities available and bragging of the progress already made. And certainly there were opportunities in the West even though the real early birds had pulled the most susceptible worms from the earth. In Morrow County the grass was no longer pristine but the farmers were learning how better to grow wheat.

The first of these publications was the work of J. W. Redington, who had returned for another round of living in the Heppner Hills. He had a firm in Portland print a 9″ x 12″ booklet on slick paper with many cuts of residents and scenes of which the community could be proud. In it he praised Ed Day and W. O. Minor for developing purebred lines of sheep and cattle; Day had improved the Spanish Merino and Delaine by buying stock in Vermont and Ohio until he was able to obtain a high price for bucks he had for sale. Minor's Mountain Valley farm featured Shorthorn cattle as he had learned that quality improved saleability and he did become the leading breeder of purebred Shorthorns in the state.

The Morrow County Land & Trust Company deserved a page and the Palace Hotel was featured with a picture of its dining room and bar. The Fair was examined in detail with an explanation of A. C. Giger's organization and merchandising theories. The First National Bank, which was really the bank established by C. A. Rhea and Maddock in 1885 and had survived the depression when the Heppner National had failed, was lauded. Minor & Company and Gilliam & Bisbee with stores in Heppner and a branch in Spray had a full page advertisement. Henry Heppner's warehouse, down by the railroad station, H. A. Thompson's Heppner Hotel and livery with a stage line to Canyon City, A. N. Slocum's sawmill on Rhea Creek were mentioned and there was a section about Ione where W. J. Blake had just completed what appeared to be a ten or twelve room house for $1800. Date of the publication was February 1901.

By the next January the *Gazette* was in charge of Fred Warnock and Ed Mitchell and they celebrated their first new year by issuing a smaller booklet, although of 30 pages. Much of the material was the same and many of the pictures for there wasn't much new to write about. Gilliam & Bisbee advertised the sale of the first combined harvester-thresher in Morrow County. Included was a list of businesses in the city of Heppner and they were good enough to include Lexington and Hardman as well as Ione. An effort has been made to identify all the businesses in Heppner by name and location for which information we are particularly indebted to Art and Otheo G. Crawford, two old timers who daily walked the streets in search of news and advertising.

On the accompanying map some of the smaller places are identified by numbers because of lack of room. By the aid of both the numbers and the script interested readers should be able to picture Heppner and form an idea of its business life.

Moderns will be appalled at the peculiar proximity of a meat market next door to a livery stable and blacksmith shops with their constant fires in wooden buildings. But moderns will be envious of the variety of the goods and services offered by the many small businessmen of Heppner at the turn of the century. One could get anything in Heppner he could get in almost any town in the state. And the compilation does not include doctors, dentists, attorneys, laundries, plumbers, dressmakers, draymen, stone masons, fuel dealers. It was probably a more complete town in 1901 than it has ever been since.

A TIME OF CHANGE

Change is constant. But change does not move at a steady pace; some years are calm and without significant events and in some years it seems that all old landmarks, people and social affairs, business, change in some way. The first decade of the twentieth century brought change and maturity to Morrow County and it brought the pressing hand of government.

One of the men who came to Stansbury flat in 1872 to open a store died just before the new century opened, Jackson Lee Morrow's passing being on September 22, 1899. Mr. Morrow was within a month of his 72nd birthday. He was a kindly man who was always popular as is shown by his quick accumulation of offices wherever he lived. In his later years he was handicapped by rheumatism in his wounded leg and he went to the hot springs often in search of relief. J. W. Redington, newspaperman who had been started in business by Mr. Morrow among others, came up from Portland to attend the funeral and write a eulogy: "These Morrow County hills seem sad today, for his brother Masons have just buried a good man—a man who gave the county its name on the maps of the world, and left a legacy of an honored reputation.

"It is warm on this treeless hillside today, and the sun beats down but the people of the city and the country have climbed up here, 500 feet above the town he founded, to pay their last respects to Mr. Morrow. Old neighbors trudged through the dust as they would not do for many other men, and his numerous friends throughout the northwest will be glad to learn that in dying as he lived, he was patient, tolerant, broadminded, and unassuming."

Early in the spring of 1901 Bill Penland died at Lexington and his body was laid away in the cemetery he had given to the city as, in fact, he had given the townsite. William Penland was a resident even before Jackson Morrow having come before 1870, also from Kentucky. Penland was an aggressive man who owned thousands of sheep to range on his thousands of acres of land, for Penland was not one to rely on the government to provide feed for his flocks forever, so he bought while the price was cheap. He had accumulated by sections or townships. Financially, Bill Penland had a great deal to do with the shaping of the industry of Morrow County and he was truly one of the founders although he held no office, had nothing to do with government, had no place named for him except Penland prairie, an open spot in the timber.

And in 1905 the labors of Henry Heppner ceased. He had been born in Prussia, March 25, 1831 and like Uncle Jack Morrow, his one-time partner, failed by about a month from reaching another birthday. Heppner would have been 74.

After a few months spent in New York City following his arrival in his adopted country he decided to go west and was soon in The Dalles, where he outfitted a packtrain to take supplies to Canyon City and then from Umatilla Landing to the Idaho mines. That occupation took him through the new land of eastern Oregon with its many opportunities. He was always interested in transportation and he was able to translate that interest to bring a good share of the trade of the John Day stock country to Heppner.

Heppner had broken his leg while baling wool several years before his death and thereafter walked with a limp. He did not have to bale wool, being owner of the warehouse, but Henry Heppner was never afraid of work, nor of handling the always odorous product from which he made his living and eventually his fortune. He got about his town in his later years in a buggy pulled by Old Sam, a bald faced bay that knew the way from the warehouse below town to the rooming house on upper Main Street where his owner lived. It was next door to Stewart's livery stable where Sam lived.

When Henry Heppner began to fail, his sisters—he was never married—had him move to the Palace Hotel where he suffered a severe stroke on Wednesday, February 15 and then another one Thursday which proved fatal. His body was embalmed and sent to Portland where it was buried in Beth Israel Cemetery.

It is still possible to hear tales of the numerous generosities of Henry Heppner, of ambitious youth sent away to school, of widows given back their deceased husband's notes, of families fed. In business he demanded and got full payment, in personal matters he was generous. But he was a grotesque figure in the town named for him, small, moustached, quick, decisive, always moving, always planning, like some detached mechanism that stimulated action.

Ellis Minor died in 1905 at the age of 73. He had come to Morrow County even before Morrow and Heppner as a butcher and had operated one of the first hotels.

Younger men of Morrow County had to take over for the elders were passing and this in itself resulted in maturity. The flood that caused so many deaths and disrupted so many families was a sobering influence. For years after that event Heppner's hills rang with the sound of hammer and saw as new buildings were put up on more solid foundations than before and closer to the hills.

The Morrow County of the nineteenth century was wild and free; the land was free to be had by homesteading or purchase at little cost, the grass was free for use by the first herd or flock to find it in the spring and with an owner strong enough to hold it. The social life was often pretty free although never unrestrained for there was always law and behind that the rather strict morality of pioneer people.

Consider the penalty for killing as imposed in three cases: all taken from the *Gazette* files. In November 1904 P. C. Creswell, who was often town marshal, shot young Frank Natter after a fight in Matlock's saloon. Creswell was arrested and taken to the city hall. Natter followed and knocked him down with a gun. Creswell fired from the floor. The jury said Natter died from wounds of unknown origin. Six months later Creswell was tried on a

charge of assault with a dangerous weapon and the verdict was guilty of simple assault settled by a fine of $200.

On May of 1907 George Horseman, a well known cattleman, shot Clarence McBroom at Potts schoolhouse where cattlemen had gathered for a meeting about new range regulations. The men had had a fight and McBroom had knocked Horseman down. Horseman shot him in the eye. The trial was held in Pendleton, already presumably, a more settled community in its regard for crime, and Horseman was found guilty and sentenced to ten years in the penitentiary. On appeal he was acquitted.

In December of 1907 Dan P. Doherty shot and killed J. O. Allen because Allen wouldn't buy a drink in a Lexington saloon. Doherty had been in business in Heppner and was generally well liked. Yet he was sentenced to life imprisonment.

In the passage of something less than four years the penalty for killing became much stiffer, evidence of a changed morality, and if one chooses to so define it, of greater civilization.

Some inventive bicycle mechanics back east had been tinkering with the theretofore unreliable gasoline engines and had attached them to a four wheeled vehicle that would occasionally run for a mile or two, so by the first years of the new century men began speculating about quicker transportation, met to talk about good roads, and planned to get out of so much hard work.

The Heppner Mining Company was headed by D. B. Stalter, a native of Bohemia, who was to lose all but one daughter of his large family in the flood. The mine was near Greenhorn and Stalter lived there every summer and mined for gold.

There was something resembling coal up Willow Creek and the Matteson family thought it valuable. Several companies were formed to exploit it and crews of men dug a tunnel several hundred feet underground. Citizens who had faith enough to put up money for the prospect were principally George Conser, who as cashier of the bank was in reality handling the Lum Rhea money and also as banker had charge of the money of many others. It was something for pioneers to dream about, a coal mine within twenty miles of town in addition to acres of grass and a population turning to the production of wheat.

The last company to be formed was the Pendleton Railroad and Coal Company in which C. A. Rhea, C. E. Redfield, C. H. Carter, C. J. Smith, J. H. Raley and Roy Raley, attorneys of Pendleton, J. W. (Billie) Morrow, T. C. Taylor and D. A.

It was right at the turn of the century that Oscar Minor, having observed that good cattle sold at better prices than poor cattle, bought some purebred Shorthorns and bred them up on his Mountain Valley Stock Farm just below Heppner. Readers who are judges of beef animals will find many good points in this prize winning bull. (Courtesy Morrow County Museum)

Herren were stockholders. It was incorporated in 1905 and prepared to build a railroad to the mine by requesting a right of way through Heppner for same. It was reluctantly granted. J. P. O'Brien of the Union Pacific said that his company would build a line to the mine if there was a guarantee of 250 tons per day of tonnage. But he also said that the coal was not suitable to make steam in railroad engines.

A lot of money that should have been spent otherwise went into the Matteson mine which resulted in total loss.

In 1905 Morrow County was still in the fair district of The Dalles but within a few years exhibits were being taken to Pendleton which had established a new fair district, one that attracted many more Morrow Countians. For by then the purebred Shorthorn herd of William Oscar Minor was taking prizes all over the state and even going to the big fairs in the East. His purebred heifers and bulls won consistently. All this to stimulate the pride of Morrow County and the fame of the Mountain View Stock Ranch just below Heppner.

And another bit of progress was the construction of a new court house in 1902, built over the expressed opposition of the residents of Eightmile and Gooseberry, cautious Swedes. It was designed by Edgar M. Lazarus, as architect, and was 52½ feet by 82 feet and had four fireproof vaults and cost just a little under $22,000. It was made of blue stone, hauled from Balm fork and is still one of the more impressive courthouses in Oregon. Soon after it was built a subscription campaign raised money for a clock to be mounted in the steeple. The steeple of the old courthouse was bought by T. W. Ayres and placed atop his house between Chase Street and Willow Creek. It was washed away during the flood and was the center of many pictures of that disaster.

In 1902 Heppner graduated its first class from a four year high school and Bessie B. Edwards was class president, W. H. Dutton, vice-president, Grace Hager, secretary and Sadie McCarty, treasurer. The class motto seems appropriate: "By Our Efforts We Hope to Rise." Nothing very cocky about that. Previously there had been classes that finished two or three years of high school work and there were two boys in the class. Morrow County was joining the world. Two boys in a high school graduation class was uncommon, education being a feminine pursuit and accomplishment. Boys were supposed to be near enough to adulthood at fifteen to handle a band of sheep or make a hand in a roundup. Boys who went to high school may have had asthma, but definitely not masculinity.

Heppner never did do a satisfactory job of keeping the Monument road in shape. The difficulties were real. Part of the road was in Grant County which had no intention of providing a road whereon citizens could go to another county for supplies. The terrain was rough and steep. Nevertheless Monument wool was hauled to Heppner far into the twentieth century but trade from areas more distant from Heppner decreased after the construction of the Columbia Southern Railway into Shaniko in 1901. Shaniko expected—and got—the stock shipments from south, clear to Silver Lake and from Crook County where sheep were sent to the Cascade range for summer pasture, but Heppner was in the running for the sheep that ranged in the Blue Mountains and it held them for a while, sharing with Pendleton. The disputed area was Wheeler County.

Although the railroad into Condon was completed in 1905 that town didn't seriously compete as a wool center. By 1909 it was reported that the storage of wool showed 4 million pounds at Shaniko, 2.5 million at Heppner, 2.5 million at Vale, 1.5 million at Lakeview, 2 million at Pendleton with some at Elgin and Baker.

As early as 1901 when Malcolm Moody was congressman he had brought a representative of the Department of Interior to eastern Oregon to look over the country for possible irrigation sites and a meeting was held at Antelope with Gifford Pinchot for a forest survey. It was customary for eastern

Morrow County's stone courthouse stands impressively on the east hill. The county grew its own rock. (Courtesy Oscar Peterson)

Heppner graduated no class in 1901, thus holding their pupils over until 1902 so they could complete a four year course instead of the three years that had been the rule for some time. Here are, from left to right, top row: Birdie Gilliam, Will Dutton, Bessie Edwards, Edna Mallory, Gus Mallory, Sadie McCarthy (Sigsbee); front row: Ona Gilliam, May Bailey (teacher), D. V. S. Reid, professor, Grace Hager (Storye). Oddly two boys finished high school; boys were usually used for a more practical purpose. (Courtesy Mrs. Elaine S. George)

Oregon papers to publish the names of sheepmen who had permits in the forest reserve, especially the ones in the Cascade mountains, which were established first. George Young and sons of Shaniko once had a permit for 18,000 head. It was November 1902 before Secretary of Interior Hitchcock decided to start a Blue Mountain Forest Reserve. It was January 1907 before anything important was done. Then D. B. Sheller came in to run the Heppner Forest Reserve. That was the end of unrestrained ranging of sheep and cattle, an important date in the taming of the formerly free Morrow County stockmen.

By February, Sheller announced that everyone must have a permit before cutting wood from the reserve. Imagine that! The stockmen were told to form two committees, one of sheepmen and one of cattlemen to work with reserve officials in determining enforcement of grazing rules. It was made clear that the government would make the rules. First there was a limit of 16,000 sheep to any one owner.

On the sheepman's committee were C. A. Minor (then bossing the Penland outfit), John Kilkenny, W. B. Barratt, W. W. Steiwer, T. J. Morrall, George Percy. On the cattleman's committee were J. D. French, George Horseman, L. B. Gilliam, L. A. Miller, R. J. Carsner, J. H. Hyland. Division was made between east and west with the Monument road the dividing line. The first thing to be decided was the trails to be used by bands going into the reserve and that was done without too much trouble although the shooting of Clarence McBroom by George Horseman may have resulted from a quarrel over some part of it.

Also in March of 1907 something was done about scabby sheep which had been a bothersome disease for some time. W. H. Lytle, a small, active, Pendleton man, was made state sheep inspector and immediately began a campaign to rid the range sheep of the wool destroying condition. A. J. Cook was named county stock inspector. During that summer T. D. Chidsey came as manager of the reserve (soon to be renamed the Umatilla) and he remained for years.

There was a lot of items in the papers that indicated the approach of a more modern way of life and it must not be presumed that many of them were peculiar to Morrow County. The doctors of the town, A. K. Higgs, N. E. Winnard and F. B. Kistner, established a hospital on Main Street below the Fair in the old E. G. Sperry house at the corner of Baltimore; the county sent an exhibit to the Lewis & Clark fair in Portland; Eightmile farmers tried to

promote a railroad from the Columbia River to Parker's mill. The government, urged by stockmen, moved to get rid of Indian cayuses, canning them for pet food or shooting them on the range. The ladies of Heppner who were most often noted in society news were Mesdames Matlock, Metschan, Blackman, Cohn, Conser, Huelat, Roberts, Redfield, Hallock who met now and then to play 500.

A bag limit for game was proclaimed which allowed 50 ducks a week, any number of geese, upland birds, 10 a day, deer five a season and elk one; haircuts were raised to thirty-five cents and baths were the same; trainloads of cattle, 2600 head, were loaded at Heppner for summer range in Montana; Jack Johnson beat Jim Jefferies at Reno, Nevada in a heavyweight bout that was heard round by round on telegraph by Heppner sports fans; Columbia phonographs, the cylinder type, were advertised in 1906. Dr. Winnard bought a five horse-power Indian motorcycle (that he soon wrecked); F. C. Marquardson advertised the Flanders automobile, 30 horsepower $1500, 20 horsepower $890. Woolgrowers were interested in a scouring mill to keep from shipping so much dirt back to Boston and Thomas Ross of Pendleton organized one with Newt Burgess, R. N. Stanfield, Joe Cunha and John Kilkenny as directors. Garfield Crawford and Percy Garrigues started the Orpheum movie house.

Wheat farming made progress also in the eventful first decade of the new century as can be gleaned from the following notes: Gilliam & Bisbee were selling combines by 1901, some attention was given to the smut problem with directions being printed for treatment with blue vitrol. The Morrow County Land and Trust Co. bought the Heppner Milling Co., increasing the stock by $35,000 to give a bit more stability to the local milling scene. In 1905 wheat production in mid-Columbia counties was given as Umatilla 4,500,000 bushels, Sherman, 1,500,000, Gilliam 1,100,000, Union 800,000, Morrow 700,000, Wasco 600,000. J. A. Woolery of Ione, who had 18,000 acres himself, said wheat farms were too large.

D. Cox advocated the raising of hogs, the papers carried stories telling about the advantages of growing alfalfa, H. W. Fell said field peas were a good forage crop, the OR&N brought a demonstration train to the county so that professors from Oregon Agricultural College could tell farmers how to grow wheat better and with what crops to diversify. None of these made much impression on wheat growers of the Columbia basin who have always grown

Old wooden hotels played a part in the settlement of the western country. There was a fire in the lobby and the kitchen. This one was at Lexington. Here sheepherders could live through the winters. Fire has brought them to a predictable end and hardly a one remains. (Courtesy Morrow County Museum)

wheat almost exclusively. In 1907 there was a little depression in money handling that caused banks to issue certificates of deposit. That slowed business for the First National Bank of Heppner, the Bank of Heppner, the Bank of Lexington and the Bank of Ione.

In 1907 the wheat farmers did get together in little combines to buy grain bags in one big order, thus saving themselves some money and it was possible to get a reduction in freight rates when the federal government was building the Celilo canal which—the railroads thought—might start a movement for river transportation. The spring of 1906 was marked by a hard blizzard that froze out much of the wheat in mid-March reducing the crop for that year, but 1907 was a very good year with warehouses full to the roofs. Winnard Bros. on Heppner flat, claimed 400 acres of wheat that made 50 bushels per acre. The threshing outfits of Peter Brenner at Eightmile and J. C. White at Lexington were both burned in one week in September of that year and far into the fall Sam Carter was still threshing near Hardman. Carter also threshed around Lexington using a new Red River special powered by a 25 horsepower steam engine. Farmers were growing a crookneck club or Walla Walla club although they all liked Bluestem, a hard white wheat that always brought a few more cents on the market, going to a dollar if the millers needed it. There were flurries of interest in other wheats like Galgallus or Gold Coin and eventually the county became uniform for Turkey Red.

The farmers were getting a pretty good break on taxes on the tillable land (187,308 acres) being

valued at $578,705 and non-tillable land (612,744 acres) being valued at $716,398. Improvements on deeded land were worth $79,087, not as much as improvements on city lots which were $130,765. The number of sheep was given as 147,884 to the assessor which was probably about half the actual number and the value was $242,414 which was considerably more than the value of the wheat farmers' horses at $88,392. The total valuation of the county was $2,617,853 but at what percentage of true cash value was not figured in those days.

Prices were pretty good at the end of the decade with flour at $6.15 per barrel, hay at $16 to $21 per ton, butter at 34 to 36 cents, eggs at 42, pork at 10½, wool 16 to 25, steers $4.75, hogs $8.75 and ewes $4.75.

Morrow County, aided by the Union Pacific, put out 10,000 pamphlets advertising its farm land; Louis Pearson, the tailor, advertised that he would make a suit of clothes for $13.00. The jury list for November 1910 included the names of 25 farmers, two stockmen, one blacksmith, one ice dealer, one lumberman and one capitalist.

Perhaps the greatest influence for repression on the social scene was the local option vote in Morrow County in the spring of 1908. There had been several murders that were laid to the consumption of whiskey but the saloon men didn't take the election seriously in the traditionally free wheeling county of Morrow and it was only in the final month before the election they began talking about how much higher taxes would be without the license money from the saloons. When the voters marked over 240 more ballots for the dry county than a wet one the saloon men were shocked. The wits sang:

"Hush, little bar room, don't you cry,
You'll be a drug store by and by."

If not a drug store it appeared that the ten saloons became ten pastimes and sheriff E. M. Shutt, who apparently made a serious effort to enforce the law, wrote an article telling of his frustrations. He said all ten were selling liquor and he had no authority to search and destroy the stocks. Local citizens would not testify and there was no law against shipping liquor into dry territory, which was proven by advertisements in the Morrow County newspapers noting that a Portland firm would ship four quarts of Cyrus Noble whiskey to Heppner for $4.90. The first attempt at drying up Morrow County didn't last long for in 1910 the wets won by a vote of 518 wet to 401 dry.

This was the era of the itinerant buggy salesman who came in to sell gaily painted buggies to farmers right on the farm, often at higher prices than the local stores asked. Small merchants suffered much from mail order trade and a common rhyme ran like this with many variants:

"The grasshoppers eat the farmers grain
The hobo steals his money
The bedbug bites his juicy back
And Sears Roebuck gets his money"

Changes came in the banking business that were dramatic and sweeping. The old First National Bank that had been started by that good Scotsman Columbus Adolphus Rhea in 1887 had gone on reliably serving the interests of stockmen, farmers and businessmen although the Heppner National had decided to liquidate in the depression of the 1890s. It was not long until the Bank of Heppner came to offer some competition. It was started by S. E. Carr of Chicago and B. F. Culp of Walla Walla, two investors and W. S. Wharton was the cashier and R. F. Hynd the assistant cashier to give it a local flavor. It was not long before W. O. Minor bought a good share of the stock and eventually became president when Carr and Culp retired.

It gradually grew in deposits but never caught up with The First National which reached $701,000 on one balance. In the spring of 1908 George Conser died. He was the long time cashier of the First National bank and a son-in-law of C. A. Rhea and presumably had the banking ability while the Rhea family had the money, owning many good acres of land along the creek named for them. The bank

had just declared a 20 percent dividend and granted Conser a 90 day vacation. Conser, however, was treasurer of the mining company that was spending money pretty fast trying to get that ill-fated venture started. He died, rather suddenly, April 2, 1908.

The directors hired T. J. Mahoney, who was cashier of the Bank of Ione, a native of Iowa with banking experience at Bonner's Ferry, Idaho to come to Heppner and take over the cashier's window. Mr. Mahoney was young and popular, once being elected state representative.

At the election of officers at the first of 1910 the directors elected Matt S. Corrigall, a sheepman from Butter Creek, to succeed Mr. Rhea. The announcement read: "We take occasion to announce the resignation of Mr. C. A. Rhea as president (after serving 22 years) and the election of M. S. Corrigall as his successor." That was a simple statement of fact without explanation or amplification.

By June 15, 1911 T. J. Mahoney as trustee brought suit against C. A. Rhea and Anna Rhea for $79,729.56 plus $5,000 attorney fees and other expenses and listed a great number of acres of land to be foreclosed. The directors and perhaps stockholders of the bank were plaintiffs, apparently acting behind Mahoney as trustee—and undoubtedly directed by a national bank examiner.

The notice stated: "T. J. Mahoney, trustee of trust estate of C. A. Rhea, an insolvent debtor. On the 17th day of November, 1909, one C. A. Rhea was indebted to divers and different persons in various sums, aggregating a large amount of money and was possessed of insufficient means or property with which to pay his debts and on said day being in an insolvent condition, and being threatened by his creditors with action and attachment, made and executed to T. J. Mahoney, serving as a trustee herein, a promissory note in the sum of $75,000 with interest on said promissory note at the rate of 10% per annum . . . . ."

Following was a long list of creditors for sums up to $7,000. The Rhea estate was lost to the family, a family that had been in the forefront of development of Morrow County. The trust went on for years with different trustees and was finally bought in the 1930s by two young investors. The creditors did not recover completely although the property enhanced in value during the twenty years the trust continued.

It was probably unfortunate that T. J. Mahoney was chosen trustee, although he was the cashier. It started a feud in the town's business that was not soon forgotten.

MECHANICAL REVOLUTION

If the first decade in Morrow County was one of change, the second was one of revolution.

Perhaps the most important was in the field of farm equipment. The combined harvester-thresher had been in use since the late 90s with gradual acceptance although the old threshing crews still operated all over the county either threshing from stacks or by the heading and threshing method, well remembered by the elders—the very elders—of present day. In 1916 McCormick and Deering (then two companies) each introduced the little eight foot cut "tin" combine that could be pulled by eight head of horses on reasonably level land and operated by two men, a driver and a sack sewer, the driver filling in as header tender and the sack sewer as machine operator and dumper of the straw. Within a year or two the company had installed a little LeRoi gas engine on them and efficiency of threshing on longer depended on a combine driver's ability to hold his team to a steady pace.

The machinery companies were advertising several types of tractors for farm use but few of them were adapted to hills or loose soil and none achieved universal acceptance. All had steel tires and growsers that caused them to bury themselves in front of a load. But every farmer, tired of the job of feeding, currying, harnessing and caring for a team of twelve horses day after day, was an interested and potential purchaser. Slowly farmer after farmer announced a sale and disposed of his often beloved horses and joined the ranks of those who talked of piston rings instead of feed grain. W. T. Campbell on Social Ridge bought a 30 horsepower track-layer in 1912 and a new type of machine came to the low lying fields of Morrow, not to be displaced for at least fifty years. Campbell already had a threshing machine and a Michigan auto.

The revolution the gas engine caused in farming was a slow one, naturally. Not every farmer believed in the noisy things, not every farmer could make them work satisfactorily, not every farmer had money enough to buy one of them nor land enough to use one efficiently. It took all of twenty years before the tractor became the accepted workhorse and the horse became the plaything, a light, limber-legged, fancy stepping beast fit only to carry a man atop him instead of pulling man's burdens

along a road or turning man's earth by the thrust of his shoulders.

The gas engine as farm power needed attention but not on a daily basis although early operators used to test the bearings with a crowbar thrust into the removable plates on the sides of the monster every time they heard a strange noise in the behemoth's innards. In the winters or during periods when field work was not being done the tractor rested in the shed or in the farm yard requiring no attention, no feed, no water.

As long as a farmer had to stay home to care for his horses anyway there was no good reason why he should not milk some cows, perhaps half a dozen if his wife would help and there was need for a cream check. And as long as he was home anyway it wasn't much trouble to look after a band of sheep, unless coyotes were too numerous. And all farmers had a penfull of shoats until early winter when he and his neighbors had a community hog butchering and put up their winter meat. In every farm yard there were chickens and perhaps turkeys and guinea hens. Gardens were a part of farm living and a farmer's wife could put a meal on the table without much aid from the village grocer. It was a time of self sufficiency.

As soon as gas engines were successfully attached to four wheels and farmers could go cavorting over

When a wheat farmer became sufficiently affluent to plow with three eight horse teams, hitched to 3-14" bottom plows, he felt very secure. It didn't come until the second generation. Film. (Courtesy Ann Bergstrom)

the dusty roads with a minimum of speed and comfort this was changed. It was no longer easy to find a farmer at home. The farmer abandoned self sufficiency. He needed money to buy fuel and oil and repairs and a dozen articles that had not been necessary on farms before. Many had to borrow it. And then the farmer became a specialist, a wheat grower for that was the cash crop—and then began the age of farm discontent.

There were other uses for the gasoline engine although it was a tricky and notional piece of machinery for years. There was nothing in a teamster's knowledge that applied to a gasoline engine; all its ailments were foreign to him, its spells of colic or indigestion—and they were many—were beyond his diagnosis. It was the young men who became the experts on transportation and who learned about carburetors, make and break ignition systems and the other knowledge of early day gas engine lore.

There were always Fords, of course, the durable little flivver, the Model T, brass radiator and the wooden boxes for the spark accelerators included. They bounced over impossible roads, leastwise impossible for a modern automobile which is a sort of aristocrat with no ability to withstand the rugged life. Fords sold for as little at $500 in Heppner in the middle of the second decade and at one time the price in Detroit was $395 for a runabout which was as roomy as a buggy. No other car attained the spidery efficiency of a flivver until the more solid jeep appeared twenty years later. Other cars were heavier, the huge Michigan, the solid Case, the Cole straight eight, the Hudson, the Dodge, the Maxwell, the Liberty and the Overland were familiar names in the teens and young men learned a new nomenclature not related in any way to that spoken by their horse driving fathers.

But what was the use of owning a shiny new automobile if one had to take it out on rutted roads? The springs were often too soft so they bent permanently or too hard so they broke also permanently. The wooden wheels were not certain to stand much of a sideways thrust either. Cars were unsafe, then as now, for in 1913 J. H. McHaley, vice-president of the First National bank was killed between Lexington and Heppner when his car overturned, becoming, probably, the first auto fatality of the county. Naturally there had to be a good roads movement.

In June of 1915 Heppner was putting two coats of crude oil on the dusty streets of the town and by 1918 the city spread crushed rock on some streets even though some had been treated to a coat of cinders previously.

The Columbia River Highway was started from Portland by the early highway commissioners and it worked its slow way up the river as its sponsors and viewers bragged about the flamboyant Vista House, the beauty of Multnomah Falls and the other sights of the hitherto little known Columbia gorge. Auto drivers, who sometimes backed their Fords up Mosier hill to keep gasoline flowing to carburetors, were among those interested in the proposed Oregon-Washington Highway clear through to Pendleton and maybe with a branch running on east.

The only towns that would benefit from a road along the river were Arlington and The Dalles. Sherman County was certain the highway would go through Wasco (and built a hotel in that expectancy), cross the John Day river at McDonald's bridge, come across to a spot somewhat south of Arlington in Alkali canyon, across to Cecil and up Willow Creek to Heppner before going via Hinton Creek to Lena and Pilot Rock and north to Pendleton. Sam Notson and R. W. Turner went to Salem to importune the legislature in 1917 to promise that route. It seemed that it was already decided and when in the fall of 1919 the state highway commission let a contract to the Huber company for grading the road from Heppner to the county line below Cecil—a road later graveled—it was considered certain. Wisdom—or was it wisdom—prevailed. Major highways were constructed to connect big towns. The Columbia River Highway was built parallel to the Union Pacific tracks down in the sand where Morrow Countians could get to it in only a few places. Thus it was early decided that highways were to be patterned after railroads and not be improved country roads.

In 1914 Bert Bowker of the Heppner Garage was selling gasoline by the case, which was $2.75 for two five gallon cans, and within a few years the price was down to 23½ cents per gallon and inventors began to make a gas pump to stand along the curb displaying a glass bowl as an indication of honest measurement.

Farm trucks were a little slower in coming to use. For wear on the roads they were little better than the old iron tired wagon for the trucks of early days had hard rubber tires that occasionally came off entirely on rocky roads. They didn't have much traction on soft fields and it was often necessary to haul wheat sacks by wagon out to the road where trucks could reload them. Motor trucks were a good ten years behind cars in the farming country, but they arrived in time to help with the revolution.

Those who remember the days of 1914 realize that all the change that occurred in that era had to be fueled by something more than the usual income from farm and forest and flock. A war started in Europe in 1914 and the price of wheat went up in expectation of a shortage of grain. The assumption was correct and by 1917 Frank Anderson was able to sell 11,500 bushels of wheat for two dollars per bushel. The price stayed high for several years and was largely responsible for an increase in the price of land from $11 to around $40 per acre.

There were other dividends; horse buyers came into Heppner and bought 96 head of horses for the English cavalry.

Harold Cohn, then an auto salesman when not going to college, traded a new Oldsmobile to John Sheridan for 100 head of ewes, a trade we guess has not been made since, mainly because Oldsmobiles have been improved more than have ewes.

The agitation for good roads in Morrow County was not restricted to desire for a through highway; Morrow County was always mainly interested in roads within the county rather than in roads that ran into or out of the county. After fifty years the original road down Willow Creek to reach the Columbia River Highway near Heppner Junction is in the same place and not much better, except for a coat of oil, than the one graded by the Huber Company in 1919. As early as 1915 Morrow County budgeted $30,000.00 for roads after learning that the year previous it had spent but $7,949.19, the lowest in the state. That year road enthusiasm was at a peak and Ione raised $1500 to be spent on roads and a meeting of citizens at the Palace with about sixty present agreed to donate money for a road program. The *Gazette-Times* had a story announcing that Morrow County had one car for 64 people which was the best in the state. Despite the road enthusiasm Morrow County defeated the road bond measure by 185 votes and a reason given at the time was that they wanted roads to their doors instead of through highways. That sentiment has prevailed.

Morrow County farmers were not easily persuaded that life was to be easier or that possession of a tractor and a little combine would solve all their problems. They had to be paid for and there was money in butter and eggs. The Morrow County Poultry Association held annual shows early in January to display a wide variety of chickens: Wyandots, Orpingtons, Plymouth Rocks, Rhode Island Reds, Hamburgs, Minorcas, Leghorns along with

turkeys and ducks and there were even a few pit games.

And farmers held meetings in school houses to talk about the dairy business and bought cows and shipped cream to Portland creameries, until some local men, particularly Frank Gilliam, organized the Morrow County Creamery with many local citizens as stockholders. It was not an expensive venture. After a few managers had come and gone the job fell to W. Claude Cox, an import from Virginia, who learned the butter making trade and drove wildly all over the country gathering up cream cans and delivering Willow Brand butter for over fifty years. (It was later called "Pride of Oregon"). His son is still at the same old stand, delivering dairy products as far away as Monument—and this in a country with no dairy cows is remarkable.

In 1917 the Farmers' Union bought the Heppner mill and went ahead with plans to install a fifty barrel flour mill to serve the county. It continued to make White Star flour.

There was reason, too, for the interest in poultry: Morrow County had something of a reputation for egg production and Ione was often called the "Egg City" in stories in the Heppner papers. Lexington was called the "Wheat City," a title it well deserved, to this day being the seat of the county's grain growers, but at one time, fifty years ago it liked to be called the egg city along with Ione.

In February of 1912 Vawter Crawford bought out E. M. Shutt who bought out Wiley Wattenburger on lower Willow Creek to raise hogs and milk cows. Country life did not long agree with the ambitious Mr. Shutt for within five years he was back to run for sheriff again, winning and taking the place of C. D. McDuffee, McDuffee who had made his reputation by shooting a would-be train robber near La Grande. McDuffee again became deputy. Shutt didn't like that very well, either, and resigned to go to selling real estate. Crawford did not long have the newspaper field to himself for along came L. K. Harlan from Condon (the starting place for several Morrow County newsmen) and started the *Herald*. George T. Pearce succeeded and S. A. Pattison followed him and remained until 1924. The town's two papers had no feuds and both reported county affairs adequately. It was said that the *Herald* was backed by the liquor interests and if so it had solid support in Morrow County.

People had a good time; they met in school houses and listened to their neighbors debate and joined in eating cake and drinking coffee later. They had visitors come to speak on almost any subject as long

Here is the famed old Heppner school that stood on top of the east hill and to which Heppnerites of mature years lay the strength of their legs for they climbed up to this fount of knowledge five days a week and then mounted the seventeen steps to the first floor. It's foundation was native rock and ample mortar and the carpenters had a peculiar idea about nailing on of siding. Date of construction was 1892. (Courtesy Morrow County Museum)

as it gave an excuse for hooking up a reliable team to the hack or starting a new car and going someplace. The coal oil lamps did not give much encouragement to readers although before 1920 nearly everyone had a gasoline lamp that gave a much whiter light than the yellow one made by a kerosene lamp with a flickering wick. They went to dances and the Palace Hotel pandered to this desire by holding a big ball on almost any publicly recognized occasion, never forgetting St. Patrick's Day. On New Year's Eve, 1912, there was a well reported dance there which was crowded. Dillard French came in from Butter Creek to call the square dances which were mixed with the waltzes, polkas and schottisches by the orchestra. The next month Gooseberry had a rabbit hunt followed by a big dinner with the losers providing the food.

Woman's suffrage had been passed and the *Gazette-Times* urged women to register so they could vote when the next election was held; women in Heppner were learning how to press their clothes with electric irons, the Heppner light plant being able to furnish enough "juice" during the daytime. The GT held a subscription contest that ran for weeks and must have resulted in everyone reading the paper. Miss Virginia Barlow won and Mrs. Earl Gilliam was second in a spirited contest. Gong Lane, Chinese restaurant keeper, whose temper caused him to have lots of trouble, decided to leave town to the delight of peace officers.

And another thing that happened in this era was the Swedes began coming to town. They had been in Ione for some time, considering that their special bailiwick, but the old country Swedes did not frequent the towns much. They stayed on their farms, tilling their gardens and faithfully attending church at Valby whenever a minister was available. But young Swedes came to town when they were growing to adulthood and had the curiosity of all young things about the world around them. Henry Peterson, son of Aaron, graduated from Heppner High School in 1917. The Swedes began to contribute their abilities to the life of Morrow. Frank Anderson, Eightmile farmer, was a director of a Heppner bank before he died in 1919.

In 1912 voters of the Heppner school district voted $40,000 in bonds with which to purchase a site and construct a new school on the hill on the east side of town. (It was just northwest of the present hospital). The directors were able to get the job completed for some $34,000. It lasted for many years, contributing not only to the mental growth of hundreds of youngsters but also to the growth of their leg muscles for there were no school busses to take children up the hill. In 1913 six graduated from Heppner High School and by 1919 22 graduated with all the fanfare they could muster, pictures, rings—the works.

There were about 350 pupils in the Heppner district at this time, different censuses showing 340 and 370. Sam Notson, who stayed on as school superintendent for years, reporting the doing in the field of education to newspaper readers, found 1497 in the county in 1915.

The agitation for a county agricultural agent was finally successful and F. R. Brown came early in 1918 partly because of the government's interest in the wheat crop and other matters it thought it should superintend. The next year Lawrence Hunt became county agent and in a couple of years C. C. Calkins moved over from Sherman County to take the job. Thus began a period of farm advice in which the image of the advisor has changed at least as much as the image of the advised. Farm discontent could be centralized and expanded, if not cured. Jobs were created to treat it and perhaps preserve it.

For all the work involved, agriculture was a pretty good business to be in during the second decade of the twentieth century. Wheat got up to $2.00 and beyond and although many lost intended profits by waiting until it reached five dollars a bushel (which it never did) that is to be expected among humans. Wool sold once for fifty cents and cattle were up to eight or nine cents. Until the First World War inflated prices coffee could be bought for 27½ cents,

pink or white beans 15 pounds for a dollar and rice 14 pounds for a dollar and bacon was twenty cents and soap six bars for a quarter.

The horse died hard and advertisements for jacks and stallions continued for the information of those who felt that horsepower would never succumb to gasoline power. The nadir was reached when E. Nordyke of Lexington offered to trade a Belgian stallion for an automobile. Farmers were being urged to try lime with blue vitrol as a preventative for smut and this was standard treatment for years as farmers soaked their seed grain for hours before hauling it out in the fields to dry a little before dumping the sacked seed into the drill hoppers. The easy life did not come to farmers until much later.

The banks were generally prosperous, the balance of the First National reached $1,091,091 at the first statement in 1917 and the Farmers and Stockgrowers reached $426,254 in 1920 before the postwar depression set in. T. J. Mahoney, after a ten year stewardship of the First National Bank, departed for Portland to take over another bank and his brother W. P. Mahoney succeeded him.

Some persons need to be mentioned for feats that would be called extraordinary or exceptional in the light of history. Frank Turner, the eldest son of R. W. Turner, a settler in Sand Hollow, left the family nest early and became the telephone operator in Heppner. He learned how to shear sheep, that being a good way for a man to pick up a few well earned dollars in the spring weeks. When sheepshearers quit the blades and devised an overhead shaft powered by a motor that could run several cutters Frank invested in an outfit and hired a crew to go around to sheep camps and denude the

Dona Barnett finds a friendly deer at Reid's Mill up in the mountains where Morrow Countians have their own recreation — and use it. (Courtesy of LaVerne Henderson)

The southern slope of the Heppner Hills is well populated with deer and some elk live in the eastern part. Morrow Countians enjoy them in front of a camera or in the pot. (Courtesy Oregon Game Commission)

woolies in rapid manner. Frank, himself, claims to have been the fastest sheepshearer in all the country around—the whole northwest, in fact—although never of the burly type physically. In the winters he worked for Gilliam and Bisbee, drove the biggest truck for commercial hauling and took on any job that promised a profit. His ambition paid off and he became a well known insurance broker.

Dr. Archibald Douglas McMurdo came out from Virginia, a young graduate from medical school and went in with Dr. N. E. Winnard in the practice of medicine. He married a local girl, Ruth Helen Hager, raised a family of three boys and spent a lifetime doctoring the ills and ailments of Morrow Countians, going to them through snowdrifts and on muddy roads if need be to set broken legs or usher children into the world. He administered the first spanking to many a Morrow County man and matron. Until 1970, full of years and wisdom, he was found in his office unless it happened to be a hunting season when he might be out after deer or birds. That was his way of death: to be lost and probably injured while deer hunting on Potamus Creek near his long occupied cabin. His body was

not found for more than a week despite a body of searchers.

Frank Gilliam was a partner, with his nephew, in the hardware and implement firm that was a sort of Rock of Gibraltar to Heppner business from pioneer times until 1968. Frank Gilliam, himself, was a man to tie to; he was county treasurer, was mayor during the most troublous time, helped start the Heppner Hotel, was a leading light in the establishment of the Heppner creamery. Any venture that could enlist the support of Frank Gilliam had more than average assurance of success.

Phil Cohn continued the business of Henry Heppner with an office and warehouse down by the railroad yards. He did not engage in public affairs, not being of that frame of mind, but he bought thousands of pounds of wool every year, supplied sheep men from Gurdane, from Long Creek and from Monument with sacks, salt, paint and other necessities and did so with such fairness that their sons still speak of him with affection. Had he not done so the wool from their thousands of sheep could have gone to Pendleton or Shaniko and Heppner would have been poorer thereby.

The Minors, William Oscar, who developed a herd of Shorthorn cattle on his ranch below town and showed them all over the west to advertise Morrow County and improve the quality of its cattle, and Art Minor who rode a horse more gracefully than he walked and ventured into many enterprises. The Minor general store was a landmark for years.

John Kilkenny was a sort of leader among the hard to lead Irish, a short, combative, ambitious son of the "ould sod" who by plunging acquired a vast herd of sheep and a large amount of land and by plunging lost a good part of it before he died in 1939. But he was a character, a man to be reckoned with as bank director, county commissioner or just John Kilkenny.

The Nobles, George and Gene, made saddles and filled local offices: W. W. Snead was postmaster, helped start new businesses, was a motivating force in the county fair and sold real estate on the side; the Crawfords, Vawter and his sons and his brother Otheo, kept the *Gazette* running steadily, quietly, with little argument and generally little reporting of the Saturday night fights that occurred around the saloons or some of the other places of amusement; the Thomsons, who kept store in Heppner as long as anyone can remember, Frank (Mike) Roberts who invested his money in solid buildings. W. B. Barratt, an Englishman who went into partnership in 1890 sheep, with Robert Hynd on a few minutes

acquaintance. He became state highway commissioner in the early twenties.

These were the men who took the place of the original settlers, the Henry Heppners, the Jackson Morrows, the Ayres, Thomas Morgan, Tom Quaid, C. A. Rhea, S. P. Garrigues, E. G. Sperry, the Mallorys and Matlocks. They were the men to see and they carried on during their generation until they were planted on the hill by those who in their turn followed them.

The first World War came slowly to Morrow County as it did to all of Oregon which was far removed from the quarrels that started it although there were German and French natives who followed the early arguments and threats closely. Spiffy little officers in high topped boots inspected cayuses in dusty corrals, the purchase of cavalry horses being one of the traditional preparations for war.

The papers were full of stories of cruelties that were shocking because people were not used to wars and the atrocities they bring, nor the stories claimed. But all this made little difference in Morrow County where the sun shone on the wheat fields and the lambs gamboled in the high grass on Penland Prairie. The government announced that this nation would never get involved in a foreign war and the people were so naive that they believed it and went on about their business of producing rather expensive wheat and wool.

Woodrow Wilson campaigned in 1918 on the plank that "he kept us out of war" and he was inaugurated for a second term March 4, 1917. Germany was sinking our merchant ships designed for England which we favored and on April 7 Woodrow Wilson declared war and immediately young men left for the front. The first to go from Heppner were two sons of Vic Groshen, Harry and Charles, Bill Durand, Elmer Presley and Ben Boone, all who joined the navy. Vic Groshen was a Frenchman.

Every young man had to register for the draft and fill out a questionnaire about his status, physical and marital, if he desired deferment. All this went on quietly under a local draft board and even before harvest was over in 1917 men were leaving in drafted contingents for Camp Lewis in the state of Washington where they were trained for killing. There were quotas nearly every month, some for half a dozen men and some for forty. In the meantime men were volunteering in the navy, the marines and in special services until Morrow County had 285 men in service (including one nurse). There were 224 in the army, 50 in the navy, 10 in the marine corps and of these 104 volunteered and 181 were drafted. Fifteen served in battle and 12 were wounded, one being killed and two dying from other causes. Morrow County's record was one similar to that of other rural Oregon counties to which a war across the world was nothing personal until it was made so by propaganda.

Morrow County dutifully raised a huge quota for the Red Cross and bought Liberty bonds to the limit of their cash or even credit. There were campaigns for Belgian relief in money or wheat. Heppner, after Art Crawford asked editorially why there was no home guard, organized one and elected Sam Notson and C. D. McDuffee as officers. Purpose wasn't to guard against invasion but to watch for incendiary fires.

The history of Morrow County's participation in the first World War can be told simply, the fatalities were few, the financial drain came from treasuries filled with war profits. Physically it was not much of a problem.

But spiritually it was something different. The people were united in a common cause to which all subscribed—as the ribald song had it, "to drown Bill the Kaiser in a bucket of Budweiser." The whole nation was going to get rid of oppression and dictatorship once and for all time, to "make the world safe for democracy." They really intended to do just that and all of that; if there were any dissenting characters from such sentiments they had better be far up in the hills when the vociferous patriots got together. There were neither Swedes or Irishmen, only Americans, and a man could speak with any inflection he liked as long as it wasn't German.

The war didn't really last long and almost no boy was in for more than two years. Farm boys learned discipline that in many cases prepared them for success; they walked with pride. And when local posts of the American Legion were formed in almost every town and when veterans turned out in their soon too small uniforms they were cheered and praised by an enthusiastic and united citizenry.

The Heppner branch railroad was built in a hurry at a time when powder wasn't powerful and a slip scraper was the accepted way to move dirt. Therefore the rails were laid right up Willow Creek, crossing it when it bent. Men knew how to build bridges before they knew how to move dirt. But bridges get old and weak and floods are destructive. In May of 1917 Engineer Sam Hanson and section foreman Frank Habelt were killed when the bridge across Willow Creek just above Morgan went out with the weight of the engine.
(Courtesy Morrow County Museum)

THE TOWN'S AFIRE

On Monday morning, May 27, 1918, Mrs. J. B. Sparks, whose husband was proprietor of the Star Theater on the northwest corner of Willow and Gale streets, came down the outside steps from the upstairs living quarters and dumped her ashes in the accustomed place and went back to her sweeping and cleaning. There was a live bit of ash that grew and grew unnoticed by any of the few passers-by and before long the house was afire. The fire department was ineffectual; it just didn't have the water nor the equipment nor the training. The fire spread to Mollie Reid's "rooming house" across Gale street and was stopped in that direction by the new building put up by Frank Roberts for the *Gazette-Times* and the telephone company.

The fire crossed Willow street to the south where it burned the city hall, the library and of all things the fire department's hose carts. It swept on south cleaning out Robert's skating rink, Clyde Wells' garage, and several storage buildings for mercantile firms with frontage on Main street. How they were saved is still a mystery. But the fire did recross Gale street and burn several residences along the hill. The Star Theater was a total loss and worst of all, for historical reasons, the photographic equipment and plates of Bert G. Sigsbee, who had stored them there.

But what happened in late May was nothing to what happened in early July. The city fathers hadn't even begun to consider what they should do about fire protection and a water system when on July 4, when many were out of town, a fire started in Patterson & Elder's barber shop, just down the street north of the Palace Hotel. It ran through Louis Pearson's tailor shop and so high were the flames they blew into the open windows of the Palace Hotel's second story and the best and most famous commercial building in town was doomed. The wind must have been blowing up the creek (as it often does) for within minutes the flames were shooting out the south windows of the hotel clear across May street where there were a number of wooden buildings, including the Star rooms, the *Herald* office, and Vic Groshen's Frogpond saloon on the corner of Main and May and some office buildings. It also reached out east to burn Gilliam & Bisbee's warehouse and G. W. Verlott's second hand store. The new First National Bank building (the present one) lost its windows but was not burned. After the fire had demolished the Groshen building it jumped Main street and cleaned the whole block south except the Natter home, the McNamee corner and south to the old Mountain House taking lawyer's offices, blacksmith shops and minor buildings in its sweep. Then it crossed Main street again and destroyed all of the buildings between August and Cannon streets except Dr. McMurdo's new home, which was saved by Jap Crawford and Phil Mahoney, two lads with garden hoses. The Heppner Light & Power Company lost 600 cords of wood but not all the machinery. Burned also was Willis Stewart's Red Front livery except for a few sets of harness and the horses. There were those who said it was about time. Stewart already had a Ford.

When Willis Stewart wanted to rebuild his livery stable the neighbors objected and said they would not put new houses close to a stable. E. L. Kirk took over the site of the old stable and the day of the horse finally ended in Heppner.

Oscar Borg had a player piano valued at $1100 which was hauled out onto the sidewalk by excited amateur firemen, who having done a laudable job, went on to other work whereupon the piano caught fire and was totally destroyed. Altogether it was a disastrous fire, both as to loss of business buildings and residences and with the May fire the town was seriously damaged. There were other troubles; the nation was at war, many families had the flu, there was not enough labor to do the work.

There was not nearly enough insurance in either of the fires to permit restarting the businesses lost and those who lost went to doing something else. The Palace Hotel insurance just about covered the mortgage on it.

Two fires almost at once caused some action among Heppner citizens to get better fire protection. H. V. Gates still owned the light and water plant and had during the war leased the Heppner coal mines up Willow Creek as a possible source of fuel in case wood became scarce. Gates said the water business had never paid and the light business had not been paying lately so he was not hard to deal with. Heppner voted 230 to 16 to get water from up Willow Creek using creek water at first but later finding some wells sufficient for the city's needs. The bond issue was for $100,000 and water was brought 16 miles down Willow Creek by gravity. Most of the pipe used was concrete pipe but three miles were of wrapped cedar, some of which can still be found. At last Heppner had its water problem solved for the time being.

The state had gone dry in 1916 and men who had isolated places back in the hills began to fill the need, nature abhoring a vacuum in the stomach as well as in the air. Sheriffs Shutt and McDuffee worked diligently at catching the offenders, but like sheriffs in all the counties in the eastern part of the state, never succeeded in reducing the supply beyond a point considered tolerable by the drinkers. When the boys returned from the war they considered it proper to hold alcoholic celebrations and the duty of trying to enforce an unpopular law came to be a contest more than a matter of moral right. It was hard to convince a jury that a neighbor would make moonshine or sell it. The law dragged on to an eventual stalemate with the careful, quiet makers of good moonshine tacitly left alone. That suited the public very well. In fact in the spring of 1920 when the weather was still cold the remark was made: "If this country ever warms up it will be by moonshine, not by sunshine."

With the old Palace Hotel gone where Metschan and Morrow had presided Joe Wilkins was unable to find enough money to rebuild. There was talk of building another one for something had to be done to accommodate travelers and put something on the barren lots. Gilliam & Bisbee bought the Vic Groshen corner and started the new two story brick hardware building, still standing. Two groups were interested in building the new hotel but after a few weeks of argument they coalesced into one. Land was bought at the corner of Main and Willow and the men who raised the money were W. P. Mahoney, Frank Gilliam, J. G. Thomsen, W. O. Minor, Phil Cohn, community stalwarts. The new hotel was 61 by 126 feet in size and was three stories high with fifty rooms, faced with white brick and looking very modest compared to the old baroque Palace.

The first name for it was the St. Patrick and the first manager was Pat Foley who had a hotel in The Dalles and who delegated the job. It was a success for several years with different managers but it never achieved the distinction of the old, ornate Palace; times had changed and a traveling man in an auto could cover the town in a day instead of a week. Transportation was quicker, and

no one bought a six months' supply on a year's credit. The time was coming when a distributor would come around in a truck, delivering and collecting at the same time. The days of long credit disappeared as gradually as spring shifting into summer; business became faster and the old time traveling salesman who had been the backbone of the country hotel business was but a pleasant and taleful memory.

In the days when history was taught in the schools, instructors used to talk about golden ages. It was a term meant to designate a period in the life of a nation or a people when they were at peace, when there were no pressing and unsolvable problems before the government or the people, when there was opportunity for a man to develop himself by taking thought.

The period just before World War I is sometimes described as such a time in rural America and it was true in Morrow County. When young men grew up and had worked a year or two on a farm or in the hills with stock they could, if of good reputation, go to the bank and borrow enough money to buy a plow and drill and some summer fallow and go to farming for themselves or they could get a band of sheep. These were character loans and collateral or the lack of it had almost nothing to do with the deal. Many an aged landowner in Morrow County started in just such a manner and in reality that was about the last generation to buy and pay for land. Land is now rented, inherited or married. If bought at all the money comes from other economic endeavor.

The social conditions were healthy; young people grew up together, many of them loosely supervised by a church. Compared to the present it was an age of innocence. When the young men went off to the first World War they learned things their fathers had never heard of.

Government was simple and interfered little with the local economy. The federal income tax was passed in 1914 and for years it was not a factor in the business of any but the most wealthy; there was almost no state laws that inhibited the freedom of the individual. The local sheriff would investigate the murders—if any—and the town marshal would hail a man before the justice of peace if he became too noisy at a dance. Society in general handled the morals by frowns, by gossip, by exclusion and in this the several churches were important factors. The Swedish preacher who came to Valby and the black robed priest at St. Patrick's and the other ministers, were men to reckon with in the matter of morals.

Almost none of the problems that beset the modern world were known in Morrow County in 1917. There were no racial problems, no burdening tax, no pollution, no traffic of consequence, no huge military establishment, and above all no worry about their absence.

And the decade of the teens was just about the last decade of hard labor. Men quit picking up a thousand times their weight in wheat sacks in a day, riders didn't stay on a horse for a sixteen hour stretch, there was machinery to pitch the hay. The gasoline engine, inefficient though it was, began to do the work, to be soon joined by electricity that needed but the flip of a switch.

And it wasn't long before men quit boasting of their physical prowess at hard labor; it wasn't stylish. Nor did it make a man popular to be able to pick up more wheat sacks or pitch more hay than his fellows. The era of physical strength and endurance ended almost suddenly and was followed by a time of boasting of social standing, clothes, personal possessions and appearance. It was socially and factually a different world, a world in which ease was honored above effort.

WANTS MAKE WOES

The nineteen twenties started on a high note with the boys returning from war, wheat and wool prices high, gas power almost ready to replace horsepower.

But it was a disappointing decade. In 1920, Morrow County had 5617 residents, presumably all working at driving teams, herding sheep or following some of the lesser trades. There were 1324 in Heppner, 439 at Ione, 264 at Lexington, 193 at Hardman. The farmers had increased their wheat acreage from 75,721 in 1910 to 102,859 in 1919 and sheep were still declining in numbers from the 322,650 of 1900 to 209,057 in 1910 to 169,204 in 1920. Prices were generally good with wheat selling at around $1.10 and wool bringing thirty cents or more.

Nevertheless the twenties were a period of discontent especially among wheat growers and being discontented is one of the things wheat growers can do very well. There were wool growers who were unhappy as they viewed the end of their day of unlimited grass. And to hasten the end itinerant sheepmen were taking over a part of the range. They were the men who owned no land and who pastured the grass along with the established sheepmen. The tramping bands that wintered on lower Willow Creek obliterated the sparse grass that grew on the sand north of Ella as they moved toward Butter Creek and the trailways that led up into the mountains for summer range. The bands and herders and packers for John Kilkenny, James Carty, Doherty Brothers, the jolly Hynd Brothers, whose sister, Mrs. T. H. Lowe chronicled the doings on Butterby Flat for the readers of the *Gazette*, McEntire Brothers, Mike Kenny, the Krebs outfit, and from farther south where the shearing was, later went Ralph Thompson, Frank Monahan, L. V. Gentry, D. O. Justus, Matt Corrigall, Frank Wilkinson and Jerm O'Connor came from farther west. The herder and packer who could find the best grass and get to it first were the men to be envied—and hired next year. The curtain was falling on the sheep business.

It was the wheat growers who made the news in the 1920s with their several schemes to get a bigger price for their product, have it hauled cheaper, borrow more money at less interest, get government aid, and find new ways to raise more of it. When the decade ended they were growing 131,536 acres of wheat, almost 30,000 more than at the start indicating that unhappiness did not affect expansion.

As early at 1921 the local farm bureau of which R. W. Turner was president and L. A. Hunt, county agent and chief propagandist, became interested in the Oregon Cooperative Grain Growers Association which was a plan to have enough farmers withhold wheat from the market to raise the price. In theory it was beautifully simple and persuasive men were hired to go about from farm to farm getting farmers to sign contracts to withhold their grain from the market on command.

Meetings were held, grain dealers denounced, millers excoriated and tempers lost. The bankers were not impressed for they had mortgages on nearly all the grain grown in the mid-Columbia basin. In 1923, which was the prime year for the Oregon Cooperative Grain Growers Association, two farmers were selected to test the contracts and the OCGGA sued F. M. Lovgren of Morrow County and P. L. Schamel of Sherman County for not delivering their grain to the association according to con-

tract. The fact was they couldn't deliver for the local bankers had taken it by foreclosure and Judge D. R. Parker of Condon in the Schamel case so ruled: that a prior mortgage had precedence over the OCGGA contracts. The comparatively few farmers who raised a crop of wheat without benefit of bankers were not inclined to hold it off the market to help their neighbors or the bankers so the scheme exploded in a rather faint cloud of dust.

Although most of the wheat was harvested by combine by 1920 farmers met annually to set wages that would be paid for harvest labor and these were generally adhered to although the Industrial Workers of the World committed some sabotage in a few instances. In 1921 common hay laborers were to get $2.00 and of course board; stackers $2.50; header box drivers $3.00; loaders $3.50; header punchers $4.00; separator tenders $8.00; tractor drivers $7.00, and other laborers, which presumably included the fast disappearing sack sewers and jigs, $4.00. Nothing was said about forkers, who were once the high priced kings of the stationary crew.

Farmers were also experimenting with new methods of growing grain. Copper carbonate was introduced and seed wheat was treated dry which held down smut better than had the old vitrol or formaldehyde treatment. It made many farmers sick but that was hardly more uncomfortable than being wet every night during seeding.

Then the wheat growers began meeting to urge passage of the McNary-Haugen bill, named for an Oregon senator and an Iowa congressman. It would have given a higher price for wheat used for domestic purposes and let the remainder be exported at the world price. It passed congress twice but was vetoed both times. Whereas farmers—all kinds of farmers—had once been in a majority in the nation and in position to dictate to politicians, they were not so favored by the time the McNary-Haugen bill was proposed. A majority of congressmen represented city people who were consumers of grain products and farmers have never been able to convince city people that an adequate supply of food at a profitable price to the producer would be to their advantage. The problem continues.

Wheat farmers had suffered a disaster in the early winter of 1924-5 when a sudden change in the weather froze out nearly all the wheat in the mid-Columbia basin. It was necessary—or thought necessary—to borrow money from the state for seed wheat to produce the 1925 crop. Delegations were sent to Salem to importune legislators and finally, because eastern Oregon had much political power in those days, an appropriation was made to loan enough money to each farmer for seed wheat. Much of it had to be imported from Montana because spring seed wheat was not sufficiently plentiful in Oregon. The crop turned out fairly well and the state recovered most of the money loaned although, it had to wait a year or two for some of it. By January 1926, it was announced that Morrow County farmers had repaid $89,305.86 of the $100,823.61 they had borrowed. The banks waived their mortgages to the extent of the seed loans.

There were bright young men working out of Oregon Agricultural College in the twenties when that school was truly agricultural in emphasis and of great influence in the development of new methods of farming in the state. William Jasper Kerr was president and he recruited Frank Ballard from Maine to head the extension service, David E. Stephens to be manager of the wheat experiment station at Moro, Edwin Russell Jackman came down from Montana to add his several abilities, George R. Hyslop was a soil and seed scientist. Don D. Hill graduated about then and immediately added his talents. And then there were Scudder and Jardine and Maris who were fluent talkers. All got around the state and held meetings and became acquainted with thousands of Oregon farmers. Somewhat later Charley Smith started as Smith-Hughes teacher at Dufur, moved to Morrow County and became secretary of the Eastern Oregon Wheat League for 15 years. These men had the ability to think and the ambition and nerve to do something about it. To them belongs much of the credit for teaching and organizing wheat growers and for inspiring others to follow in their footsteps.

Late in 1925 they began talking about a convention of wheat growers to be held in Moro in February of 1926 for the purpose of discussing the problems of the wheat grower in detail. Many committees were appointed and nearly every wheat man who was discontented was on one. About 250 men met and talked about tillage methods, freight rates, taxes, alternate crops and world markets. It lasted three days and out of it came the Eastern Oregon Wheat League that, under that name or another, has been the leader in wheat grower activity to this day.

The 1927 crop was one of the best, there being 2,894,085 bushels grown in Morrow County according to estimates. At Cecil there were 94,375 bushels (indicating that the sand area grew a crop), 330,000 bushels at Jordan, 100,000 a Echo, 213,000 in the Farmers warehouse at Lexington and 393,000 bushels at the Collins warehouse at Lexington; 315,000 at Ione elevator and 283,000 at the Collins house at Ione; 117,000 at Macnab, 150,000 at the Brown warehouse at Heppner and 420,000 at the Heppner elevator; 81,000 shipped independently and 395,000 bushels still on the farms for feed and seed.

Herbert Hoover was elected president in 1928. He appointed Alexander Legge, head of the International Harvester company, as his secretary of agriculture. Legge soon discerned that the problem was one of too much production and not enough sales, but he had too little power to influence either. A farm board was established and from it grew the North Pacific Grain Growers, a huge cooperative that pretty well controls the grain market and does much of the exporting. However, because it was soon a monopoly it did away with the private exporters who had made the market.

Nevertheless, wheat growers were buying out their neighbors and it was getting harder to find a wheat ranch to rent. The price of land was steadily going up and the days of $11 land were gone. Discontent didn't seem to be hurting the wheat business.

Compared to the hyper-activity and excitement of the war times the decade of the twenties seemed drab and dull. Farmers were selling horses and buying tractors and they usually put out more money for the tractor than they obtained from the horses. Debt survived the day of $2.50 a bushel wheat and business was generally poor. Gilliam & Bisbee, the hardware and machinery dealers with a new building to pay for, advertised a little plaintively: "In 1921 our business died. Now she's dead again. We don't know where she's gone to, only trust for the best. But trusting won't do; that is what caused her death. Bring some money instead of flowers to the funeral."

Social activity was normal or more so; young men home from the wars turned to thoughts of love and married the waiting young women in great num-bers. They did other things too. An American Legion post was formed and the members put on smokers and dances and held big meetings to tell of the things they had seen, the vin rouge they had drank, the madamoiselles they had met, all tinged with enough imagination to make it interesting. They also started a swimming pool on Willow Creek near where Krug's laundry had been.

The bank balances held about equal, the First National varying from $800,000 to a million and the Farmers & Stockgrowers running from $300,000 to half a million. The Heppner *Herald* published its last issue in April of 1924, Gurdane & Son quit and moved to Bend, John Hiatt took over the Cash and Carry Grocery and soon took in Dix and then joined M. D. Clark to enter the Red & White chain. The Peoples' Hardware, which also sold machinery, advertised a sale to close out stock but LaVerne Van-Marter became manager and it remained open. During the sale disc harrows went for $103 instead of $175 and Winona wagons for $128 instead of $160, 3-16" bottom plows for $120. This is at a time when the demand for horse drawn equipment was coming to an end.

In 1927 the Bank of Ione suspended and there were several farm sales by the administrator; that same spring the bank at Stanfield closed having lost its one biggest depositor and in December the Lexington State Bank closed its doors voluntarily, setting aside enough money to pay 80% to depositors. In those days the stockholders were responsible for the deposits and when a bank closed the whole community suffered, not some distant Federal Deposit Corporation.

Judge W. T. Campbell was beaten by Judge R. L. Benge without noticeable change in public policy. Both attended nearly every meeting of the state highway commission where for 1921 and 1922 sat W. B. Barratt, one of the county's most prominent sheepmen. After the road down Willow Creek was graveled interest turned to the completion of the Lena-Vinson section of what was called the Oregon-Washington Highway, it still being set in the minds of citizens that the new highway was going to follow the stage route of the 1870s. It took years to get the connection made, long after the road over Franklyn hill was finished. Then the attention of county officials, especially George Bleakman, who could be elected county commissioner, but not county judge, turned to the Heppner-Spray road. This was in itself a compromise. Heppner could not or did not build or maintain a year around road to Monument and although, there was occasionally a bit of public conversation about the Heppner-Ritter road it was never fit for much use.

The reason for the Heppner-Spray connection was that the John Day highway had been built and it was the thought of Heppnerites that the Monument trade would drive down the north fork of the John Day to Kimberly and then down the John Day's main stem to the spot four miles east of Spray where the Heppner-Spray road entered and thence up over the hill to Heppner through now almost deserted Hardman. Some traffic did come that way but Heppner was in competition with Condon for the business it once could have had exclusively.

H. V. Gates still owned the Heppner Light and Water Company, complaining every month that he was losing money. In 1927, he sold the electric light plant to the Sherman Electric which brought current from DeMoss Springs and which quickly sold out to the Pacific Power & Light Company to become part of a central system, less subject to local breakdowns and capable of giving continuous service. The rates were less, too.

Many of the pioneers who had come to Heppner as young men and women in the seventies and eighties died during the nineteen twenties, having finished their three score and ten. Most died at home. And there were also many deaths of old teamsters and old sheepherders who often lived alone in shacks about town. Few applied for public assistance, being too proud. There was a little work they could do repairing a garden fence, looking after a ranch a few days; there were more little jobs fifty years ago. The *Gazette-Times* noted the end of one such by announcing the death of Anson Hooker Currier, about 70. "The Baron," a brick mason, follower of John Barleycorn found dead in his cabin by Marshal Devin and S. E. Notson.

Getting up the hill to the cemetery in all kinds of weather — for death does not wait for a dry period—was a constant problem until Mayor Gene Noble called for all citizens to get out and build the road into a better condition. The county lent its grader and eventually the road was graveled which ended the day of straining hearse horses unable to pull their load or motorized vehicles from getting stuck when the passengers were in their best clothes to attend a funeral.

In 1926 a thousand persons went to Wells Spring to dedicate a plaque to Colonel Cornelius Gilliam who had been accidentally killed there during the Cayuse war of 1847. Leslie Scott was principal speaker and the always venerable George Himes, secretary of the Oregon Historical Society attended. Wells Spring was the main claim to fame of Morrow County in the days of the emigrants. It has pretty much gone unnoticed since that day in May of 1926.

Instead of all the businesses in town being locally owned, outside interests came in. Red & White was connected with Wadhams & Co., of Portland although, not owned by it; it was a buying combine. MacMarr Stores bought out J. F. Stone's grocery, Henry Collins owned some of the best warehouses in the county, the Tri-State Terminal Company bought a local warehouse, the federal government organized a Joint Stock Land Bank to do some of the local financing. J. C. Penney opened a store in 1929.

One man needs mention. Dwight Misner farmed all the land he could get down in the level country north of Ione. Misner, according to his story, frequently told, harnessed 38 head of horses every morning while his wife cooked breakfast. They hooked them up and she drove them until they were tired—one hitch a day—while he did the chores and repair work around the ranch. They used a combine hitch. In 1929 Misner bought a Holt 30 which ended his distinction and his wife's horsemanship and within a few years they had departed the county.

The Heppner water system had never been satisfactory. It depended on the water in Willow Creek. In January of 1930 the city hired A. A. Durand to drill for water and in April he struck artesian water at 210 feet that ended the water problems for the town for many years when properly piped and distributed.

The Heppner Rodeo attracted good crowds every September with due praise given the best cowboy and advertisement of western clothes for bankers and bookkeepers to wear during the celebration. By 1929 the Crosley company and C. H. Latourell, the Ford dealers—and trap shooter—brought in a microphone to give the announcer's voice a little help. Gradually a wool and grain products show was added to the rodeo and it became as much a fair as a rodeo.

Altogether it was a poor decade, not that the crops were poor, for they were average, the sheep industry slipped farther, taxes were raised to build highways for the steadily increasing automobiles. Although, there is no readily available record, the personal debt of Morrow County citizens increased tremendously in the twenties. Young men went into debt to buy a car, older men had trouble meeting the interest and payments on their land. There was a reaction from the free spending days of big wartime prices and certainly Morrow County put out more money than it took in during the nineteen twenties. That could only lead to one thing — and it was upon them.

THE GREAT DEPRESSION

It wasn't only a depression, to many it was disaster. Probably the greatest reason was the wheat crops which were uniformly bad during nearly all of the thirties, especially in the first few years. The crop in 1934 totalled 490,960 bushels and much of that was so low in quality it could be sold for nothing but feed, and poor feed at that. Some sold for as low as 18½ cents a bushel which was all it was worth.

There was a shortage of money all over the western world, big banks closed and big bankers jumped out of windows. There were many more potential borrowers than there were depositors; depositors were afraid of banks and for good reason. Money was safer in almost any hip pocket than in a bank. In 1932 the Farmers & Stockgrowers were down to a balance of $192,240 with loans of $134,360 and deposits of $114,599 and the First National had a balance of $585,636, loans of $395,456 and deposits of $244,214. This was less than half the balances these banks had had for years.

The Heppner Farmers Elevator assigned its resources to its creditors early in October of 1932, followed shortly by the First National on a Friday. The Farmers & Stockgrowers held out until the following Tuesday. A general bank moratorium was declared and all banks were closed by federal edict. J. L. Gault was sent into manage the affairs of the banks.

Moderns cannot imagine a condition in which there is no money. Debt, partly caused by World War I and partly by the excesses of living beyond incomes had caught up with the United States and Europe. Those who had kept out of debt were not inclined to lend to those who had been less provident and who had spent their money. It didn't seem good business to lend to a man who had proven himself a failure. Besides the ones with a little money had very little, not enough to lift a mortgage, merely enough to live on and perhaps hire an indigent neighbor for a few days.

The spendors—as is the habit of spenders—had been somewhat arrogant and boastful, feeling that a dollar borrowed was as good as a dollar earned. There was not much inclination on the part of those who had saved to bail them out of their predicament.

Morrow County farmers were made eligible for drouth loans early in the spring of 1931 because the crops had been poor. It gave them an opportunity to borrow up to $300 for seed and was welcomed. Fortunately there was a gas war going on in Portland and farmers drove down in every vehicle that could contain gas and filled everything on the ranch.

W. P. Mahoney, the banker, Charley Cox and Henry V. Smouse, farmers, were appointed to administer the loans for farm relief. The wheat problem was not new; it had begun back in the teens, perhaps it began when business became more profitable than agriculture as a way of life and farmers borrowed to maintain their social standing. In any event it had been preceded by several years of wheat grower discontent. Charley Smith, as county agent and administrator of the farm program that was hastily formed in the spring of 1933, said that the $163,899 wheat men would get in the spring of 1934 was more than the value of the entire crop.

In payment for the money from the government wheat growers had to reduce their acreage, which was the remedy advocated by Alexander Legge of the Hoover Farm Board, only the new plan was made mandatory for all practical purposes. (If you didn't join in you couldn't sell your wheat). The weather stayed dry so a reduction in acres didn't make a great deal of difference; there wasn't much wheat grown anyway.

Men were out of work and emergency relief was given. Local clubs started the program by donating money for long wanted improvements but it was soon expended. The Reconstruction Finance Corporation was set up but its funds did not trickle down to the hungry fast enough to prevent distress. There was no vast federal bureaucracy in 1932 able to distribute funds quickly; there was no tradition of distributing federal funds to citizens; no machinery for it and, in fact, no stockpile of funds to distribute. And would you know, this was the time Henry Ford announced the manufacture of a new V8 automobile.

The first of the unemployed were put to work on the highway below Lexington and some were put out on the Spray road and another crew rebuilt the cemetery fence. It was made work, but it would buy beans. In time the Civil Works Administration started and the Works Progress Administration and Public Works Administration all designed to provide work when there was not always work to do.

Almost every farmer was in debt. He had to borrow operating money from the bank and when crops were poor he could not pay up in the fall after his harvest and needed to start borrowing again to put in a new crop. This sort of business has never appealed to bankers. Those who had more than one source of income were considered better risks. Many farmers who had bought land during the prosperous war time were still in debt and were unable to pay their interest and much less make the payments. Some were very good operators but the banks were unable to lend them any money because the banks had almost no depositors. They relied on Portland banks for credit but city banks stopped providing funds for local banks and the only solution was foreclosure.

Historically taxpayers organize after the money is spent and when the bills come due. This was true when the Morrow County Tax Conservation League was formed. Its purpose was to get lower taxes but property owners could not pay taxes already levied. Prime movers in the organization were R. B. Rice, Carroll Kennedy, R. I. Thompson, P. W. Mahoney, Jack Hynd, Ralph Akers and W. F. Barnett.

One minor source of income almost became major; Claude Cox announced that the Morrow County Creamery had paid out $60,000 in cream checks the year before. Milking cows was as profitable as anything else for Glenn Jones sent a deck of hogs to Portland and received five cents a pound and for a deck of lambs he got $3.50.

Even the county's interest in other means of getting income seemed doomed as the mill on the old Slocum site on Caplinger Creek burned with a loss of $35,000 and some jobs.

Groceries were cheap: flour cost $4.25 a barrel, ordinary canned goods could be bought at ten cans for 98 cents and beans were 25 pounds for 95 cents at MacMarrs. But it took money to pay for them and the stores had to have cash in order to restock. In the fall of 1932 it was possible to gain admission to the Heppner Rodeo for a sack of wheat.

In December the mercury dropped to 14 degrees below zero and the men who were working on the Spray road and in a camp had to quit. The cold weather damaged the wheat crop which was poor anyway, having been sown with some very poor seed.

In the fall of 1932 the nation elected Franklin D. Roosevelt as president. They wanted a change of some sort and he promised rigid economy and a cut of at least twenty-five percent in federal expenditures. There was a feeling that economy was the key to most of the trouble. Those with federal jobs and what seemed to others as very high salaries defended their salaries by every argument. State and local officials were less fortunate. County officials' salaries were reduced and the county imposed a limit on school teachers' salaries of $100 in grade school and $115 in high school. In addition to the other troubles there was a flu epidemic and many were ill and schools were closed for a month at Christmas time. The *Gazette-Times* advertised that it would take chickens, beef, vegetables, almost anything edible in exchange for subscriptions.

Where was all the money that had powered the war and the boom that followed? The movement of money is often more important than the volume; a dollar that changes hands four or five times a day can generate a good bit of business; a dollar that hides in a pocket or a bank vault, afraid to venture out, is almost useless to business.

After January 26, 1933 when the national bank examiner took control of both Morrow County banks it was possible to get a little money on good collateral.

As a stop-gap Dean Goodman persuaded the Lions club to issue scrip which was to circulate as money in limited amounts locally. It would be backed by county and school district warrants. A teacher could draw a ten dollar warrant—never his full salary—and get scrip for it. He could spend the scrip for groceries or face powder if of the face powder gender. The warrant was negotiable and could be used to pay taxes, when and if anyone became sufficiently prosperous to begin paying taxes. It was a sheer stroke of genius that caused the Heppner scrip to be printed on sheepskin. The novelty of that made it in such demand that well more than half of it was kept for souvenirs and was never turned in to the committee for redemption. The Lions club backed $5000 in scrip in amounts from 25 cents to $10 and to make it official Mayor Gay M. Anderson appointed Charles Thomson, Earl Eskelson, J. J. Nys, Lucy Rodgers, Josephine Mahoney and Spencer Crawford to help Goodman with the project. Other communities followed the lead of Heppner by issuing scrip and there were several kinds circulating in Oregon.

By spring when Roosevelt was inaugurated there began a gush of laws from a subservient congress that eventually brought the federal government into nearly every home and every phase of the life of all citizens. Verily, it was a new deal, wiping out the good along with the bad in what had been an independent economy. The federal government reached down to control wages and prices, controlled the acreage of wheat, the rate of interest, nearly everything economic and even social. Within a few months an independent citizenry was turned into serfs, subservient, willing, even enthusiastic serfs.

In January of 1934 the First National Bank of Portland opened a branch in Heppner and it was possible to get money again if one had the right credentials. The deep depression had lasted only a few months but a man gets hungry by hours, not days or months. It had been a trying ordeal that no one ever forgot.

When the new deal came to the job of deciding the number of acres and bushels Morrow County was permitted to raise it was done through a local committee working under strict and unchangeable rules. Morrow County was allowed a base of 119,688 acres of winter and 6,103 acres of spring wheat which was figured to be the average for the previous five years. The regulations became more complicated as time went on.

When growers were paid three years allotment for two years production there was money again in the land.

The government paid up to $20 a head for cattle to be slain although the average obtained by the owner was six to $13 a head and sheep were shot for a payment of $3.00 each and the meat used to poison coyotes by an expanded body of government trappers.

The Agricultural Adjustment Administration went on with its program for some months until the plan eventually was taken to the supreme court which threw it out as unconstitutional. There was consternation among those more concerned about their income than the constitution and there was rage at the men on the supreme court and an attempt to expand the court.

But the men in the AAA were not without imagination. Payments were attached to soil conservation and new agencies devised to manage that program. The next year, 1937, Frank Anderson started strip cropping on his wheat ranch near Eightmile. Soil conservation was an ideal that was approved by the court.

It will not be possible to assess the economic and social effects of the new deal until all of the generation that was a part of it has gone to their eternal rest on the hill. It was an emotional matter and not to be judged by normal standards and it was so popular that Roosevelt was elected four times to the presidency. The voters thought he was indispensible—a god.

The main thrust of the new deal was to raise prices. The National Recovery Act established prices for almost every service and arrested any who worked for less. Acreage of farm crops was reduced and domestic animals shot to reduce the number. The old concept that American industry would and should produce more of everything until everyone could have enough was thrown away for a program of scarcity. High prices were substituted. Eventually the class to derive the most benefit was labor.

As an uplifter of confidence or a sop to sadness the government legalized beer and within a short time it was possible to buy whisky but there wasn't much money to buy it with.

Gay M. Anderson, county clerk and mayor, and very popular, was acquitted of misappropriation of funds, but the bonding company made up the difference which existed. Anderson moved to California.

The Townsend plan advocates were never as enthusiastic in Morrow County as in some although there were regularly organized clubs that met and listened to speeches about the advantages of retiring at 65 on an income of $200 per month. Even the most enthusiastic could not have believed that it would come to pass or that the scheme would contribute to the condition that reduced the hoped-for $200 to a value of around $80 in 1935 values.

Within a year or two J. L. Gault had made good progress with bank liquidation and the Farmers & Stockgrowers paid out in full and with some additional interest to depositors for the time their money had been tied up, even the stockholders were repaid. The First National was in a less fortunate position. It paid out 85.35 percent. But inasmuch as payments had been made periodically shortly after the examiner had taken charge the settlements of the banks added a lot of money to the county's exchequer.

The Civilian Conservation Corps was organized to take young men off the streets of eastern cities and put them near little western towns where they were expected to build trails, repair farmers' fences, poison sage rats, dig ditches and do other work not generally done and not considered necessary. About 200 New England boys were located on the fair grounds at Heppner and other camps were located up in the mountains. The reaction was generally good and a crew did succeed in draining Ditch Creek into Willow where the water is more usable.

The Taylor Grazing Act finally came into force in 1936 and this eventually reduced the number of itinerant sheepmen in Morrow County and the state. It made it necessary for a man to have a home base before he could run stock in a government reserve.

Morrow soon became an excellent example of the need for soil conservation. The land north of Ione has never been very stable and the summer-fallow system as practiced in 1934 was not conducive to keeping the land in place when the winds began to blow. And they blew in 1934. In 1935 they blew harder. The west wind swept across the flat land sifting the finer parts of the soil into the air where they were borne away for miles. It was possible to work the soil with spring-tooth or several other implements and halt the blow at least for a time. Not every farmer wanted to do this. The blows would work toward the direction of the wind, thus constantly moved westerly. The blow moved west into Gilliam County and much of Shuttler flat was moving at one time. The ground was dry on top in the spring and if crops were planted the seed was blown out. Dust piled up around machinery, covered fence rows and there was a pile in Bert Johnson's yard higher than his house. People could not stay home when the wind was blowing;

the finer particles of the soil sifted into any house, floors were covered three or four inches deep and lace curtains became half an inch thick. Everything was gray, including the prospects.

Joe Belanger was county agent, having succeeded Charley Smith, who had been called to higher duty in Corvallis. What was wanted was a law to force a man to work his summerfallow so it would not blow. It was realized that it might be a continuous operation so long as the winds persisted. But farmers wanted to have everything done that might help. Ernie Fatland of Condon had been elected state representative and he took up the problem and with others worked out a bill that was passed by the regular session of 1935. Most fortunate of all was that the extremely hard winds of 1934 and 1935 did not continue thereafter. Soon the style of farming changed as trashy fallow was introduced.

In 1939 a more comprehensive bill was designed, one to establish a state soil conservation district, instead of merely a wind erosion district. Henry Smouse, R. B. Rice, Omar Reitmann, Frank Saling and Louis Marquart, who had worked on the wind erosion district were also interested in soil erosion. It was the first soil conservation bill in any state and Morrow County had the first soil conservation district in the United States. And the general terms of the Oregon law prevail throughout the nation.

Lexington farmers had already started an oil cooperative which they considered successful and in 1940 Morrow County Grain Growers began to acquire warehouses and elevators all over the county until they were—and are—in almost complete control of the grain storage business in the county. And also in that year farmers incorporated the Columbia Basin Electric Power Company to buy electricity from the Bonneville Power Administration and distribute it locally and in adjoining counties. Cooperative endeavor seems to have more than average appeal to Morrow Countians. It may be the influence of the Swedes.

Depression or no depression Heppner youth insisted on having a swimming pool and after one built by the American Legion on Willow Creek proved something of a hazard during a small flood on Balm Fork it was condemned. The Pacific Power & Light Company owned some property just south of the old Heppner plant on August street which it donated to the city. It is almost in Shobe canyon and occasionally gets filled with run-off water but it has been the city swimming pool for thirty years.

Of course Morrow County's prominence in the wool industry caused several of its prominent sheepmen to be elected president of the wool-growers, Garnet Barratt being one of the more active ones. Mrs. W. P. Mahoney, wife of a former president, became head of the national auxiliary and in that same year Mrs. Ralph I. Thompson was state president (later national) giving Morrow County a prominent spot in wool promotion.

W. T. Campbell wrested the county judgeship from R. L. Benge (these two men were neighbors in the Social Ridge area) and with George Peck and George Bleakman as commissioners Campbell took up the job of spending county, state and federal funds on the roads as such funds were made available. The Spray road was Bleakman's especial interest, he being a resident of Hardman, and he eventually saw it completed.

There was no boom in education in the depressive thirties, it not being then considered necessary to finish high school to exist. Graduating classes increased from 19 in 1931 to 25 in 1939 although the population of the county decreased from 4941 to 4337.

The price of land went down and Joseph T. Peters, a Portland capitalist, bought the Duran land in Blackhorse for $18 per acre and he also built the one story brick building at the corner of Main and Willow. When Charley Smith moved away he sold a half section of land for $15 per acre.

Morrow County became directly involved in a labor dispute as early as 1934 when Cornett Green, going to Portland with a load of wool, had to run a gauntlet of teamsters to deliver his load to the terminal.

Agricultural producers who hauled to Portland continued to have trouble delivering their loads as teamsters tried to make farmers pay a teamster to take their produce from the city limits to ultimate delivery. In the 1937 legislature a bill restricting such aggression was defeated by a small margin so rural shippers initiated a measure for the 1939 ballot. The Eastern Oregon Wheat League was directly involved, and Morrow County was especially so as George Peck was president of the league that year. The campaign was a rough one with nearly every citizen involved before the election. The bill carried in every county but two. It was a battle that drew agricultural producers closer together than they had been before.

The thirties were not all depressive even though the economics of the nation never were in good shape until the second World War. The Bridal Veil Lumber company came to Heppner and looked around for a site for a sawmill on which to saw some pine lumber into box shooks for the Kraft Cheese Company. Local citizens offered their help and pledged some money but it didn't work out. H. O. Wray, a small operator with a little money, bought some land from Frank Parker just below town and put up a little mill of his own, doing most of the work himself. It burned up. Orville J. Smith came over from Naches, Washington to help out and was soon in the lumber business, not only box shooks but lumber for there was a heavy demand for soft pine to crate war material for overseas shipment.

The mill prospered and was soon hauling timber from Grant County around Monument and on Cottonwood Creek. After some years of remarkable prosperity it was sold to the Kinzua Lumber Company which had been buying timber in the mountains for several years, since 1937 in fact, when they had bought the Blue Mountain Ranch of 1800 acres from W. H. French.

Ben Swaggert, of a family whose occupations varied from keeping a saloon to lecturing and preaching, moved out into the Black Horse country and developed a breed of horses he called the Creamoline, some being sold to movie actors. They were beautiful and proud and often with more rounded hips than this one. They were definitely not Palomino; they were Creamoline and a horseman can pick out a horse with that blood in him even unto this day and Ben Swaggert has been gone for many a year. (Courtesy Oscar Peterson)

Eligible men were forced to register for another war in 1940, just as a precaution, it was said. But men were not surprised; they had long expected war. And the government had already taken land in the north end of the county as a bombing range over the protest of Judge Bert Johnson who said the county was losing a tax resource.

Despite government payments for not growing wheat, despite easier credit, despite the heavy and protecting hand of government the number of farmers dropped from 638 to 539 in the depression decade and the size of farms increased.

In 1934, C. A. Rhea, the first banker who lived to be 89 years old and discredited, died at the home of a son in Stanfield. And George Mossil Vinson, also 89, a pioneer of upper Butter Creek where he had been since a boy, passed away.

In 1937 Morrow County lost its chief advocate. Samuel Edward Notson, who had served Morrow in so many ways, died and was buried in Portland. He had first come to Lexington as a school teacher, soon became mayor and then moved to Heppner as county school superintendent. Early papers carried his reports of different schools and the progress they were making toward following the recommendations of the superintendent, especially in the matter of lighting and ventilation.

Notson went to reading law with Gilbert Phelps in a little office on Main Street above May and soon was admitted to the bar while Phelps went on to be circuit judge. Notson became district attorney and held the post until old age caused him to decline another nomination. He occupies a peculiar spot in Morrow County his-

tory. He wasn't much like them, at least not like the wilder and free-wheeling ones. He was a religious man who often preached in the Methodist Episcopal church and at any gathering of Christians. He made no enemies for he didn't do anything to create enemies. He was spokesman for Morrow County, the man who was sent to the legislature to plead for a bill, the man who attended meetings of sheriffs and law enforcement officers, who spoke at picnics and other gatherings of people, who was a leader in the campaigns for navigation on the Columbia and irrigation of the sand. He was the county's workhorse, modest and unassuming about it all. For years he saved copies of the local papers and filed them away in the court house and this history—and any history that is ever written about Morrow County—will depend to a great extent on the papers on which is stamped S. E. Notson.

Nothing ever kept Morrow Countians from going up into their mountains to gather berries in the fall, to fish in the spring and especially to hunt deer in the fall. There were always many little parties composed of a family or two going up to some spring or open glade for a Sunday holiday or a week of camping. And Lexington for years held a pioneer picnic that brought out a crowd to listen to a prominent speaker.

Recreation was not a commercial enterprise thirty years ago and no one made money out of it. Morrow Countians have always enjoyed their county, much more than most it seems, and perhaps that is a heritage of the almost poetical status that John Watermelon Redington heaped on his beloved Heppner Hills.

THE FORTIES WERE TERRIBLE

Preparations for war began in 1940 before the decade of the thirties was properly over and men were going to the army camps all during 1941, not in dribbles of three or four, but by the dozens. Mr. Wilson's first world war was a quick and was thought decisive conflict that the nation entered with a sort of enthusiasm and the survivors remembered with pride. They saw many new things.

Mr. Roosevelt's war was a replay in that the same allies were opposing the same enemy, resentful over an unworkable peace. Whether headed by a Kaiser or a commoner the Germans were out to

conquer Europe and the United States was not going to allow it. Speculation about the wisdom of it still goes on in philosophical and political circles and will until the final history is written.

Russia was drawn in and the carnage on the eastern front was astounding; wonder was that enough of what was called the civilized world remained to start another one. And when the battle of Stalingrad ended the western front exploded and death came to millions. At the end Russia insisted on a division of Germany that may end that nation's aggressiveness. The result will not be in this history.

The official start of war against Germany and Japan was made on December 8 when congress declared war against them after the Japanese had bombed Pearl Harbor and sunk the Pacific fleet whose rusting frames may still be seen protruding from their graves. America was angry and badly hurt militarily.

This is a history of Morrow County, Oregon, a comparatively small, rural county whose citizens were drawn into war activities so completely as to absorb all their energies until long after the peace. They spent no time in reasoning why; they sent men, they gathered scrap; they sold bonds; they did without sugar and other commodities; they supported the Red Cross; they submitted to daylight saving; they did all these and many more in a spirit of patriotism without questioning.

The history of Morrow County during most of the 1940s is a history of the nation at war so completely were Morrow Countians involved. Naturally people died and were buried, children were born—although in reduced numbers—and life went on but it was a strange life.

When it was over all trace of the ebullience of early Morrow County was gone. Men looked to the government for guidance and help in all endeavors. It was war that subdued the pioneer spirit. It was not depression; depression tested it and strengthened it.

It would be impossible to or at least improper to write the history of Morrow County without explaining the reason for this subservience.

The government came in 1940 to buy a part of the north end of the county for a bombing range, range where Hynd Brothers and others had some grazing land. The price offered was $1.25 per acre which the Hynds succeeded in having raised to $1.42. Krebs Brothers enlarged their holdings by buying 22,000 acres of grass land from Smythe. During this decade Hynds further reduced their holdings by selling the Sand Hollow land to Orville Cutsforth. Prices were low because of the long depression of the thirties, beef roasts for 21 cents, Fels Naptha soap (for those who remember) at ten bars for 45 cents. But wheat was a pretty good price and after something like ten years of poor crops the rains came to Morrow County and the land produced wonderfully for over twenty years.

The rule was that if farmers voted by three to one for government controls they could borrow from the government on their wheat at a specified price that was always generous. Farmers made money during the war, made so much money that the price of land

soared and the elderly or inefficient sold out, reducing the number who enjoyed the big income.

In September of 1941 organizers for the sale of bonds came through the county and P. W. Mahoney was chosen the first chairman with Lucy Rodgers, Ralph Jackson, J. Logie Richardson, Jasper Crawford, Judge Bert Johnson, to aid him. Thus began a movement that drew many dollars out of the county for the war.

And in October the advocates of the new hospital appointed a committee to further that enterprise; they were Judge Bert Johnson, Harold Cohn, Harvey Miller, Ralph Jackson, Lucy Rodgers, Garnet Barratt and J. O. Turner. One can see who were the leaders in the county in the early forties.

The Catholics dedicated a new brick church downtown in November of 1941 and it was one of the last improvements to be made for five years. Wheat marketing had to be changed for these was no jute for grain bags so the old flat houses were hurriedly cribbed to hold bulk wheat. Farmers piled up enough scrap to make 13 light tanks according to an offhand estimate by someone who had probably never seen a tank.

Those who held farm sales advertised on the sale bills "Bring Your Own Sugar" for the Office of Price Administration was in control of all commodities and it was a terrible thing with power over everything from which there was no effective appeal. If a citizen thought the local administrator or his committee was prejudiced there was nothing he could do except holler and hollering was unpatriotic and unheeded. Most administrators were honest and efficient to judge from the overall record, but the system of setting quotas and establishing limits on prices and labor is one so far reaching and uneconomic that even the federal government cannot do it with equity.

One needed points for red meat, for many common foods, for tires, for fuel oil, for gasoline. Merchants could not get supplies nor sell them freely. Safeway left Heppner to concentrate in bigger towns—and has not returned. M. C. Clark closed his grocery. Had the war been a holy war it could not have governed the people more completely.

Victory gardens, tin can drives, scrap paper, rationing stamps, tons of clothing for the valiant Russians; so many activities in the name of patriotism that the people were confused. Morrow and Sherman Counties ran a close race for the honor of dedicating a landing craft, the Fon du Lac, in the Portland shipyards, and Mrs. B. C. Pinckney and Mrs.

Orville Smith, wives of two bond workers went down for the occasion.

Germany was finally pinched between the hordes of Russians marching through Poland and the forces of the Allies moving across the Rhine and with Hitler apparently self destroyed the war on the western front ended in early May of 1945. Roosevelt died and was succeeded by the decisive Truman who gave the order to bomb Japan with atomic bombs which ended resistance on the Pacific front in August of that year. Mr. Roosevelt's war lasted longer than did Mr. Wilson's and the repressions on the people were more sweeping; its end brought relief, not elation.

The Heppner plant of the Morrow County Grain Growers burned during the late forties and was replaced by one with a capacity of 234,000 bushels in solid concrete.

When the war was ended farm trucks were released for purchase by farmers relieving a very serious situation; soldiers returned to flood the court house with discharges to be registered and prove they were free men again although the society into which they entered was hardly more free than the service they had left.

The older citizens who had carried on with all the war work during the five years of war were anxious to turn the jobs—the jobs that still needed doing—over to the returned men and these men never wanted to take another order again or conform to another regulation. It was some time before the succession was made. Yet, Bert Mason at Ione, who had been faithfully keeping store for 45 years, took advantage of war's end to close up shop. Lexington used the interest in flying to clear the level land north of town and establish an airport that was used for many years. Farmers had been raising wheat so long they never wanted to do anything else and were in search of some product that could be made from wheat and sold. Orville Cutsforth spent some of his time talking up Dextrose although starch can be produced more cheaply from plants other than wheat.

It had, of course, been impossible to buy a car during the war and dealers had a hard time keeping their priorities straight after cars became available, but eventually everyone with money had a car and the dealers began advertising their product instead of advertising patience.

By 1947 it had been decided that the Heppner Rodeo and the Morrow County Fair were entertainments that could properly be held together and Garnet Barratt, Orville Cutsforth and A. C. Hough-

ton (one of the first men from the north end of the county to be appointed to anything) were named to the fair board. The Rural Electrification Administration's local agency, the Columbia Basin Electric, with a two percent loan from the federal government, began planning again, operations having been postponed during the war.

Work also started on the new hospital that was to be built on the brow of the hill on the east side of town. Garnet Barratt donated the land and arranged preliminary grading. The county had $189,-000 on hand to build the hospital and were able to contract the building for $167,000 with a Portland firm.

There were two developments in the forties that have made a direct effect on wheat farming. One was the use of weed killers applied in a spray which was said to kill weeds; it has been used steadily since then without decisive effect. The other was the use of nitrogen fertilizer which had, especially at first, a surprisingly beneficial effect on the wheat crops on the better land. Thus, two new expenses were added to farming and in as much as the use was so general it is difficult to judge what the effect would have been without them.

Only a small part of the artisans who had gone to the shipyards or other war work returned to Heppner or to any of the other small towns and rural America has been short of men with mechanical skills since. The last storekeeper at Hardman went off to do war work. War demands boosted wages—and labor unions, with the encouragement of government, accelerated the process—until the hourly wage is often too high for a rural economy to pay. It is a part of the pinch between rising costs for labor and a price for wheat established by a government controlled by consumers.

Farmers had grown accustomed and adept at complaining but their problems since World War II are more serious than before and they have fewer resources and less political strength with which to oppose them.

O. G. Crawford, then editor of the Gazette-Times, was concerned lest war be used as an excuse to perpetuate a bureaucracy—and never was editor more prophetic.

Morrow County was concerned in 1942 about its railroad for the federal government made a move to take up the tracks of the Columbia Southern in Sherman County and send the rails to Russia. That plan was thwarted and Morrow County's fear subsided.

Morrow County women aided the war by "adopting" men in hospitals. Mrs. Ralph I. Thompson raised money and gave comfort to the men in McCaw hospital in Walla Walla.

Ralph Jackson anticipated the end of the war and a revival of farm implement business by starting a machinery store in Lexington, a venture he sold later in the decade to Braden-Bell, a sort of chain of the implement trade. It was time, for inventors had developed a self-propelled combine that could be operated by one man. This made it possible for a man and wife to harvest without hired help if the wife could drive a truck—and many of them could and did. It was a far cry from stationery threshing.

Politically the "balanced" plan was put on the ballot in 1949 as a substitute for the "federal" plan of legislative representation. Either would have saved legislative strength for the producing areas of the state. It was defeated by city votes and the political power of eastern Oregon has declined until it is but a small part of its economic importance.

Pioneers died on a regular—but private—schedule, wars having on effect on their longevity. But it seems proper to speculate on the last recollections of Franklin Dee Cox, who lived on Hinton Creek since 1877 as he contemplated the restrictions that had replaced the freedoms he came to enjoy, or of Mrs. Paul Reitmann, mother of eight sons and two daughters, or of L. A. Florence, one of a family that settled on Willow Creek before there was a county or a town and only a self made trail to his cabin, or of Leon W. Biggs, the county treasurer, who died at 90. He had kept books for Heppner & Blackman. Is it possible that they were content to leave a world so different from the one in which they knew how to act, in which they were free to act?

There are those who say that more people make more laws necessary, which is not, we think, a polite commentary on the quality of humans. We seem to cherish ease above effort and this certainly accounts for many of the changes and may be the key to mans' eventual enslavement—to whom or what, we would not hazard a guess.

MODERN TIMES

Progress, said the English biologist, Thomas Huxley, is the movement from heterogenity to homogenity. He was saying that the more things became alike the faster we were moving ahead. The writer does not subscribe to that theory.

Nevertheless in the last twenty years Morrow County has made some great strides toward progress if Huxley be correct. The individual and the community have decreased in importance, have lost power to make decisions, have smaller part in history and the state and federal government have grown fearfully in authority. And Morrow County accepts it with grace and gleans what money it can from the ever-flowing pot. In fact Morrow County is adept at obtaining federal and state money.

The economic life of the county is vigorous with many entrepreneurs trying new methods and raising new crops. It is the social, the public life of the county that has become repetitious and custom-bound. Spontaniety is gone, the spontaniety that made pioneer life so interesting Moderns seem like automatons in comparison.

Each year the county or someone in it selects a conservation man of the year and like the old ditty about Lydia Pinkham "the papers publish his face"; according to rules laid down by some distant board the county chooses a stockman of the year and only once did it vary it by selecting a woman for the

The first farm well for irrigation was drilled in 1944 and this crop of hay was the product of the additional water it provided. (Courtesy Orville Cutsforth)

In contrast to the bleakness of the homes of original homesteaders as depicted in the picture of the Duvall first home is this picture of Cutsforth Corners, site of the Cutsforth holdings northeast of Lexington. Subsidies and fertilizers have raised the price of land and farm incomes and now farm establishments are centers of far reaching activity and many look like it. All the amenities of modern living are available in Morrow County farm homes and the average of them is superior to the average town or city home.
(Courtesy Orville Cutsforth)

honor; high school classes move relentlessly from first year to last like well trained troops, grade schools observe closing ceremonies with no more than a few giggles; holidays are noted as a solemn duty; reunions gather the ever-growing aged to a session of reminiscence; lodges and club meetings are held as a ritual; five girls are chosen as fair princesses and one becomes queen in a mock imitation of royalty. Life that should be an adventure becomes a repetition of the obvious to all but the very young. We know of no cure for such ennui. Wouldn't it be fun if a bunch of cowboys rode down Main Street on the run, or if John and Frank Kilkenny came to town with their sheepherders and knocked a few men through saloon windows? Or even to watch Les Matlock bet against two pairs behind a set of threes?

The federal government was the major influence on Morrow County in the last twenty years. After the conclusion of World War II and the signing of

the peace which was with Stalin and was not observed by the Russians, it was only a few years before the decisive Mr. Truman involved the nation in a conflict in Korea. Allies deserted and the country had a rather serious war on its hands, the start of the nation's concern in the affairs and politics of southeast Asia that was to last at least twenty years, taking many thousand lives, billions of dollars and create emotional and political disturbances at home that will have a long lasting effect on the nation's history.

This directly affected Morrow County which furnished a steady stream of young men as soldiers and contributed many millions of dollars to the public pot for war, to say nothing of bond sales and drives for various causes. The nation gave with a grudging hand to wheat farmers to get them to balance their production to meet the nation's need and took away, with apparent glee, a sizeable share of everyone's income. The county and the cities, thus deprived of income, came to depend more and more on handouts from bigger governments and the pioneer spirit of do it yourself or do without was stifled.

Government, big government, has made local governments almost superfluous or at least petty. And that is reason enough to doubt Mr. Huxley.

In January of 1951 the soil conservation district reported that some scientifically advocated practices were being observed, such as strip cropping: 8,984 acres, and stubble mulch: 14,266 acres. That spring there was the first real interest in rain making and Dr. Irving P. Krick, the chief advocate of cloud seeding to cause rain to fall, came to Heppner and a meeting. Many farmers were convinced and much money was spent in the next few years in some form of inducing rain to fall on command. Wheat farmers consistently voted by huge margins for a continuance of government controls and government subsidy. Most of them felt there was nothing else to do—and maybe there wasn't—nothing else was seriously debated. Who would shoot Santa Claus?

The Morrow County Grain Growers, of which Al Lamb was the manager, shipped the first barge load of wheat from the Paterson ferry site in December of 1954. Farmers formed committees to reappraise the land of the county because of a state law that was based on the well founded assumption that assessments in the state and county were not equal as between individual owners nor between counties. And in Morrow County the job was done with little argument. There were good years and bad in the wheat business with most of them being good as to yields and prices, especially in the early fifties when President Truman did not invoke quotas nor cut payments, giving wheat growers large incomes.

The number of grain growers diminished gradually but certainly as neighbor swallowed neighbor. The reason was more often age and affluence than poverty. Despite its cost there is a surplus of machinery in the county for each grower desires independence. Result is that it takes a pile of money to buy a wheat spread and few have the cash to do it and, unless in possession of other lands, are without the credit to do it. The forming of corporations to buy wheat land is not yet common. Wheat growers complain that they make no money and can often prove it by arithmetic, but they go on with the same huge expenditures, drive expensive automobiles and display few evidences of poverty.

A large part of their income comes from the federal government in one way or another, the details

of which are too complicated to be explained here, mere possession of wheat land gives them an income independent of other sources. Even the wheat market is secondary and the banker is not so final a figure as he once was.

The organizations the wheat grower has developed to combat the economics and the government have not been effective; the grange is more a social organization, bound in ritual and devoted to the consumption of most excellent cake; the Farmers' Union never caught on in the Oregon wheat belt; the Farm Bureau has at times had an active following but its national policies have not recently concurred with local desires; a new group, the National Farm Organization, sometimes withholds farm products from the market by dumping milk and by similar practices attempts to raise the price by inducing scarcity. It arranges to ship grain overseas directly to obtain a higher price. It could become a union of farmers that set prices instead of accepting them although that concept is so far from the usual marketing methods as to not be accomplished without the passage of much time and perhaps the passage of many agriculturists.

For the greater part of the two decades since 1950 agriculture has moved along with little change; wheat farmers did what the government told them to do and they were generally prosperous so they gradually quit being farmers and turned into wheat growers, selling the milch cows, eating the flock of chickens, plowing the pig lot. They became specialists in the growing of wheat, using more fertilizer, spraying for more weeds, and of necessity buying more machinery which grew in price until a combine sold for $24,000 and a big tractor for as much or more. It was considered imperative for each farmer to have hay balers, new type grain drills and other auxiliary equipment until many a wheat grower has an investment in excess of $100,000 in machinery alone. His annual budget makes the banker scringe, but the farmer is not hesitant to ask for loans based on anticipated income from wheat and government. When he fails his neighbor will buy him out without buying additional machinery. His only skill is growing of wheat—and he is good at it.

Neither has it been conclusively proved that specialization is the organization of the future. The farmer with a modest sized farm who does his own work, does not attempt to keep up with the latest style in machinery, keeps a flock of sheep, a small herd of cattle and who has eggs to eat and sell, may eventually prove that diversification is a better way

Shirley Rugg is a modern sheep raiser, probably the state's most modern. She has but minor use for grass as sheep feed, preferring forbs and weeds. Her methods would scare the whiskers off an old time sheepman — but they work. (Courtesy Shirley Rugg)

to the good farm life than specialization. Perhaps another Alexander Pope will sing:

> "Happy the man, whose wish and care
> A few paternal acres bound
> Content to breathe his native air
> On his own ground."

It is being reported that but three percent of Americans are active producers of the food we eat and certainly the tendency has been downward for many generations. The problem leaves the area of economics and becomes social. What occupation will the non-food producers follow? How many lawyers, gasoline pumpers, hair dressers, doctors, salesmen can the producer support in the style the ever-present television tells everyone is necessary? Who will pay the taxes for affluence when affluence comes more and more from other peoples' taxes? Or will we just print more money and take the short route to national bankruptcy?

Specialization came to other fields also. After the thirties the number of sheepmen in Morrow County gradually declined. The thirties were dry and the government, through the Bureau of Land Management and the Forest Service, held that overgrazing was the cause of depleted ranges. Permits were gradually reduced and sheepmen of necessity reduced the number of sheep. This chart shows the history of Morrow County agriculture:

	1890	1900	1910	1920	1930
Wheat A	26,094	43,389	75,721	102,459	131,556
Cattle	10,746	8,746	6,161	13,388	7,961
Sheep	169,971	322,650	209,057	169,214	193,568

	1940	1950	1960	1970
Wheat A	72,661	115,620	115,835	111,964
Cattle	10,632	22,195	29,953	27,147
Sheep	110,624	51,397	44,325	10,617

The numbers of cattle and sheep for adults or cattle over six months and ewes of approximately the same age. Wheat is for acres. Most of the figures are for agricultural census years which are for one year before the decennial census of humans. Also it was not (especially in early days) expected that a stockman have a perfect memory or an exact count when talking to an assessor and it is likely that in its heyday Morrow County had around a half million sheep.

There are really more than 10,000 sheep in Morrow County. The only local operator is Shirley Rugg who has 5300 ewes but Krebs Brothers take several bands to Montana every spring and Morrow County cannot assess them full time.

Shirley Rugg, whose savvy of stock comes naturally, she being the daughter of Frank Wilkinson, as wise a stockman as the county ever knew—and his companion on many a range ride—is a specialist. As she rides her range, owned and leased, atop her purebred Appaloosa, she observes her sheep and what they eat. She knows as much about it as do the sheep.

These are the five "potato circles" on the D. O. Nelson farm north of Lexington, down by Finley Butte. Each circle comprises 130 acres and is given all the water the plants can use during the growing season. In the center is a huge motor, up to 400 horsepower, which turns the irrigation heads at a speed determined by the operator. The camera was pointing south. This is the most modern way to raise potatoes and the production is tremendous for the soil is adapted to potatoes. (Courtesy D. O. Nelson)

A far cry from the header and the crew that piled grain in a stack to await the threshing machine is this modern battery of self-propelled combines that can travel around a wheat field from sun up until dew fall without stopping for food or water and only an occasional halt for another tankful of fuel. They can reduce a whole section of grain into stubble with the straw all spread, or piled, and the grain in the elevator in a few hours. Verily, the wheat farmer operates a manufacturing plant as surely as does a man whose machinery is within a closed factory and the wheat farming business is among the world's most efficient—witness how it is still feeding the world although the number of workmen has been reduced to a mere fraction of its numbers a half century ago. (Courtesy Morrow County Grain Growers)

Among old sheepmen it was the assumption that the way to make a ewe happy and her lamb to grow to saleable weight by mid-July was to run them on a cool mountain where there was frequent water and where some of the fescues grew thick and lush. Shirley Rugg finds that forbs and weeds are better than grass for sheep, having observed that her ewes prefer that fodder. She moves her bands so skillfully over her range that they never follow one another and they arrive at the cutting pen and the weighing shed on a schedule unhurried and never excited. And they weigh much better than 110 pounds. The forest management people have recently permitted her to run 200 cows along with her sheep and it is the cows that eat the grass; the ewes fatten on dry sunflower leaves. In this day lambs are produced for mutton and are sold to be killed immediately, quick frozen, and trucked to New York before their bleating mothers have moved five miles.

Shearing is done in early February, before lambing, which eliminates tagging. Winter headquarters are near Boardman. The wool is a valuable adjunct, but not the major concern. Losses are kept low and the 1970 lambing was over 130 percent. Bill Penland or John Kilkenny, should they rise from their graves and observe the care taken of the Rugg sheep, would not recognize the industry that made them both famous and rich.

D. O. Nelson is a specialist, growing potatoes on his former wheat farm north of the base line where wheat is not always as successful a crop as farther south. In 1969 he had 237 acres of potatoes from which he took 20 tons of potatoes each and hauled them away to a processing plant in Hermiston. In 1970 he and his partner, Tucker, had five "circles" of potatoes and built a plant at Boardman to handle the crop. Water comes from three over 2000 gallon per minute wells and the "circles" are powered by a 400 HP electric motor. It may be that the question will not be how many potatoes can Morrow County produce with sufficient water, but how many can be sold.

Allen Tom, down in Sherman County, may not be a specialist on chickens but he is in fair way to be with over 300,000 laying hens due to a new facility now being built in what used to be his barnyard. Instead of adding to the surplus of wheat as he used to do on his Sherman and Morrow County wheat ranches he expects to buy 500,000 bushels to feed his chickens every year.

Almost adjoining Morrow County is the hog raising and feeding establishment of Hansell Brothers, who produce a big part of the seven percent of locally grown hogs Oregon is said to eat. The others are bought from the middle west. As specialists the Hansells have to rate high on anyone's list. They are not farmers.

A man who wanted to be a farmer and self sufficient on a farm would find ample opportunity and invitation on any of the numerous creeks in Morrow County—Willow, Rhea, or the two Butters being the largest. On them can be grown nearly every crop except fruit (berries do well) and in recent years the farming on these creeks has improved marvelously. All the water is used, over and over, and where once sand blew on Willow Creek, now all the bottom land is in crops, alfalfa or permanent pasture, and cattle loll in the shade of trees in what appears to be the height of cow comfort. New houses and outbuildings indicate prosperity.

In keeping with a trend that seems to have swept the state new school houses have been built, following a type of architecture that has been variously described, seldom in praise. Modern schools are one story and rambling, both safety features and laudable, except for the gymnasium which is often the largest part of the building—and some critics say, appropriately so.

In 1953 Heppner wanted to build a new grade school and the plan was to put it some place near the high school which then occupied the building on the east side of the creek. Three sites were suggested, one being the Tum-A-Lum business property on Main Street and across the creek from the school but voters didn't like that much, neither did they like the George site. Finally, after several votes and the resignation of L. E. Dick from the board, a new grade school of ten rooms was built on the Prock-Devin site at a cost of $272,000. Voters were willing to float bonds for something they wanted but it took a long time. Then in 1961 the school board was prevailed upon by the state to buy 32 acres on the hill west of town for a new high school building, the number of high school pupils reaching up toward 200. Bonds were voted and the structure built, a product of the automobile age, surely, for it is doubtful if anyone, man or child, has ever climbed to it on his own two legs.

Ione developed, too, in its own quiet fashion. It drilled a new well that produced an ample 700 gallons per minute, evading in one stroke Heppner's well and water problems. In 1953 Ione built a new school almost right in town, on the level valley floor. Ione has a knack of being contented.

Eventually, after the county was made into one school district the Lexington High School was

A modern press drill seeding in the fall. Some farmers operate more drills than three, but the method is the same. With lights on the tractor this outfit can run day and night and put in a crop while conditions are the best. (Courtesy Morrow County Grain Growers)

closed, the last class graduating in 1959, all nine of them, and the long struggle of Lexington against Heppner was nearly ended. The headquarters of the county school system was moved into the old school building which is a sturdy structure, capable of many years use.

With the advent of the John Day dam Boardman was to be flooded and the many army engineers were charged with moving the town and rebuilding the public buildings. This entailed the construction of a modern high school a half mile east of Main Street, a rather different looking building, new and functional.

Heppner continued to spend a lot of money for a sufficient water supply and the council was issuing new bonds for improvements every few years until they have enough to meet the demands of a city that cherishes green lawns and high shade trees as well as clean water in the tap and adequate fire protection. In 1952 Heppner citizens voted 252 to 51 for a new sewer system which was built and put into operation before the newer and more expensive state engineers came to the fore. It works—the prime requirement.

Before the John Day dam was started hearings were held to hear arguments for a high dam or a low one and people attended although most of them knew that the engineers would build a dam just high enough to cause slack water to the foot of the McNary dam, which is exactly what they did. Nearby Arlington was moved to higher ground and the business section made over and many new houses built and all of them moved to the hills.

Boardman, being on land but little above the river, had to be moved further inland and as there were few houses worthy of being moved the town is almost entirely new, along a new highway and railroad track, modern in every respect and entertaining ideas of growth and grandeur that may, with luck and perseverance, come to pass. Blalock Island, a long strip of sand and gravel that lay in the middle of the river and provided a temporary home for thousands of wild geese every fall, was

submerged except for a point or two that old timers can point out to interested visitors. The new high water did another thing: it resulted in the taking of desert land claims that were soon to be nearer the river and there was quite a bit of speculation over them. The government also auctioned off many hundreds of acres of land to buyers who believed successful irrigation to be imminent.

The state or the forest service oiled roads into the timber, and road building was already a function of bigger governments than counties. The Bank of Eastern Oregon, an Arlington corporation, moved into Heppner and eventually Ione to offer some competition to the First National.

The Morrow County bombing range is a 96,000 acre plot of land lying in roughly the center of the north end of the county along the Columbia River. It was not considered valuable except for some early sheep feed when it was established and private owners were offered $1.25 per acre for their holdings within the boundaries, although Jack Hynd held out and eventually got $1.42. Mark Hatfield, then governor, developed the idea that so much land lying along a stream that was navigable by barge and backed by a productive farming and timber area, should be of some commercial value. The nation's wars were not very competitive at the moment and the navy was not using the land to practice bombing.

By legislative enactment he caused the site to be purchased by the state (using veterans' funds) and leased the west part to the Boeing company for $60,000 per year which at that time had a contract to build rockets, which it needed to test. Latest is that Boeing may use the site to test Super Sonic Transport engines and planes if the government continues its subsidy to private companies for research on that project and Boeing gets the contract. The state was to pay the taxes on the land to Morrow County, it being the owner, technically at least. The price of the land immediately rose to what seemed astronomical figures to some as local citizens believed—or at least said—that the land was fine farming land and extremely valuable. The taxes soon rose to a figure near what the state derived from the

Boeing lease. It was a fine hassle for those who like to fight and eventually the state invoked a law that permitted assessment of farm property on the basis of income instead of ad valorem value as set by the county. In the meantime Boeing's rocket contract expired and it does not at present have much use for the tract whose future is not predictable.

More constructive things were happening. Mrs. Harry (Amanda) Duvall, whose husband and daughter had recently died and whose ranch was sold, decided that a good use for a part of her money would be to build a museum and library and dedicate it to the county in the name of her departed family. The south end of a tract along Willow Creek on Main Street was chosen by the city and a contract let for approximately $65,000 to build a neat brick structure where the artifacts and memorabilia of the county are kept. An addition has since been built. It was certainly a landmark in the history of a county and rates as the most important social contribution made to Morrow County by any citizen.

In 1963 the Columbia Basin Electric, an REA affiliate, agreed with the Pacific Power & Light Company, a private utility, on a division of terri-

tory. The CBE took Heppner and the southern end of Morrow County, the southern part of Gilliam County and all of Wheeler County as its part and the private company took the territory along the river including Arlington and Boardman. At the time of writing competition between public and private power is not keen, neither having any surplus to sell.

The famed Christmas flood of 1964 did great damage at Ione. It was a peculiar flood, the warming trend coming from the south and Heppner snow went off more quickly than at Ione causing a flood. The destruction in most mid-Columbia counties was very great, not only to roads and bridges, but to land. Morrow County received $402,000 in federal funds to repair roads, indicative of considerable damage.

At no time has the agitation for a dam on Willow Creek immediately above Heppner died completely. When it quiets for a few weeks an engineer is brought in to talk to the Chamber of Commerce, someone writes a story of the supposed benefits therefrom; business men smack their lips over the prospect of profits during construction and occasionally a delegation goes back to Washington, D.C. to visit their congressman. The project has been on the U. S. Engineer's list for many years but apparently other projects have a higher priority. Perhaps a vote within the county would settle the problem definitely.

In 1954 Orville Smith, principal owner of the sawmill below Heppner, said that Maurice Hitchcock and Dant & Russell were now owners. In 1959 it was sold to Kinzua Pine Mills whose owners live in Seattle, but which owns a good part of the privately owned timber in the south end of Morrow and in Wheeler County and has a big mill at Kinzua.

There were more personal matters of public interest such at Dr. McMurdo being named "doctor of the year" for Oregon in 1957; there was a wind of an estimated 100 miles per hour that demolished the towers of Bonneville Power Administration along the Columbia; Orville Cutsworth developed a park up Willow Creek and donated it to the public which uses it for skiing, swimming, hiking or hunting. The Pacific Gas Transmission Company dug a ditch for a pipeline diagonally across the county and

built a sub-station near Ione, to add a goodly sum to the county's tax roll. It pumps gas from Canada to California. And just recently the Hynd family moved out of Morrow County, the older generation having died and the younger grown too old or affluent. For many years Hynd was a name to figure on in the stock business.

We have now recorded a hundred years of the history of Morrow County about which there is written record. There will be more, of course, but we doubt if it will be as dramatic or even as interesting. It is our private speculation that the repressions of World War II years are the cause of the social disturbances of the present years. It is possible that youth will reassert itself and become as self-reliant and as independent as their ancestors of a hundred years ago, as willing to pioneer in ideas as grandpa pioneered in land and occupations.

But it is the function of a historian to recount the past, not speculate on the future.

"Whatever will be, will be
The future's not ours to see
Sirrah, Sirrah"

MISCELLANY

In the writing of history there always seems to be some pertinent information that should be included in the record although it doesn't fit in any particular place. This chapter is of such material. Like a word in a dictionary it is not important until you want to know what it means.

For instance the population of Morrow County by decades was: 1890, 4205; 1900, 4151; 1910, 4357; 1920, 5617; 1930, 4941; 1940, 4337; 1950, 4783; 1960, 4871; 1970, 4465.

Heppner has had an estimated 318 in 1880; 675 in 1890; 1146 in 1900; 880 in 1910; 1324 in 1920; 1190 in 1930; 1140 in 1940; 1648 in 1950; 1691 in 1960; 1492 in 1970.

In a democracy the original concept was that public officers were not to be important in that their function was to do the bidding of their constituents, not necessarily to initiate programs of their own. Surely it has always been true that many of the actions of government come from private citizens and elected officials administer them. But elected officials are often prominent enough and popular enough to be elected by the people to perform a specific service and are entitled to the honor accorded.

In early Oregon government, before there was a state of Oregon, delegates were going to Oregon City to try to bring some order into the territory that was literally without government with authority. Many were able men and worthy of recognition. James K. Kelly, an able lawyer, was on the state council in 1853 and Orlando Humason, a lawyer, county judge and printer, was on the council in 1854 and N. H. Gates, a merchant, was the delegate in 1855 and Gates and Aaron Wait represented Clackamas and Wasco, and yet to be born Morrow County in territorial government and Robert Mayes was there in 1859.

The sole representative of all eastern Oregon in the constitutional convention in 1857 was Charles R. Meigs of The Dalles and he tried to have the eastern boundary of the state set at the top of the Cascade Mountains, saying that the then estimated 1100 persons in eastern Oregon would be better off to be under the domination of the federal government until they achieved sufficient population for statehood than to be forever under the domination of the more populous Willamette Valley whose people had, nor would have, an understanding of

113

the problems of the vast area beyond the mountains. Meigs, east Oregonians must admit, was something of a prophet.

After Oregon became a state in 1859 it was only until 1862 before Umatilla County was established and its men represented Morrow until 1885. It has since had representation of its own, almost always in conjunction with others of the small counties in the mid-Columbia basin, which are designated by initials that will be easily interpreted by the informed even though U stands for both Umatilla and Union, W for Wasco and Wheeler, and G for both Gilliam and Grant. The legislature met in alternate odd years, meeting in September, until 1901 when the sessions were changed to January. Each who served, of a certainty, suffered the frustrations attendant to getting his way among others and those who served the longest must have achieved some success in this regard. Public opinion undoubtedly affected their opinions and a few, perhaps, were able to affect public opinion. In the light of a hundred years no legislation by Morrow County men seems to have changed the trend of state politics, except possibly Jackson Morrow's barbed wire fence law and the soil conservation district act that became the model for national legislation.

State Legislators from 1860 to 1969

	HOUSE	SENATE
1860	Robert Mayes W	J. S. Ruckle CW
1862	O. Humason W	James K. Kelly CW
1864	L. F. Lane U	L. Donnel W
1866	H. A. Gehr U, T. W. Avery U	Nathaniel Ford U
1868	A. L. Kirk U	Nathaniel Ford U
1870	J. Thompson, U, F. A. DeShiel U	T. T. Lieuallen U
1872	Geo. A. LaDow U, James Curran U	T. T. Lieuallen U
1874	T. Roe U, U. Jackson U	Chas. L. Jewell U
1876	J. L. Morrow M, J. M. Partlow U	Chas. L. Jewell U
1878	Lucian Everts U	S. M. Pennington U
1880	P. J. Kelley U, John Q. Wilson U	S. M. Pennington U
1882	J. B. Sperry U, Benj. Stanton U	S. M. Pennington U
1884	J. L. Morrow, M, special	S. M. Pennington U
1886	L. B. Cox, MU, H. C. Gay MU	J. P. Wager MU
1888	T. E. Fell M	J. P. Wager MU
1890	J. C. Thompson M	H. Blackman GHM
1892	J. N. Brown M	H. Blackman GHM
1894	J. S. Boothby M	A. W. Gowan GHM
1896	J. N. Brown M	A. W. Gowan GHM
1898	E. L. Freeland M	J. W. Morrow UMU
1901	A. B. Thompson MU	J. W. Morrow UMU
1903	Gilbert W. Phelps MU	W. M. Pierce UMU
1905	W.C. Cole MU	W. M. Pierce UMU
1907	W. B. Slusher MU	W. C. Cole UMU
1909	T. J. Mahoney MU	W. C. Cole UMU
1911	T. J. Mahoney MU	C. A. Barratt UMU
1913	R. N. Stanfield MU	C. A. Barratt UMU
1915	R. N. Stanfield MU	C. A. Barratt UMU
1917	R. N. Stanfield MU	C. A. Barratt UMU
1919	C. N. Woodson MU	Colon R. Eberhard UMU
1921	C. N. Woodson MU	Colon R. Everhard UMU
1923	Alfred J. Smith MU	H. J. Taylor UMU

	HOUSE	SENATE
1925	A. R. Shumway MU, C. A. Tom GMSW	H. J. Taylor UMU
1927	Joe N. Scott MU, C. A. Tom GMSW	Fred E. Kiddle UMU
1929	Joe N. Scott MU	Fred E. Kiddle UMU
1931	Joe N. Scott MU	Fred E. Kiddle UMU
1933	E. W. Snell GMSW, J. O. Turner GMSW	Fred E. Kiddle UMU
1935	E. R. Fatland GMSW, Paul Lynch GMSW	Jack E. Allen UMU

in special session that built burned statehouse G. L. French was in the house and J. G. Barratt of Morrow was in the senate

	HOUSE	SENATE
1937	E. R. Fatland GMSW, G. L. French GMSW	Rex Ellis UMU
1939	E. R. Fatland GMSW, G. L. French GMSW	Rex Ellis UMU
1941	G. L. French GMSW, E. Harvey Miller	Rex Ellis UMU
1943	G. L. French GMSW, H. E. Peterson GMSW	Rex Ellis UMU
1945	G. L. French GMSW, H. E. Peterson GMSW	Rex Ellis UMU
1947	G. L. French GMSW, H. E. Peterson GMSW	Rex Ellis UMU
1949	G. L. French GMSW, H. E. Peterson GMSW	Rex Ellis UMU
1951	G. L. French GMSW, H. E. Peterson GMSW	Rex Ellis UMU
1953	J. P. Steiwer GMSW, Allen Tom GMSW	Rex Ellis UMU
1955	Allen Tom GMSW	S. Hardie, J. P. Hounsell, G HR MSWW
1957	Allen Tom GMSW	Ben Musa G HR MSWW
1959	Frank M. Weatherford GMSW	Ben Musa G HR MSWW
1961	Frank M. Weatherford GMSW	Ben Musa G HR MSWW
1963	Jack L. Smith GMSW	Ben Musa G HR MSWW
1965	Irvin Mann UMGSW	Ben Musa G HR MSWW
1967	Irvin Mann UMGSW	Ben Musa G HR MSWW
1969	Irvin Mann UMGSW	K. Jernstadt G HR MSWW

As recounted George Stansbury was the first postmaster of Heppner having moved the office from Butter Creek. The date of the appointment was June 3, 1872, John Vinson served the Butter Creek office. David A. Herren was postmaster on September 22, 1875, being succeeded by Cassius M. Mallory on June 13, 1878. It is likely that the change in postmasters in early days was governed by political affiliation.

Anyway Oliver H. Hallock succeeded Mallory on January 27, 1880 to be followed by Elisha G. Sloan, May 28, 1885 and then Mallory, the elder, Augustus, took over on May 17, 1889 and Joseph P. Williams on May 8, 1894. Benjamin F. Vaughan was postmaster from July 19, 1898 until he was drowned in the flood and W. W. Smead took over

as of June 14, 1903 to serve until August 12, 1913 and was reappointed June 17, 1930. W. A. Richardson was appointed August 12, 1913 and Smead again January 30, 1922. The Democratic sweep brought in Charles Burton Cox June 30, 1930, who stayed until his death in an accident October 18, 1945. Joe Aiken was an interim appointee until James H. Driscoll returned from the service and resumed his postal service July 1, 1946 and has been putting out the mail ever since.

Of postoffices and postmasters Morrow County has had many for in a faraway day transportation was slow and there were no mail routes. As listed by a postal employee in Salem this list is inclusive until 1955.

NAME	County When Established	First Postmaster	Mail Sent to	Est.	Disc.
ACTON	Umatilla			7/11/1879	6/19/1888
ADAMSVILLE	Umatilla	Silas Miles	Hardman	4/9/1884	6/30/1885
ALPINE	Umatilla	G. H. Parsell	Galloway	10/3/1884	7/27/1894
ATWOOD	Umatilla	H. Thompson		10/22/1883	11/20/1888
BOARDMAN	Morrow			7/13/1916	still
CASTLE ROCK	Umatilla		Boardman	8/3/1883	5/16/1926
CECIL	Morrow	Louis Balsiger		7/1/1902	
CECILS	Umatilla	James Rast		10/3/1867	8/17/1870
COYOTE	Morrow		Irrigon	6/17/1904	5/15/1912
DAVIDSON	Morrow	G. Davidson	Eightmile	4/26/1893	8/27/1897
DOUGLAS	Morrow	L. Morgan		12/31/1890	2/27/1906
EIGHTMILE	Umatilla		Heppner	9/10/1883	3/4/1941
ELLA	Umatilla	Frank Oviatt	Ione	4/24/1882	9/30/1910
FARRENS	Morrow	Lillian Page		5/9/1908	1/21/1909
GALLOWAY	Umatilla	J. J. Galloway	Echo	7/31/1886	9/30/1915
GOOSEBERRY	Umatilla	I. R. Esteb	Ione	10/3/1884	1/31/1918
IONE	Umatilla	Aaron Royse		5/26/1884	still
HEPPNER	Umatilla	G. H. Stansbury		6/3/1872	still
IRRIGON	Morrow	Frank Holbrook		11/16/1903	still
HARDMAN	Umatilla	out 9/30/43 to 4/16/46	now out	6/15/1881	
LENA	Umatilla	C. E. Hinton	Heppner	6/11/1873	8/31/1942
LEXINGTON	Morrow	Nathaniel Yeats		11/11/1885	still
MORGAN	Morrow	A. C. Morgan,	was Saddle Ione	2/27/1906	1/31/1955
MOSADA	Morrow	Alice Albright		9/23/1915	rescinded
PARKERS MILL	Morrow	Mr. Maxwell	Hardman	6/4/1907	12/15/1925
PETTYS	Morrow	S. P. Jones	Ione	11/9/1900	5/15/1901
PETTYSVILLE	Umatilla	A. C. Pettys		12/24/1878	3/19/1887
SALINEVILLE	Umatilla	Mrs. Benefield	became Lexington	1/9/1884	4/2/1886
SEPANEK	Morrow	Bertha Sepanek	Echo	8/2/1917	9/14/1918
SINNOTT	Morrow	S. Osborn	Lexington	4/29/1916	2/28/1918
STOKES	Morrow	D. Dailey	Umatilla	5/26/1897	4/25/1899
STRAWBERRY	Morrow	J. C. White		3/7/1904	12/31/1908
WILLOW FORKS	Umatilla	A. C. Pettys	Ione	6/3/1872	12/24/1878

When it is considered that Morrow has been a county for 85 years, it has not had very many officers, most of them remaining in office until they retired from age or boredom.

When the county was formed, the governor appointed the new officers most of whom did not suit the electorate who chose different men at the first opportunity. However, many of them were chosen again at subsequent elections. Augustus Mallory was the first judge and he didn't care much for the

job although he was an original settler. Besides he was terribly tormented by John W. Redington who ran the *Gazette*. William Mitchell succeeded him and Julius Keithley moved in from the ranch to be elected judge—and drowned in the flood that also washed away his excellent garden. Then came A. G. Bartholemew, who had a fine house in the south part of town and is said to have looked the part of judge. T. W. Ayres tried it for a term and C. C. Patterson tried it for two. W. T. Campbell retired from a farm on Social Ridge, moved to Heppner, and became judge, to be defeated by Ralph Benge a former neighbor on Social Ridge, but Campbell won the job back again. Both were very diligent at road building and consistently attended meetings of the state highway commission.

Bert Johnson, an intense little man from Ione, was judge for a couple of terms and Garnett Barratt was elected for two terms but resigned because of illness and Oscar Peterson was appointed to take his place. Peterson was followed by Paul Jones. Some were Democrats and some Republicans, the voters not seeming to care about political affiliations. County judges have often worked conscientiously at their job and have often dominated the court although there have been commissioners who were elected judge by the process of opposing the incumbent. J. W. Becket was an early commissioner, George Bleakman served long in that capacity, Garnet Barratt served as commissioner before becoming judge and Ralph I. Thompson put in many years on the county board as did George Peck.

The county clerks have usually served a long time. Sadie Parrish is the incumbent. Some sheriffs have distinguished themselves for various reasons, George McDuffee having shot an attempting train robber in Union County although he was not an old-time gunslinging sheriff, serving much of his time as deputy to E. M. Shutt, who quit the newspaper business to become an officer and chase bootleggers.

But the sheriff who achieved the most distinction is Clarence J. D. Bauman, who served forty of the county's 85 years of existence. He served in the Marines in World War I, boxed and wrestled his way to wide acquaintance and was elected sheriff in 1929 and served continuously until 1969, although he took leave of absence for World War II to serve in the navy. His local interests are many and he still serves the county.

The assessor's office has been changed by state law recently and the duties are much different than in the old days when he was charged with personally determining the number of sheep and cattle owned in the county. Land, once on the tax roll, was often unchanged in value for years, whereas it now must be reassessed every four years. The job is more under the direction of the state tax commissioner than of the local electorate and moves are being made to make him a state officer.

Many good men have served as treasurer. W. J. Leezer was the first and he was treasurer of many things in his time. Both Nobles, George, the elder, and Gene, both saddle makers, were county treasurers as was the reliable Frank Gilliam and Leon W. Briggs would have completed forty years in that office could he have but lived a little longer. Lucy Rodgers, after long service as county school superintendent, became treasurer for a change and served until she decided she didn't like it. Altogether Morrow County has been served well by the men it has chosen for public trust and even the few exceptions barely cloud the record.

It seems that no history should fail to include the names of the men who served in the armed forces and were killed in that service. They not only served their country, but were representing Morrow County also. The three who died while serving in World War I were Arthur Chapel of Hardman, Golder A. Collins of Monument and Elmer Presley of Heppner.

The records of World War II have not been so carefully kept but in 1967 the Morrow County Pioneers listed the names of honored war dead which generally agrees with other records, although more inclusive.

Earl K. Akin, Tench B. Aldrich, Ione; Eldon L. Allen, Irrigon; Raymond Allen, Irrigon; Roger J. Arndt, Nalbro Cox, Heppner; Herbert R. Davidson, Ione; Clyde Edwards, Lexington; Alfred Emert, Ione; Cecil Espy Jr.; Kay Fergusen, Heppner; Ernest Forbes, Heppner; Elbert M. Gibson Jr., Heppner; Clarence T. Harris, Ione; Norton King, Heppner; Bobbie Morgan, Ione; Donald Myles, Boardman; Paul V. Reitmann, Ione; Jerry Settles, Heppner; Oswald Sika; James Stevens, Hardman; F. E. Stillwell; George Wallise; Kenneth E. Warner, Lexington; Stanley Way, Lexington; Dow Worden, Boardman.

Morrow County has had some famous sons, the first perhaps being "Pap" Hayseed McAlister of Lexington who was a famous center for early day Oregon State College football teams. Johnnie Beckett was a tackle on the University of Oregon football team that went to the Rose Bowl in the teens and "Skip" Ruhl was a headline making linebacker for Oregon State University in more recent times.

The present chancellor of higher education in Oregon, Roy Lieuallen is an Ione product and John Kilkenny, associate justice of the U. S. Court of Appeals in San Francisco is a Morrow County native and proud of it.

IRRIGATION

When the emigrants drove their weary oxen across the northern part of Morrow County in the eighteen forties they saw it as a country covered by grass that was dry after a hot summer. There was a short, quick growing grass and occasionally there was what the travelers called sage that might have been rabbit brush. In addition there were some forbs to give the area an appearance of fertility although not near enough to appeal to the emigrants, many of whom came from fertile Iowa and Illinois and were used to grass two feet high.

After crossing Butter Creek, a mile or so down stream from where the present Lexington-Echo road turns east, the emigrant road angled south and west to reach Wells Spring where the emigrants arrived late in the evening, hot, tired and dry enough to drink the brackish water of the series of springs that ooze from a little depression in the even plain. Unless they were among the first to cross that way there was little grass for the cattle; the sparse grass of early spring grew but once. But early in the morning they could fill their barrels and hurry on toward Willow Creek before the sun and the dust made life seem intolerable and the squeal of the wooden axled wagons a steady and annoying accessory to the lonesome desert around them. Never on the trip had some of them felt so abandoned by God and man.

They drove a little north of present day Ella, being at that point on or about two townships north of the as yet unestablished base line (which, incidentally is not on a true parallel) and moved around a low hill to reach Willow Creek for the night and some fresh creek water that ran a pretty stream.

No one of these parties gave thought to irrigating the barren waste they described. Irrigation was an agricultural aid unheard of in 1840. It was not until 1870 that Michael Hanley, near Jacksonville, tried irrigation on a commercial scale although there are other claimants to the title. Probably the first irrigator was some observant housewife with a shovel and ambition to direct the creek through her withering corn patch.

But since men have first written about the north end of Morrow County there have been many schemes to irrigate that low lying stretch of land between two north of the base line and the Columbia River. Editorials about the eventual flowering of what was once called the "sands" have filled many a page in local newspapers and promoters and men able in business have planned ways and means of wetting the now barren ground.

There was a time, before the sheepmen had eaten—or worse, trampled—the shallow rooted grass and edible forbs, when the desert was green in the spring and early lambs gamboled over low Finley Butte and played in the heads of shallow Six Mile and other canyons. Consider, however, that sheepmen had been in the county many years before farmers came and the warm winters along the Columbia appealed to them and the grass that came up early there made it a good place to lamb. In lower Sand Hollow, much farther east than Ella, several very successful sheepmen started, to mention only W. B. Barratt and Robert Hynd and John J. Kilkenny, who built a fine house on his headquarters ranch where the grass must have been much more prolific than in present days.

Even into the twentieth century itinerant sheepmen wintered on Willow Creek and drove their bands across the sands to Butter Creek before starting south to the mountains on the pre-determined stock trails. Because of the usually mild winters it was possible for them to be ready for the mountains in time to establish a range that had not been preempted.

The forest service gave out allotments to stockmen in 1905 and the Taylor Grazing Act eliminated the itinerants in 1936. The itinerants were men who had sheep or cattle and no land for a home base.

The first scheme that had any success started on the eastern boundary and used overflow irrigation water from the Umatilla River. The Bureau of Reclamation introduces its story of the scheme in these words: "An irrigation system to serve lands in the Hermiston Irrigation District was approved for construction December 4, 1905, and water was made available for the first unit in 1908. Demand for land was good and private land in the brush sold for $50 to $250 per acre. Public lands were laid out in 10 and 40 acre units and disposed of rapidly so that in two or three years a resident entryman was living on practically every homestead and desert claim and much of the privately owned land was settled. Most of the settlers came from the Midwest. Many of them had sufficient capital to buy land and build improvements, set out orchards, and pay water costs during the development period. The few with little or no capital worked for those who had capital and were thus able to survive the "development period."

It was all a promotion of the Oregon Land and Water Company of which John W. Cook, president, and Willis Maguire, secretary, both of Portland and W. R. Walpole, Jr. of Irrigon was treasurer. They used the usual promotion tactics, showing pictures of already developed irrigation lands on lower Umatilla River and Butter Creek. By 1907 the company was broke and the corporation was dissolved in 1915.

Until the early 1920s there was a boom in the Irrigon and Boardman areas. Then the rate of abandonment exceeded the rate of new units being settled. The West Extension District was added to the original district in 1917 and its ditch reached west and south of Boardman. The Hermiston district (Irrigon) was planned for 20,000 acres and the West Extension for 16,300 acres of irrigable land, but neither reached such figures.

Probably it would be impossible among all the reclamation projects in the United States to find a more abject failure of attempted irrigation. Yet the climate is favorable, the winters being usually mild, the growing season long and the number of crops possible being varied and numerous. But the promotion was too good and the residents became discouraged. Farmers could not pay the cost of the land, nor the interest, nor even the cost of the water and the federal government has reduced the payments and written off thousands upon thousands of dollars. By 1948 the district owed the government in excess of a million dollars. By 1968 there were but 25 full time farmers and 131 part time farmers on the West Extension. But an arrangement has been made that may eventually resolve the problem and let the occupants of the farms own their land.

To detail the history of the two projects would require a bulging volume. Perhaps the original fault was the settlement of the area without a soil survey to show what crops were possible, a marketing study to show what could be sold—and where. The area does produce the very best watermelons.

In 1970 much of the irrigable area was used for pasture by stockmen who had bought the land for summer range or who rented it for the same purpose. It is apparent that it is not fulfilling its best use.

The east end of the project starts at the Umatilla River from which the water is obtained; for the first few miles the project is very narrow, less than half a mile wide in places. The soil is heavy sand, Quincy by geological title, and is often underlaid with alkali. The sand is very productive and early settlers poured on water which caused the alkali to rise to the top of the ground where it prohibited growth of any kind. Fruit trees were planted and fruit trees are less adaptable to alkaline soils than almost any plant. Modern occupants of the land have learned to leach the alkali off the soil and into lower places or into the river, but that is a process not accomplished in one year or, in this case, within the financial ability of many settlers.

Few pioneers of the project are still alive and still residents; the rate of change was high. Archie McFarland was the first chairman of the three man board that managed the project, in the time when knowledge was insufficient to the success thereof and the government still expected to be repaid. W. R. Walpole was a businessman and land owner who stayed until his death. Paul and Frank Partlow also remained until their end came and left progeny to continue the battle. Adolph Skoudo and D. R. Brownell served on the board for years and R. V. Jones and Bob Smith have been consistent residents and boosters of the Irrigon section. E. P. Dodd was a power in the area far into old age. Elmer Perry Dodd was a small man who came to the area in time to be elected to the 1919 legislature from Umatilla County for he always lived at Hermiston. Nevertheless he adopted the Hermiston and West End projects and was the final authority on them for years, right up to his death in 1959 at the ripe age of 90. His little office was stuffed with books and papers pertaining to the development of the Columbia River and the project.

The area between Irrigon and Boardman consists of low lying sand dunes that may eventually be irrigated when sprinkler irrigation is well enough developed to keep it wet until a crop is growing.

The first real engineer to take charge of the project was A. C. Houghton who managed it for many years, until his death in fact. He is responsible for much of the progress in irrigation, so much so that the new school (to the sixth grade) is named in his honor. The heyday of Irrigon was about 1910 when settlers were flocking to the new land, digging out the sagebrush and building homes in what looked like desert — and was except for the narrow ditch filled, providently, with sufficient water for all. It was then that Addison Bennett established his little and financially precarious weekly, the Irrigon *Irrigator*, and brought a temporary fame to the town until the promise of steadier finances drew him away. Max Jones is now the project manager and the man to see in Irrigon.

The history of Boardman is different. It was almost ten years after water was put on the Irrigon land before the ditch was extended on to Boardman. And the soil watered by the West Extension (Boardman) project is alluvial soil, the kind that is found in river and stream beds, the kind of soil that is naturally wet and productive when irrigated. How this comparatively small patch of alluvial soil happened to be out in what is otherwise a desert (less than ten inches of rainfall) we will leave to the geologists and the soil conservationists, who are probably as much in a quandary as are historians.

Boardman was first settled by Sam Boardman (Samuel Herbert Boardman), a native of Lowell, Massachusetts, born December 13, 1874, who homesteaded in 1903 before congress had passed the act authorizing the Irrigon project. He settled near the river on a stretch of level sand. He was a civil engineer who had worked for railroads in the middle west and in Oregon. Sam Boardman was still a young man in 1903 and he was vigorous; he decided that the barren sand dunes along the river should be growing trees, so he set them out, watering them at first with a little cart. When the state built a highway through the country that was an invitation to Sam Boardman to plant trees along it and to make little parks where travelers could stop and rest in the shade. He was so successful at it that in 1919 the State of Oregon hired him to be the first parks superintendent, a position he filled until his retirement by which time Oregon had 151 parks containing 61,500 acres and the start of what is perhaps the most ambitious and extensive state park system of any state. He was a man of delightful and persuasive personality and the town he first settled is appropriately named for him.

"Yesteryears of Morrow County" credits C. H. Dillabaugh with being the first homesteader after water was made available in 1917. He was followed by about forty who became residents. Some stayed a long time and others—less well financed—left before their incomes were sufficient. Among others mentioned were Buster Rands, R. Wasmer, Frank Otto, W. H. Mefford, Ed Kunze, for whom a road is named, Charles Wicklander, John Pruter and his wife. There was a regular change of residents.

There was a North Morrow County Fair held for some years starting about 1921 where was shown the products of the project. Only in recent years has Morrow County in general given much attention to the small number of citizens who live along the narrow streak of land wet by the ditch, but recently a county commissioner has been elected from that region and there have been at least two county clerks from Boardman.

L. L. Harlan came in 1917 to start the Boardman *Bulletin* but his newspaper was short lived although his sheet was a means for C. C. Paine to advertise his Boardman hotel, E. W. Mark and J. S. Ballanger to tell about their lumber, C. H. Warner his auto livery. In 1921 Mark A. Cleveland started the Boardman *Mirror*, which lasted four years before combining with the Arlington *Bulletin* as a first step toward oblivion. Most of the advertising came from out of town, but the building businesses were still able to advertise along with the inevitable real estate agents.

Irrigon and Boardman, like many another pair of small towns—and big ones too—did not agree on many things and they have spent much of their energy in intercity battles. That stage seems over and the first six grades of the area are educated at Irrigon and the last six grades in the new Riverside, junior-senior high school near Boardman. Irrigon had a postoffice in 1903 and Boardman not until 1916. Boardman's population has ranged from 100 to 159 and is presently a prosperous 228. Irrigon has always been larger having 246 in 1960.

When the U.S. Engineers built the John Day dam the waters flooded old Boardman and the town, schools, business houses, public and private buildings, even the cemetery, were moved almost a mile south to higher ground where a new town was built —the public buildings with federal money. And the Boardman that Sam Boardman knew is under water and not even a buoy marks the boundaries of his 80 acre homestead.

Some geography here is necessary. Ella is the point in northern Morrow County where cultivation stops. When Johan Troedson lived here for 41 years and raised his family, sending them to the little school up the dry creek a mile or so, and tilling his acres year after year; he planned continually to leave next year. But Mrs. Troedson, seeing her sons grow tall and strong, was content, so they stayed until old age took them to retirement in Ione near their sons who had acquired better land than the thin acres their father farmed.

It is almost correct to say that no one went farther north than Ella to take up a homestead, or to live on it long enough to prove up on it if he did, but

Johaness Troedson (no relation to Johan) had a half section and Phil Doherty a quarter. There was less than two sections of homesteaded land when the bombing range was bought and leased. Practically there was nothing north of Ella.

But in the spring it was green for a time and the sheepmen pastured it and drove their bands east across it to get to the driveway into the reserve. The marching of sharp footed sheep moved the sand and disturbed the shallow rooted plants and soon the soil began to blow. And when the west wind blows across the barren plain the sands move with such violence as to destroy every growing thing except the tough little sage.

Here it appears we cannot continue without a few words about geology. Under many of the soils in the drier parts of the United States, including the great plains, there is a calcareous layer formed by the accumulation of soluble salts. These are usually the carbonates, chlorides and sulphates of sodium, magnesium and calcium. These are alkali soils and because the alkali is soluble it will rise to the surface of the land when too much water is applied and the land is useless until they have been leached away. Calcium chloride becomes a cement like material called caliche which when broken up and spread on roads makes a good base. In agricultural land it is sometimes found useful and the good lands of the mid-Columbia basin often have such a calcareous layer at a depth of four or five feet that keeps moisture from going on down beyond the reach of wheat roots. It does not—in dry land agriculture—get wet enough to dissolve and come to the surface—a condition, however, that might occur in Morrow County wheat land if over irrigated.

A soil survey is now being conducted of the bombing range and it is expected to solve some problems and determine, possibly, how much of the sands are suitable for irrigation. The presence of alkali under the land, however, does indicate that the bursting of the perhaps fabled Lake Mazula that flooded the Columbia valley may have been but a prelude to long eons in which the north part of Morrow County was the shore of an inland sea into which streams brought all kinds of soluble material.

The second attempt to irrigate the wide band of land between tillable wheat land and the Columbia River came in 1916 and although preceded by an official report by state engineer and federal reclamation service was—and even is—as fantastic a dream as an engineer might have after a night of smoking hash-hish.

The 1916 effort was the ill-fated John Day project, the report on which was written by John T. Whistler of the U. S. Reclamation Service and John H. Lewis, state engineer of Oregon. Briefly the scheme was to dam the John Day River at the picture gorge about five miles below Dayville, flooding 2800 acres of fine bottom and, and convey the water down the John Day to a spot below Thirtymile called Bull Basin. There a diversion dam would be built and the water conducted by ditch along the east bank of the John Day to a little north of the base line from where it would be moved across Schuttler Flat and across Eightmile and Willow Creek above Rhea siding by trestle and conducted to Carty Reservoir (named for Jim Carty an early day sheepman). It was to be near the head of Six Mile canyon and an 85 foot high dam would have (in theory) kept the water from running down that canyon to the river.

W. L. Powers and C. V. Ruzek, two soil scientists from Oregon Agricultural College were obtained to conduct a survey, but the financing was not sufficient for them to do a complete job. They found the area to be sand, coarse sand in the western part heavy enough that the prevailing winds had not moved it, and finer sand farther east. Much of the sand was found to be very deep and therefore only irrigable with great care and much expense for fertilizer. Powers and Ruzek did not report on the amount of the area where basalt protrudes from the surface, nor where the native rock is covered with a layer of sand less than three feet thick and that subject to instant removal in case one of the unpredictable winds prevalent in the area finds conditions right for a blow.

Their final conclusion was: "altogether it does not appear feasible or reasonable use of time, money and water at the present from an agricultural standpoint to develop this project at the estimated cost, yet it may prove a feasible project in the future."

The cost, in that pre-war and pre-inflation day was estimated at $15,240,000 or $124.92 per acre for 122,000 acres.

Many objections have been discovered by observant citizens who are less polite than Powers and Ruzek. Among them are that there is little or no water in the John Day River, that the 2800 acres of bottom land to be flooded near Dayville would be worth almost as much as the land to be irrigated, there was no highway up the John Day River in 1916 but there is now and it runs right through the picture gorge where the dam was to be built and relocation would be very expensive, the canal from

Bull Basin to the spot where it reached the level land would have to be cemented for the terrain is so rocky and undependable as to foundation, the crossing of Eightmile and Willow Creek by trestle would be at a high cost and there was doubt that the projected site of Carty Reservoir would hold water, there being sand in the area.

But the idea did gain credence among optimistic men of affairs in both Arlington and Ione. In fact there was a case at law that went to the supreme court to decide whether Art Minor and Art Wheelhouse were elected to the board of directors over C. C. Clark and Ed Reitmann. It was to be partly financed by a tax on the land to be irrigated, most of which belonged to the government and the Northern Pacific Railroad grant lands. Finally the project was dropped under the weight of so much evidence and John H. Lewis, as engineer for the plan, sued Morrow County for his fee and the suit was compromised to the satisfaction of no one.

But there was life in the people of the north end of Morrow County and throughout the depression 1930s they went on trying many crops, none of which were very successful, partly because of the diversity that made marketing difficult. At one time there was quite a bit of dairying, and some tried to raise fruit which was generally ill-adapted to the soil. Irrigon and Boardman engaged in many quarrels over prestige, schools in the manner of small unsuccessful towns. Nearly all of the available energy of the area (the towns are eleven miles apart) was spent in fighting one another. Wars came and went, nuclear energy was used to destroy and finally domesticated after a fashion. The U. S. Engineers built dams on the Columbia so spaced that the overflow from one fell on the upper pool of the other and every drop of water contributed its mite to make hydroelectric power for a good half dozen times before it reached the ocean after falling as snow in the high Rockies. The Bonneville Power Administration sold the electricity to aluminum plants or sent it away to California.

Water from the higher river that flooded Boardman made a smaller impression on Irrigon.

In the deal between the federal government and its agencies and the state, the navy did preserve some 47,291 acres east of the Boeing lease for use in practice bombing. It contains Juniper canyon. The navy is expected to end its lease on this property in 1974 or 1975 upon which action the land is expected to revert to the Bureau of Land Management which has already sold its other holdings in Morrow and Umatilla Counties to local citizens—

and others—who are able to bet on future irrigation.

Because Bonneville Power Administration has sold so much power to aluminum companies, an industry that hires few men or develops few other companies, the power of the Columbia is being used for purposes that do little to develop the growth of population or of industry in the northwest. The fumes from aluminum plants have caused innumerable law suits by farmers who claim damage to tree fruits and even cattle and who often collect damages for that reason.

Therefore there is demand for the construction of nuclear plants to supplement the hydroelectric power so recently considered a panacea for all the economic ills of the northwest, because, even with all the huge dams there is a danger of a power shortage in the northwest. This is the condition in 1970 and it may sound absurd at some future time.

It takes time to build a nuclear plant, partly because so few have been built that no one knows exactly how to go about it. The fish and wildlife people are greatly concerned because a nuclear plant as now planned will require millions of gallons of water to cool the process and if it is dumped back into a river may eradicate fish life even faster than the dams themselves. Agriculturists have developed a plan to use this warm water to irrigate land before it eventually (in part) flows back into the river. It is said to make it possible to produce crops earlier when market conditions are better.

It is a fact that the east end of the sands area contains the finest sand and the most irrigable and on the navy's bombing range it is even mixed with fine soil. It might be possible to irrigate it successfully and boosters are encouraged by the success of D. O. Nelson, whose ranch is but 14 miles south of the Columbia and near the bombing range. He is south of the lands recently sold by the Bureau of Land Management but since he discovered water in deep wells that produce in excess of 2000 gallons per minute he has raised 20 tons of potatoes per acre. No one knows how long the water will last, whether it comes from the Blue Mountains or whether it comes from the Columbia River, but three 16 inch wells each pumping in excess of 2000 gpm must have a source somewhat remarkable in a semi-arid country. Without irrigation the Nelson land must be farmed so as to keep trash on top of the surface to prevent wind erosion.

If there was power available the buyers of Bureau of Land Management land a few miles south of the river would certainly have bought pipe and put in irrigation system by now. Many of them have money, are willing to gamble and a cooperative organization should not be hard to organize.

A nuclear plant, located near Boardman, would solve the problem of power. But nuclear plants cost great sums of money and if local people were able to get the federal government to build one (which would take a lot of time for political manipulation and more for construction), the power would be controlled by Bonneville Power which might sell it to an aluminum company or export it to Los Angeles. How to get a plant built that is locally controlled is not easily solved. Engineers are almost unanimous in stating that it takes a lot of power to pump water onto land through pipe.

But Boardman has been facing impossible situations since Sam Boardman homesteaded in the sand beside the river and gave the town its name and the citizenry are undeterred by difficulties. This is particularly true of the Port of Morrow County whose board consists of Oscar Peterson, Dewey West, Gar Swanson, J. Richard Krebs and Lawrence Lindsay, with Rupert Kennedy as co-ordinator.

In their favor is the by now generally accepted theory that the land in much of the bombing range and east to Butter Creek on the Umatilla County line is irrigable and would be productive of crops in demand. It is warm, it has a 200 day growing season, and with water from a nuclear plant might exceed that. Sprinkler irrigation would probably remove the danger of alkali.

And Boardman has more than agriculture going for it. It is planning an industrial park, has a park laid out to receive any industry that aspires to use the facilities, a planned port area. It might well be a center for processors of agricultural products. In fact, there is a plant for pelleting alfalfa already built and Nelson and his partners, the Tuckers, have a new shipping plant to handle their potatoes. The railroad runs nearby, the river barges pass every day, there is a sizable airport, the tourist traffic on the double lane freeway is fast and numerous. Why not?

INDEX

Names appearing only in charts or maps not indexed.

A

Abernathy, George, 14
Abrahamsick, Abe, 61-69
Adkins, James, 10
Adkins, Nora, 69
Adkins, Wm., 64
Akers, Ralph, 98
Akin, Earl, 116
Aldrich, Tench, 116
Allen, Eldon L., 116
Allen, J. O., 77
Allen, Raymond, 116
Allyn, J. T., 10
Anderson, Arthur, 10
Anderson, David, 24
Anderson, Frank, 85-87
Anderson, Gay M., 99
Andrews, Arthur, 10
Andrews, Mrs. Ida, 75
Arthurs, Ione, 59
Arndt, Roger, 116
Ashbaugh, Ed, 61
Ashbaugh, Mose, 63
Ayres, John, 10
Ayres, T. W., 10-19-24-25-34-53-62-67-69-89-115
Ayres, Wm., 10-24

B

Backett, W. J., 10
Bacey, Alton, 39
Bailey, May, 79
Ballard, Frank, 94
Ballanger, J. S., 119
Balsiger, Paul, 59
Barlow, Virginia, 86
Barnett, Donna, 87
Barnett, J. L., 61
Barnett, W. F., 97
Barratt, J. Garnet, 101, 103, 104
Barratt, Wm., 10-20-61-80-88-95-117
Bartholomew, A. G., 10-66-115
Bartholomew, Harry, 69
Bartholomew, Mrs. Herb, 69

Bartholomew, Herb., 62
Basey, _____, 25
Bauman, C. J. D., 116
Beach, Elsie, 60
Beach, Karl, 60
Beagle, _____, 25
Beard, James, 75
Becket, J. W., 116
Belanger, Joe, 100
Belshaw, Maria, 13
Benefield, J. I., 34
Benge, R. L., 95-100-116
Bergstrom, Bill, 50
Bergstrom, O., 49
Bergstrom, Rudie, 50
Bernard, Frank, 27-28
Bewley, Lorinda, 14
Bisbee, T. H., 10
Bishop, Ed R., 48-50-53
Blackman, Henry, 10-39-40-42-53-54
Blair, Wm., 37
Bleakman, George, 101, 116
Blake, W. J., 75
Boardman, S. H., 119-122
Bond, May, 41
Boone, Ben, 89
Borg, Oscar, 91
Borg, P. O., 25
Booher, B. M., 34
Borcher, Chris, 67
Bowker, Bert, 84
Brayman, Mason, 52
Brant, Mrs. Wm., 67
Breden, A. J., 19
Breeding, A. J., 25
Brenner, Peter, 81
Briggs, Leon, 105
Brock, Mrs. G. W., 60
Brosnan, Jerry, 46
Brown, F. R., 87
Brownell, D. R., 118
Buffalo Horn, 26-28
Burgess, Newt, 80
Bushee, J. P., 25

C

Campbell, W. T., 83-95-101-115-116
Cantwell, Lee, 66
Carle, T. J., 59
Carr, S. E., 82
Carsner, R. J., 80
Carter, C. H., 77
Carter, Sam, 81
Carty, James, 93-120
Cartwright, C. H., 35
Cecil, Wm. Y., 19-20-21-24
Chapel, Arthur, 116
Chase, Bishop, 24
Chase, Isaac, 25
Chidsey, T. D., 80
Clark, C. C., 121
Clark, M. D., 95-103
Clark, Oscar, 19
Cleveland, Mark A., 119
Cluff, Ed., 59
Coffey, J. W., 48-54
Coffey, V. J., 49
Cohn, Harold, 85-103
Cohn, Lilly, 67
Cohn, Phil, 62-63-69-88-92
Conser, George, 10-39-43-62-63-66-69-75-77-82
Cook, A. J., 80
Cook, John W., 118
Corrigal, Matt, 52-93
Cox, Charles, 97-115
Cox, F. Dee, 80-115
Cox, Nalbro, 116
Cox, L. B., 34
Cox, W. Claude, 85-98
Collins, Golder, 116
Collins, Henry, 96
Crawford, Arthur, 55-72-75-90
Crawford, Garfield, 80
Crawford, Jasper, 55-91-103
Crawford, Otheo G., 55-72-75-104
Crawford, P. V., 13
Crawford, Spencer, 55-99

Crawford, Vawter, 55-75-85-88
Creek, Bob, 69
Creswell, P. C., 77
Crook, George, 19
Crook, Joseph, 21
Crooks, Ramsey, 13
Crow, D. C., 34
Culp, B. F., 82
Cunha, Joe, 80
Cunningham, Chas., 20-34-45
Cunningham, W. B., 53
Currey, George, 15
Currier, Anson H., 96
Cutsforth, Orville, 103-104

D

Davidson, H. R., 116
Davis, John, 21
Dawson, Mrs., 62
Dawson, Perry, 61
Day, Ed, 10-19-75
Day, John, 13
Deaton, Virginia, 55
Dennis, _____, 25
Devin, M., 96
Dick, L. E., 110
Dillabaugh, C. H., 119
Dishaway, J. D., 25
Dodd, E. P., 118
Doherty, B. P., 46
Doherty, Dan P., 77
Doherty, J. G., 20-46
Doherty, Phil, 120
Douglas, James, 14
Douglas, O. T., 25
Driscoll, J. H., 115
Driscoll, Tom, 69
Drouillard, George, 13
Durand, A. A., 96
Durand, Bill, 89
Dutton, Will, 10-79
Dutton, W. H., 78
Duvall, Mrs. Amanda, 35-112
Duvall, Harry, 35

E

Edwards, Bessie, 78-79
Edwards, Clyde, 116
Ehegante (Egan), 27-28-52-53-54
Ellis, W. R., 36
Elder, John, 10
Elder, Mrs. Lloyd, 67

Estes, Bill, 69
Estes, David, 22
Emerick, George, 59
Emert, Alfred, 116
Eskelson, Earl, 99
Espy, Cecil Jr., 116
Evans, J. & M., 34

F

Farnsworth, O. E, 10-20
Fatland, Ernie, 100
Fell, H. W., 80
Fell, T. E., 36-48-59
Fergusen, Kay, 116
Fields, Hugh, 10-24-41
Five Crows, 14
Florence, Al, 10
Florence, L. A., 105
Florence, S. P., 10-20-24-53
Flory, A. M., 31
Foley, Pat, 92
Foor, G. W., 67
Forbes, Ernest, 116
Freeland, Gene, 39
French, Annie, 24
French, John H., 19-24
French, J. Dillard, 80-86
French, Lee, 46
French, Pete, 27
French, Uzz, 46
French, W. H., 101
Fritz, James, 61
Fuller, J. L., 36

G

Galloway, Mike, 67
Garrigues, Percy, 80
Garrigues, S. P., 25-36-42-69-89
Gates, H. V., 42-91-95
Gates, N. H., 113
Gault, J. L., 97, 100
Gay, H. C., 10-20
Gentry, L. V., 93
Gibson, Elbert Jr., 116
Giger, A. C., 62-69-75
Gill, J. K., 25
Gilliam, Birdie, 79
Gilliam, Cornelius, 14-96
Gilliam, Earl, 43-44-86
Gilliam, Eugene, 68
Gilliam, Frank, 10-20-36-39-66-75-
    85-92-116

Gilliam, Jackson E., 44
Gilliam, Lou, 43-80
Gilliam, Ona, 79
Gilmore, John, 25
Glidden, Joseph, 24
Goble, Frank, 25
Goodman, Dean, 98
Gray Eagle, 14
Groshens, Charles, 89
Groshens, Harry, 89
Groshens, Vic, 89-93
Gunn, A. M., 53-62-63-75

H

Hager, Grace, 78-79
Hager, Ruth, 88
Haguewood, Wm., 49
Hale, Milton, 21
Haller, Mrs. G. O., 16
Halley, T. W., 37
Hallock, Homer, 53
Hallock, O. H., 24-25-29-52-53-
    115
Halvorson, Matt, 59
Hamilton, Lois, 75
Hanley, Michael, 117
Hardman, David, 20-51
Harlan, L. K., 85
Harlan, L. L., 119
Harper, J. B., 27
Harrington, G. W., 36
Harris, Clarence, 117
Harris, M. C., 33
Harrah, W. K., 49
Hart, R. C., 10
Hatfield, Mark, 111
Hawker & Munkers, 25
Hayes, James, 10
Hayes, John, 10
Head, W. W., 55
Heard, Charles, 55
Heppner, Henry, 10-22-23-24-25-
    38-39-40-42-54-75-76-77-89
Herren, Dave, 10-24-25-67-77-115
Hewison, _____, 25
Hiatt, John, 95
Hicks, A. H., 54-55
Higgs, A. K., 66-80
Himes, George, 25-96
Hinton, Charles, 53
Hitchcock, Maurice, 113
Hoover, Herbert, 95

Horseman, George, 72-80
Houghton, A. C., 104-118
Howard, O. O., 27-28-52
Howard, T. R., 36-61
Hughes, John, 10
Hughes, Wm., 10-34-45-46
Humason, Orlando, 113
Hunt, Lawrence, 87-93
Huxley, Thomas, 105
Hyland, J. H., 80
Hynd, Annie, 20
Hynd, Charles, 20
Hynd, David, 20
Hynd, Jack, 20-98-110
Hynd, Jennie, 20
Hynd, Margaret, 20
Hynd, R. F., 10-20-62-69-82-117
Hynd, Thomas, 20
Hynd, William, 20
Hyslop, George, 94

I

Isaiachalakis, 15

J

Jackman, E. R., 94
Jackson, C. S., 35
Jackson, Henry, 112
Jackson, Ralph, 103-105
Jenkins, John, 69
Johnson, Bert, 100-103-116
Johnson, Felix, 50
Jones, Elsie, 75
Jones, Henry, 10
Jones, James, 10
Jones, Josie, 44
Jones, Max, 119
Jones, Nelson, 48
Jones, Newt, 43-49
Jones, Paul, 116
Jones, Pearl, 63
Jones, R. V., 118
Jordon, John, 19-21-24
Justus, D. O., 10-93

K

Kamiakin, 15
Kathan, Wm., 25
Keeny, Lou, 68
Keithley, Julius, 20-25-36-62-63
Keithley, Mrs. Julius, 75
Kelley, Bruce, 69

Kelly, James K., 15-113
Kelly, Norman, 10
Kelly, Ora, 75
Kennedy, Carrol, 98
Kennedy, Rupert, 122
Kenny, Mike, 20-34-46-93
Kerr, Wm. J., 94
Kiamasumlin, 15
Kilkenny, Frank, 46-106
Kilkenny, John, 46-80-88-93-106-117
Kilkenny, John F., 46-53-116
King, Norton, 116
Kenney, Alfred, 25
Keenan, J. M., 74
Kintzley, George, 62
Kirk, Charles, 10
Kirk, E. R., 91
Kirk, J. C., 10-20-25
Kistner, Dr., 69-80
Klokamas, 15
Krick, Bob, 50
Krick, Irving P., 107
Krebs, J. Richard, 122
Kunze, Ed., 119

L

Lake, C. H., 66
Lahonde, Steve, 10
Lamb, Al, 107
Lange, George, 86
Latourell, C. H., 96
Lazarus, Edgar M., 78
Lee, H. A. G., 14
Leezer, W. J., 18-25-36-53-116
Legge, Alexander, 95-97
Lemons, K., 21
Leonard, Daniel G., 21
Lever, W. H., 18
Lewis, John W., 120-121
Lewis & Clark, 12-13
Lichtenthal, Matt, 10-25-49-65
Lieuallen, Roy, 116
Lincoln, Abraham, 19
Lindsay, Lawrence, 122
Lippset, W. W., 62
Lockley, Fred, 65
Locknane, J. D., 25
Looney, Press, 10
Lowe, Mrs. T. H., 93
Loutrelle, George, 59
Lovgren, F. M., 93
Lytle, W. H., 80

M

Maddock, Frank, 22-24-25-28-53
Maddock, J. G., 34-41
Maddock, Louis, 41
Maddock, Lucy, 24
Maguire, Willis, 118
Mahoney, Josephine, 99
Mahoney, Phil, 91-98-103
Mahoney, T. J., 82-87
Mahoney, W. P., 87-92-97
Mahoney, Mrs. W. P., 101
Mallory, Augustus, 22-29-36-53-62-115
Mallory, C. W., 25-115
Mallory, Edna, 79
Mallory, Geo., 79
Mallory, W. L., 62
Mark, E. W., 119
Marlatt, Thomas, 10
Marlatt, Wesley, 10
Marquart, Louis, 100
Marquardson, F. C., 80
Mason, Bert, 59-64-66-104
Matlock, Cas., 10
Matlock, Dee, 66
Matlock, E. L., 10-35-50-69
Matlock, James, 61
Matlock, Les., 44-64-106
Matlock, Thomas, 10-20-24-61
Maxwell, M. S., 59
Mayes, Robert, 113
McAlister, Pap, 116
McAllister, J. F., 24-31-48-60
McAtee, Dave, 65-66-69
McBean, Wm., 14
McBride, Ralph, 25
McBroom, Clarence, 77-80
McCarthy, Sadie, 78-79
McDougall, M. C., 42
McDuffee, C. D., 85-90-116
McFarland, Charles, 37-59-60
McHaley, J. H., 84
McMillen, H. B., 31
McMurdo, A. D., 88-91-103
McSwords, P. B., 62-63
McVey, Jack, 60
McVey, H. R., 49
Meacham, Mrs. A. B., 52
Meacham, Nellie, 54
Means, George, 43
Meek, Joe, 14
Mefford, W. H., 119
Meigs, C. R., 113

Menefee, _____, 19
Merritt, Coreleis, 54
Metschan, Phil., Jr., 42-65
Michell, Ed, 54-55-75
Miles, Evan, 28
Miller, Harvey, 103
Miller, L. A., 80
Minor, C. A., 10-65-80-88
Minor, Ellis, 10-19-24-25-42-53-61-63-75
Minor, W. O., 10-63-69-75-78-82-88-92
Misner, Dwight, 96
Mitchell, Wm., 115
Monahan, Frank, 93
Moody, Malcolm, 78
Moody, Zenas F., 36
Morgan, Bobbie, 116
Morgan, Thomas, 19-42-51-53-87
Morrall, T. J., 80
Morrison, E. E., 62-69
Morrow, Jackson L., 10-22-23-24-25-28-35-38-42-53-54-61-69-76-89-114
Morrow, J. W., 10-42-49-77
Morse, Wayne, 112
Mulkey, D. B., 25
Myles, Donald, 116

N

Natter, Frank, 66-67
Natter, J. B., 42-50-53
Nelson, D. O., 110-121
Nelson, Thomas, 54
Nesmith, J. W., 13-15
Noble, Gene, 88-116
Noble, George, 20-24-42-62-88-116
Noble, Mrs. George, 69
Nordyke, E., 87
Norelius, Eric, 45
Notson, Samuel E., 67-84-87-90-96-102
Nys, J. J., 99

O

O'Brien, J. P., 78
O'Conner, Jerm, 93
Ogden, Peter S., 14
Oglesby, Roscoe, 25
Oller, Perry, 24-25
O'Meara, Paul, 59
Otto, Frank, 119
Oviatt, Frank, 59

P

Padberg, Henry, 10-20-37
Paine, C. C., 119
Palmer, Joel, 19
Palmer, Sam, 50
Parker, Ben, 10-19
Parker, Frank, 101
Parker, D. R., 94
Parrish, Sadie, 116
Parrish, Samuel, 27
Partlow, Frank, 118
Partlow, John, 119
Patterson, A. W., 50
Patterson, Ben, 62
Patterson, C. C., 115
Patterson, John, 62
Patterson, Otis, 39, 54
Pattison, S. A., 85
Pearce, George T., 85
Pearson, Louis, 91
Peck, George, 101-116
Penland, Bob, 55
Penland, Jane, 24
Penland, Wm., 10-20-21-24-25-34-36-37-60-75
Pennoyer, Sylvester, 42
Percy, George, 80
Peters, Joseph, 100
Peterson, Aaron, 87
Peterson, Don, 112
Peterson, Henry, 87
Peterson, Oscar, 112-116-122
Pettys, C. Ammanuel, 10-21-22-24
Peu Peu Mox Mox, 14-15
Phelps, G. W., 62
Pinchot, Gifford, 78
Pinckney, Mrs. B. C., 103
PiUte Joe, 27-28
Polk, James Knox, 14
Ponder, W. D., 16
Pope, Alexander, 108
Powers, W. L., 120
Presley, Elmer, 89-116
Price, Byron, 112
Pruter, John, 119

Q

Quaid, Mike, 22-46
Quaid, Patt, 22-46
Quaid, Tom, 10-12-34-42-46-49-66-89

R

Raley, J. H., 77
Raley, Roy, 77
Rands, Buster, 119
Rasmus, A. W., 61
Rasmus, Henry, 54
Rasmus, John, 66
Rast, James, 21
Reaney, Andrew, 34-37-49
Redfield, C. E., 62-77
Redington, J. W., 52-53-54-75-76-115
Redington, Mary, 52
Redington, Patrick, 52
Reed, Dol, 19
Reeves, S. R., 37
Reed, D. V. S., 79
Reid, Mollie, 91
Reitman, Paul V., 59-110
Reitmann, Ed, 121
Reitmann, Omer, 59-100
Reitmann, Mrs. Paul V., 105
Rhea, Columbus Adolphus, 10-19-25-34-41-42-43-61-75-77-82-102
Rhea, Josie, 43
Rhea, J. P., 10
Rhea, Mrs. Lum, 69
Rhea, T. A., 10
Rhea, Waldron, 49
Rhoden, Alex, 27
Rice, R. B., 93-100
Richardson, J. Logie, 103
Richardson, W. A., 115
Rinehart, W. V., 27
Robbins, Orlando (Rube), 27
Roberts, Al, 66
Roberts, Frank (Mike), 43-44-66-69-88-91
Roberts, James, 25-62
Robinson, James, 19
Rodgers, Lucy, 99-103-116
Rood, Andrew, 10
Rood, Harvey, 10
Roosevelt, F. D., 98-102
Ross, Thomas, 80
Rounds, Ed, 51
Royse, Aaron, 59
Royse, John, 26
Rugg, Shirley, 108-110
Rush, Ed, 10
Ruzek, C. V., 120

S

Saling, Frank, 100
Saling, Peter, 24
Saling, W. L., 61
Scholl, Louis, 15
Schamel, P. L., 93
Scott, Leslie M., 65-66-96
Scott, Thomas, 24
Settles, Jerry, 116
Shiach, W. S., 38
Sheller, D. B., 80
Sheridan, John, 85
Sherman, Wes, 55
Shipley, John, 21
Shipley, Lewis, 25
Shippey, G. W., 19
Shobe, Allan J., 24-25
Shutt, E. M., 39-54-55-61-66-75-82-116
Shutt, Sloan P., 54
Sigsbee, Bert, 71-91
Sika, Oswald, 116
Skoudo, Adolph, 118
Sloan, Elisha, 115
Slocum, A. N., 75
Slocum, E. J., 62
Smead, W. W., 88-115
Smith, Bob, 118
Smith, C. J., 77
Smith, Charley, 94
Smith, Orville, 101-113
Smith, Mrs. Orville, 103
Smith, Will, 67
Smouse, H. V., 97-100
Spalding, Frank, 69
Spalding, H. H., 13
Sparks, Mrs. J. B., 91
Spencer, Taylor, 24
Sperry, Elisha Green, 10-24-43-50-53-56-59-89
Sperry, J. B., 42
Stalter, Dan, 62-69-77
Stanfield, R. N., 80
Stansbury, Elizabeth, 24
Stansbury, George H., 22-24-25
Steiwer, W. W., 80
Stephens, D. E., 94
Stevens, I. I., 15
Stevens, James, 116
Stevenson, A. J., 25
Stewart, David, 13
Stewart, George, 24
Stewart, Willis, 91

Stillwell, F. E., 116
Stine, J. H., 53-75
Stone, J. F., 96
Swaggart, Ben, 101
Swaggart, G. W., 25-53-62-68
Swanson, Gar, 122
Swinburne, E. R., 25-42

T

Tamahas, 15
Taylor, J. C., 77
Tedrowe, George, 50
Theodore, W. E., 25-53
Thompson, Alec, 10-35
Thompson, H. A., 75
Thompson, Henry, 10
Thompson, Holland, 10
Thompson, J. G., 92
Thompson, O. F., 10
Thompson, Press, 10
Thompson, Ralph I., 43-93-98-116
Thompson, Mrs. Ralph I., 101
Thomson, Charles, 99
Thornton, H. M., 49
Tillard, Low, 50
Tilouyaikt, 15
Tom, Allen, 110
Troedson, Johan, 119
Troedson, Johannes, 120
Turner, Frank, 87
Turner, J. O., 103
Turner, R. W., 84-87-93

U

Umapine, 24

V

Van Cadow, Will, 42
Van Duyn, C. W., 50
Van Marter, LaVerne, 95
Vaughn, B. F., 61-115
Verlatt, G. W., 91
Vey, Joseph, 24-34
Villard, Henry, 26
Vinson, George, 19-102
Vinson, John, 19-24-115

W

Wait, Aaron, 113
Wallice, George, 116
Walpole, W. R., 118

Walton, Wm., 62
Waltenburger, Wiley, 85
Waltronburger, J. W., 61
Warner, C. H., 119
Warner, Kenneth, 116
Warnock, Fred, 54-55-67-75
Warren, Mrs. William, 25
Wasmer, R., 119
Way, Stanley, 116
Webb, Nat, 10
Wells, A. J., 61
Wells, Abraham, 25
Wells, A. S., 19-28
Wells, Clyde, 91
Wells, Mrs. Clyde, 75
Wells, Wm., 62
Welsh, Mrs. H., 52-62
West, Dewey, 122
Wharton, W. S., 82
Whistler, John T., 120
White, J. C., 80
Whitman, Marcus, 13
Wicklander, Charles, 119
Wilbur, Father, 15
Wilkinson, Frank, 93-108
Wilkins, Joe, 92
Williams, James, 10
Williams, Joseph P., 115
Wills, Mrs. James, 63
Wills, Robert, 59
Wilson, Woodrow, 87
Winnard, N. E., 80
Winnemucca, Lee, 27
Wister, Owen, 54
Woodward, John, 43
Woolery, J. A., 39-59-64-65-80
Worden, Dow, 116
Wray, H. O., 101
Wright, A. E., 10
Wright, Albert, 10-19-25
Wright, George, 50
Wright, Silas, 10-50
Wyland, James, 10

Y

Yeager, J. A., 66
Yeager, Ora, 66
Yeck-a-tap-em, 13
Yellippit, 12
Young, George, 80
Young, Jake, 33-50

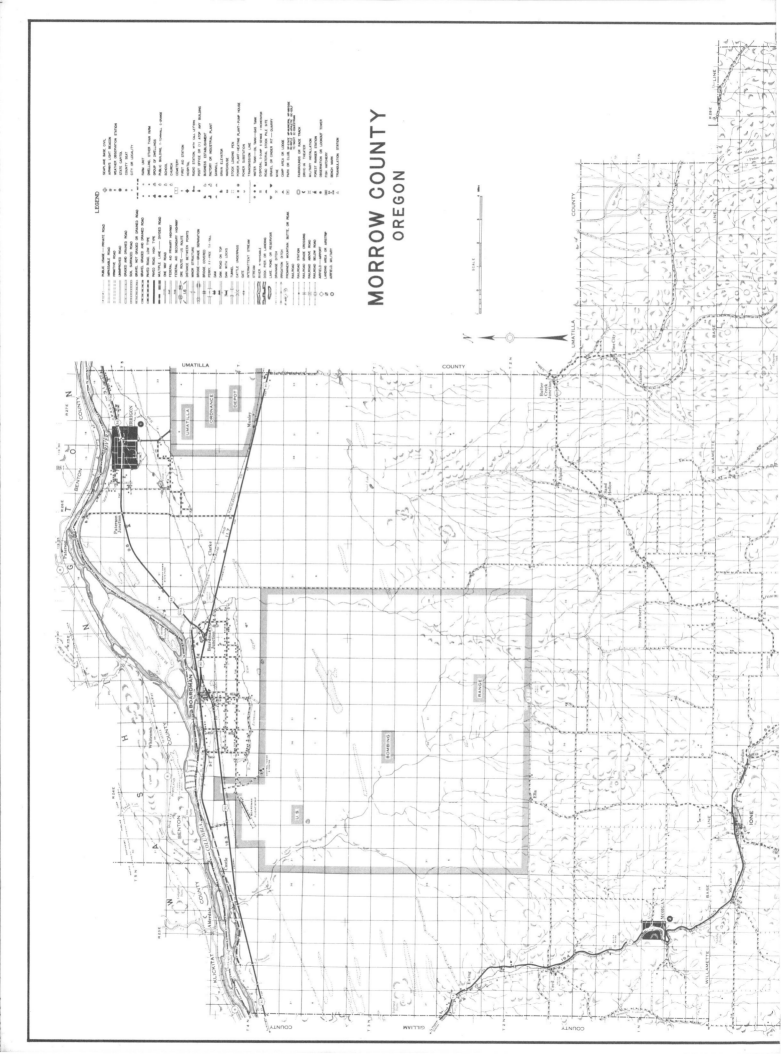

MORROW COUNTY
OREGON

LEGEND

SEAPLANE BASE, CIVIL	
AIRPAYS LIGHT BEACON	
WEATHER OBSERVATION STATION	
STATE CAPITOL	
COUNTY SEAT	
CITY OR LOCALITY	
FARM UNIT	
DWELLING, OTHER THAN FARM	
GROUP OF DWELLINGS, T-TOWNHALL, G-GRANGE	
PUBLIC BUILDING	
SCHOOL	
CHURCH	
CEMETERY	
HOSPITAL	
FIRST AID STATION	
RADIO STATION, WITH CALL LETTERS	
POST OFFICE OR (*) ATOP ANY BUILDING	
BUSINESS ESTABLISHMENT	
FACTORY OR INDUSTRIAL PLANT	
SAWMILL	
GRAIN ELEVATOR	
WAREHOUSE	
STOCK LANDING PEN	
POWER SUBSTATION	
TRANSMISSION LINE	
FOREST RANGER STATION	
WATER TANK—OIL TANK—GAS TANK	
DISPOSAL, D-DUMP, S-SEWAGE, I-INCINERATOR	
ROAD MATERIAL STOCK PILE SITE	
GRAVEL OR CINDER PIT — QUARRY	
MINE	
CAMP AREA OR LODGE	
PARK, OR CLUB, M-SITE OF MEMORIAL, MB-BRIDGE RC-RACE, AC-ATHLETIC, GC-GOLF	
FAIRGROUNDS OR RACE TRACK	
DRIVE-IN THEATER	
MILITARY INSTALLATION	
FOREST RANGER STATION	
OBSERVATION OR LOOKOUT TOWER	
FISH HATCHERY	
BENCH MARK	
TRIANGULATION STATION	

PUBLIC USAGE — PRIVATE ROAD	
IMPASSABLE ROAD	
PRIMITIVE ROAD	
UNIMPROVED ROAD	
GRADED AND DRAINED ROAD	
SOIL SURFACED ROAD	
GRAVEL, NOT GRADED OR DRAINED ROAD	
GRAVEL, GRADED AND DRAINED ROAD	
PAVED ROAD, LOW TYPE	
PAVED ROAD, HIGH TYPE	
MULTIPLE LANE — DIVIDED ROAD	
ONE WAY ROAD	
FEDERAL AID PRIMARY HIGHWAY	
FEDERAL AID SECONDARY HIGHWAY	
ONE ROUTE — US ROUTE	
DISTANCE BETWEEN POINTS	
MINOR STRUCTURE	
BRIDGE, COVERED	
FERRY, f.f.-FREE, T.f.-TOLL	
DAM	
DAM ROAD ON TOP	
DAM WITH LOCKS	
GATE	
CATTLE UNDERPASS	
TUNNEL	
STREAM	
INTERMITTENT STREAM	
RIVER, VARIABLE	
DOCK, PIER, OR LANDING	
LAKE, POND, OR RESERVOIR	
DRAINAGE DITCH	
IRRIGATION DITCH	
PROMINENT MOUNTAIN, BUTTE, OR PEAK	
RAILROAD STATION	
RAILROAD GRADE CROSSING	
RAILROAD ABOVE ROAD	
RAILROAD BELOW ROAD	
LANDING AREA OR AIRSTRIP	
AIRFIELD—AIRPORT	
AIRFIELD, MILITARY	

SCALE

N